Adolescent Social Development: Dynamic Functional Interaction

Adolescent Social Development: Dynamic Functional Interaction

Vivian Center Seltzer
The University of Pennsylvania

LexingtonBooks
D.C. Heath and Company
Lexington, Massachusetts
Toronto

Library of Congress Cataloging in Publication Data

Seltzer, Vivian Center.
  Adolescent social development.

  Includes index.
  1. Adolescence. 2. Socialization. I. Title.
HQ796.S4253   305.2′3   81-47001
ISBN 0-669-04511-x   AACR2

Copyright © 1982 by D.C. Heath and Company

Second printing, March 1983

Published simultaneously in Canada

Printed in the United States of America

International Standard Book Number: 0-669-04511-x

Library of Congress Catalog Card Number: 81-47001

Contents

Contents

List of Tables

Part I
Introduction

1

Formulations toward a New Outlook

The study of adolescence is more than a study of change: it is a study of changing. A rich adolescent literature gives us a picture of an individual who lacks a framework, who suddenly finds old supports insufficient and new supports undefined. Generally, the existing literature treats adolescence from the vantage points of the major developmental domains—biological, cognitive, and affective. The theory of Dynamic Functional Interaction, (DFI) as introduced in this book, addresses adolescent development from a fourth dimension—that of social development.

Excellent work on adolescence from differing perspectives has created a mosaic of the period and an appreciation of the tasks and challenges it presents, but a feeling for the individual adolescent and his or her immediate psychosocial milieu has been less than clear. Knowledge of growth, both as a function of internal determinants and as something occurring in a social context, has not given an understanding of the actual processes and the cause-and-effect relationships involved in growth. Additional theoretical work seemed necessary that would emphasize the crucial impact of social interactions between adolescents on individual development and would offer formulations of specific functions and processes of these interactions and their relation to successful passage through the adolescent period. Dynamic Functional Interaction is an attempt at this theoretical integration.

The process of framing conceptions about adolescent social development gave rise to a sense of the fundamental and defining difference in functions served by individual adolescent peers and those fulfilled by the adolescent peer group. The adolescent peer group emerges as a purposive congregation of individuals experiencing identical conditions of physical, emotional, and cognitive change as well as sharing the developmental position of anticipating and seeking self-definition, integration, and prescription. Since no other assembly at any other point in the life cycle appeared so closely defined, it followed that the interactions of adolescents would be unique. Thus the theory of Dynamic Functional Interaction highlights the central role of adolescent peer groups as a peer arena and the impact of this arena on adolescent social development. Our conception deals with the value of adolescent peers to one another in their varous and varying postures and relative movements as members of a peer group rather than as individual peers. Together, they stimulate a functional interaction.

3

The adolescent period itself has long been recognized as idiosyncratic and puzzling. The literature on adolescence reflects both heightened and reduced theoretical and empirical exploration. Current life-span literature charts the course of life as a series of developmental transitions or passages, each specific period having its own beginning, middle, and end, with the ending of one usually heralding the onset of the next. Adolescence, however, has long been regarded by the literature as a period of transition between child and adult functioning, with the emphasis on the various domains involved in change on an individual basis. Dynamic Functional Interaction, however, emphasizes the interactional dynamics of adolescence as a developmental stage and the process of individual changes in the context of a peer arena. It describes the interactional functions and processes within the peer arena during each of the two peer-group periods of adolescent development. The first of these is the period of the large aggregate primary peer group; the second is that of the smaller and more selective secondary peer group. Each set of group interactions has unique but related functions and processes. These interactions advance the completion of the tasks of self-understanding and clarification; the ultimate result is self-integration and a setting of direction. To date, the literature on the adolescent peer group has delineated and described functions, tasks, roles, behavioral manifestations, and outcomes. This theory presented here delineates the dynamic processes of adolescent interactions in peer groups and the functions these serve in advancing social development.

The occurrence of biological puberty has been considered the onset of adolescence. Its end is marked by the achievement of psychological identity and a life direction toward which to channel one's expanded intellect and energies. Accomplishment of the tasks essential to leaving behind the dependencies of childhood and assuming the responsibilities of adulthood, both personal and communal, are the societally distinguished cornerstones first of entry into, and later of departure from, the period. As various orientations and perspectives in the rich adolescent literature address the question of what an adolescent is, how adolescence can be appropriately defined, and what occurs during the long period of adolescence, we find new questions heuristically framed. Nevertheless, a view of the adolescent does emerge: at first, rootless and at sea; later, expansive, changeable, and unpredictable; finally, less scattered and in greater equilibrium.

Casual observations of adolescents, newspaper accounts of their mass activities, and everyday commentary yield a generally distinct portrait of individuals who travel together, have similar eating habits, spend leisure time in characteristic activities, and support group interests. Individual differences are apparent, but for the most part adolescents have differentiated themselves from generational elders through dress, custom, and even language. Together, they appear to be having fun and pursuing leisure activities. Individually, however, they manifest a more serious, goal-directed, and future-oriented dimension. Earlier empirical studies (Seltzer 1975) on reference-group preferences of adolescents supported these ancedotal observations by yielding unexpected findings that pointed to pragmatic and functional actions by adolescent peers. Friends and reference figures seemed to have been selected for specific purposes. Findings from exploratory interactional studies (Seltzer 1975) suggested that interactions in the peer group were not at all casual or otherwise undiscriminating, but were precisely directed. Thus adolescent friendships were not as cavalier as a passing observation would indicate but gave evidence of functionalism, a structural brace to the adolescent interactions. Even more surprising, however, was the apparent high rate of activity and its intensity. These findings seemed to demand further theoretical attention, suggesting that the peer group was neither merely tangential to the adolescent period nor a random social product. On the contrary, the observed interactions hinted that the peer group characterizes and defines the period.

Through a conceptual blend of pertinent theory from the diverse fields of adolescent development and social psychology, a new perspective on the process of adolescent social development was conceived. The theory of Dynamic Functional Interaction suggests that the active period of adolescent participation in the peer group is crucial to smooth development. This book describes in detail the dynamic functions and processes that occur during this important period and the ways they contribute to the completion of adolescent tasks. Peer groups in different contexts are conceived in combination as arenas in which development takes place through the interactions that occur. Our conceptual structure provides two major peer-group stages during the adolescent period—primary and secondary—appropriate to the sequence of developmental progression. Both primary and secondary arenas are conceptualized as composites of any and all of the interactional activities of the varying peer groups in which the adolescent participates during that period. Interactions in each of these two sequential peer-arena periods are functional. Regardless of setting, similar dynamics occur. The objectives of the two periods are related but differ, as do the functions and processes involved. This sequential peer-arena model identifies adolescence as a developmental period in which the social organizations are unique and qualitatively different from those of any other period, are sequentially ordered and traversed, and are functional to developmental passage toward adulthood.

The impressive forces, the concurrent activities, and the functional emphasis serve as criteria for selection of the term *Dynamic Functional Interaction* for the theory of adolescent social development presented here. The theory presumes an adolescent status of developmental readiness for the sequential developmental functions, occasioned by the onset of puberty and by maturational advances in the cognitive, emotional, and biological domains. This new perspective on adolescent social development assumes that the end of the parent-child primary-nurturance period is marked by adolescent entry into the primary peer group, and that major psychological movement away from parenting adults has taken place. Dynamic Functional Interaction suggests a transformed nurturance need that can be filled only by peers. A peer-arena experience is seen as a central factor in meeting this unique need and thereby in maximizing potential for smooth adolescent developmental progression. The confounding and changeable attitudes and behaviors of the adolescent are seen generally as overt, often displaced, manifestations of responses to interactions with peers. It is not the peer group but the parental home (now a field of only secondary relevance) that is the haven. The peer group now is the arena.

In attempting to identify the precise functions and processes of interactions, the theory necessarily conceptualizes both actions and consequences. The sheer volume of actions—many of them simultaneous, parallel, and concurrent—may be confusing at first. A nomenclature has been devised and a number of mechanistic similes used in an attempt to reduce confusion. Only through occasional redundancy and repetition of terms can we be sure to identify antecedent factors and to distinguish between actions and interactions that overtly appear similar. Indeed, this overlap and repetition itself is characteristic of the adolescent in the primary-group period, and within limits we have defined the scene in order to describe the action. Despite a host of new terms and suggested dynamic functions and processes, however, the developmental period of adolescence is characterized by a linear progression and a simplicity of composition.

After introducing the theory, the book attempts to frame a context within which the theory applies. Therefore, varying views are presented from the adolescent literature of the domains of adolescent cognitive, emotional, and social growth as well as various perspectives from the literature on peer groups. Within a context of social-psychological reference group theory, we then reconceptualize the peer group as reference group and go on to suggest a more expansive reformulation. The next nine chapters describe the new theory in detail, beginning with socially based external forces that mesh with psychologically rooted inner states to provide strong motivation for affiliating with a group of peers. Characteristics of the members that determine the uniquely adolescent composition of the groups of the primary peer arena are described. The functions and processes of the primary peer group are detailed in relation to how they serve *latent structure* needs, and the unique and paradoxical milieu of the primary peer group is delineated. Finally, the growing momentum toward leaving the primary peer group is traced, as is the transition to the secondary peer group. The functions and processes of the secondary peer group and the dynamics that signal completion of adolescent tasks and that stimulate the forces for leaving the peer arena comprise the final segments of explication of the theory proper. The last of these chapters details specific irregularities in development that may result from partial or complete deprivation of the peer-group interactional experience. Part IV structures some beginning models for practical application of the theory to parenting, education, and diagnosis and therapy.

Nature or nurture notwithstanding with respect to preadolescent development, Dynamic Functional Interaction takes a developmental view of the interactional dynamics of a peer arena suggesting that major adolescent social development occurs within the arena. In preparation for adulthood, each adolescent brings to the arena his or her own developmental outline, which can be fashioned idiosyncratically and carefully refined with appropriately integrated hues and colors. Interactions with enough other adolescent members of sequential peer groups provides the raw materials. Each adolescent is his or her own unique creator.

2 Seeds

The adolescent's initial entry into life is indeed a period of innocence and helplessness. In juxtaposition to the Darwinian perspective of the survival of the fittest, Loren Eiseley (1946) adopts the position that human beings evolved to a higher order as a function of delayed development that allowed for nurturing. By virtue of tender, slow care—allowing the organism to be exposed gradually to environmental elements necessary for development—the brain matured over a longer period and man reached his ascendant position among the primates. Sigmund Freud's theories (1938) have emphasized careful nurturance of the instinctual organism in the crucial early period of life lest restrictive patterns and responses take hold that will negatively affect the handling of environmental stresses and demands in adult life.

Physical appetites must be fed for physical growth. Emotional warmth and commitment of the caretaker likewise are seen to support growth. In early childhood, although primary emotional nurturance continues to come from parents, the developing child accomplishes psychological separation sufficient to permit physical separation from the mother for periods of time necessary for education and socialization. Of necessity, as the young child continues to develop, the nurturer continues to be a generational elder. Likewise, interaction in the social world necessitates a mediator. The organism that enters adolescence, however, possesses advanced biological and cognitive skills on which to draw in order to transact with the social environment. He has benefited from his gradual introduction to negotiating the practical aspects of the immediate social environment. Now, however, he must deal no longer only with his environment, but also with his world. Therefore, adolescence is regarded as a period in which the organism not only attempts to go beyond psychological separation from the original object, but also tries to embark on real independence.

Theoretical notions from the literature about the precarious biological, affective, and cognitive status of the adolescent, coupled with our observations of groups of adolescents as changling youths huddled together, devoid of their former guides and guideposts, have prompted questions about the precise nature of this group interaction. Why do adolescent groups form, and why do they persist? Why does age exclusivity remain a constant? Why does this appear an automatic transitional move? Which transactional processes do occur? The attribution of causation to influences such as mass media (Bandura 1964) or parental unavailability or exclusion (Bronfenbren-ner 1970) appeared insufficient, as did earlier conceptions of escape from burdensome unconscious libidinous drives (Freud 1938). The group itself stood out: That membership in the group might be a strong need, perhaps even instinctual, seemed apparent and hence worth pursuing.

Accordingly, the focus here is not only on a chronological period separate from early life. The theoretical formulations also point to a developmental span during which the component essential to successful growth is nurturance not by parents, but by peers. This perspective suggests that adolescent membership in a peer group has dimensions and depths not yet recognized. The literature to date has generally followed the lead of formulations that frame the peer group as an available and important forum in a transitional adolescent period, serving functions of refuge from parents and the adult world and/or of experimentation with roles (Josselyn 1952; Erickson 1968). Little or no attention has been paid to the specific interactions occuring within the peer group itself. Dynamic Functional Interaction suggests that the type and quality of the interactions among members of an adolescent peer group are most important—the necessary source of adolescent nurturance. In fact, the extent to which the adolescent derives the essential and relevant nur-ture from these interactions is prominent in determining whether passage through adolescence proceeds smoothly, is inhibited, or is cut short.

* * *

Some of the basic tenets of Dynamic Functional Interaction may be traced to the science of ethology as well as to the work on infant behavior of John Bowlby (1969). Bowlby has posited an instinctual need in infancy—the at-tachment need of infant and mother—as prototypic of future relationships. He holds that successful attachment aids in a smooth progression of physical and psychological development. Interruption of this attachment has ramifications, possibly leading to maladaptive growth. Dynamic Func-tional Interaction suggests that in adolescence, as in infancy, a need for at-tachment surfaces. In adolescence, however, it is a need to attach to similar others in preparation for future adult life. This adolescent attachment proc-ess differs from earlier modes. In Bowlby's formulation, attachment is seen as a one-to-one relationship. Successful satisfaction of the attachment to the original object, usually the mother, facilitates formation of close rela-tionships to others in the family, such as the father and siblings, and, later, to other children and to one's own children. By puberty, the adolescent has already experienced physical separation from the mother, has been able to form close relationships with the other parent and with siblings, has gone on to develop child-child relationships, and then has been able to handle simul-taneous relationships with a number of children. In adolescence elements of both infant and adolescent postures emerge or reemerge. The ability to relate to a number of others is active; simultaneously, however, the impulse to attach seems resurgent. These two needs synthesize in the imperative to interact intimately and closely with a group.

Conceptualizations about adolescence were also stimulated by ideas from the science of ethology and the study of following behavior in animals (Lorenz 1965). Such observed behavior has been hypothesized to be instinctual and served as a model for Bowlby in formulating his own notions of the instinctual nature of attachment in humans. In the neonate we can assume a condition of helplessness and a sense of danger as stimulants to the instinct to attach. The question, then, was whether the sense of precariousness experienced by the developing adolescent may in fact stimulate following behavior similar to that of the duck or chick. Indeed, Anna Freud (1958) and followers of her psychoanalytic orientation see adolescence as precarious enough to be likened to near-psychosis. Is it possible that the adolescent undergoes a reactivation of the intense vulnerability experienced by the neonate, which restimulates instinctual attachment behavior? (Of course, with humans other than neonates, when a cognitive dimension is added, there is always the question of the extent to which the behavior is instinctual as opposed to cognitive copying). For the adolescent, reactivation of the original object (the mother) would be regressive. By the time the individual reaches adolescence, he has gone far beyond that one-to-one relationship and is able to negotiate many relationships.

Therefore, it can be theorized that the attachment need, newly reexperienced (or reactivated), presses the adolescent to find a suitable, relevant object appropriate to the psychological growth that has already taken place. However, since the changing adolescent organism is not yet developmentally ready to attach to another solo object, the attachment must be to *figures* rather than to *a figure*. Furthermore, these figures must be relevant to the adolescent's immediate concerns. Only adolescent cotravelers meet this description. Accordingly, it follows that the period of adolescence demands interaction with cotravelers. As in the Darwinian formulation, wherein organisms deal with the challenge of the present, so does the adolescent. He has not yet developed the full cognitive structures necessary to a future orientation (Piaget and Inhelder 1958), and his new biological powers still give rise to emotional uncertainties. Although he may cognitively anticipate the future, the adolescent experiences an attraction toward a forum peopled with others in similar condition. The step-by-step passage from childhood to adulthood seems to produce a need to travel a road peopled with chronological peers in coaction.

Although adolescent allegiance is generally viewed as in transit from parent to peer, influential formulations have reinforced earlier notions of abrupt parental rejection stimulated by the changes accompanying the advent of puberty. The formulation offered here departs from this consensus.

Movement away from parents and toward peers is regarded as occurring "in service of" developmental growth and is described as continuous, rather than discontinuous, with prior attachments. Adolescent allegiances must be considered as existing within a spectrum of change, not as falling at either end of a peer-parent dichotomy. The notion of the primacy of the adolescent peer as the "current relevant other" is introduced and extended to a concept of "progressive relevant others" within progressive peer groups. Dynamic Functional Interaction holds that the quantity and type of interactions with peers are crucial to whether the adolescent emerges from this transitional travel equipped to continue functioning alongside both chronological peers and adults of all ages.

*   *   *

A word is in order on the evolution of a new view of the significance of the adolescent peer group. Since no other assembly of individuals at any other point in the developmental cycle contains members with so many identical attributes, it follows that their congregation and their interactions also would be unique. We theorize that these dimensions are functional and goal directed. But rather than serving irretrievable decision making, this social environment is used dynamically to further idiosyncratic developmental prerogatives, one by one. The adolescent members engage simultaneously in parallel tasks that focus their interactions and stimulate the unique dynamic of their association.

Dynamic Functional Interaction is a pioneering attempt at a revisionist view of the adolescent peer group from the vantage point of the dynamics of the processes of interaction. The adolescent literature has generally pictured the adolescent peer group as formed in a movement away from elders and as a passive entity to be acted on at will for whatever idosyncratic needs the individual adolescent might have. The present view suggests that it is more proper to view the peer group as active—in fact, as an energizing system. The interactions occurring in the peer group are seen as dynamically functional to developmental process. Hence, the peer group is considered here to be the essential forum in which adolescents sharing identical conditions of physical, emotional, and cognitive fluctuation and position in time express developmental imperatives.

One cannot achieve or maintain membership in the group without becoming involved in its functional properties. Hence, a group characteristic prevails that crystallizes a group phenomenon of functional interaction that is more than the sum of its parts. Although future orientation is its salient characteristic, the group function determines its rationale and definition. The premise of Dynamic Functional Interaction is that the peer group congregation draws its character from its function. No interchange is casual. Interaction is functionally rooted in the individual's ultimate goal of self-definition, integration, and self-prescription.

In conquering the developmental challenge, each adolescent appears to use familiar skills to integrate new capacities. He goes back to the basic skills he has commanded from infancy and to those mastered in earlier developmental periods. The entry into life of an instinctually motivated and satisfaction-seeking human organism is accompanied by the complementary initiation of the activity of the five senses in the early struggle for life and survival. These five senses are used in the sensorimotor period of intellectual development—to cope with new stimuli (Piaget 1952). The newborn, in a strange, new environment, uses the senses of sight, hearing, touch, taste, and smell to acquaint him- or herself with that environment. The achievement of the ability to form and retain mental images means that sensory impressions can be stored and later retrieved for use. The advent of language is dependent on this storage; verbal communications become prominent as humans expand their capacities to learn more about their world. As development continues, the individual moves further and further up a complex ladder of skills by which socialization takes place and the child takes on the role of a member of society. The senses cease to function exclusively, operating instead in conjunction with intentional strategies for coping.

The literature suggests that a second intense period of insecurity and doubt occurs during adolescence. It seems natural to speculate on the fundamental function of the senses—specifically the eyes and the ears—in this period when, abruptly, the developing individual is once again assaulted from within (emotionally, physically, and cognitively) and from without by the shock of new and insistent stimuli. The infant used the equipment that came with birth—the basic senses—to become acquainted with a new environment and to begin to handle himself in it. Like the infant, the adolescent is called on to learn to handle an abruptly entered new environment. The key word here is *learn*. The notion will be offered in later chapters that the adolescent moves between periods of regression and those of integration. This regression is different from that offered by the proponents of psychoanalytic theory. It involves a dialectical process of regression and integration occurring in rapid action.

To understand the adolescent developmental period/process, it is helpful to consider again the role of the basic senses—specifically sight and hearing, behaviorally distinguished as looking and listening. The adolescent transition from child to adult is characterized by the cessation of traditional, parent-centered guides and guideposts. Abruptly the adolescent finds himself left to search out through his own volition a frame of reference by which to structure his goals and actions. It is logical, then, that individuals might return to basics and use those tools that, in infancy, introduced the outer environment and were instrumental in the handling of the earliest survival forays. The regression to those first helpers—the senses—is followed by an integration of the information yielded by those senses, which in turn stimulates a new form of questioning. Looking and listening—the product of the information gained yields a new integration and perhaps a reinitiation of the process through several sequences or until the need is satisfied.

Maturational advances move the adolescent away from a concern only for the concrete present to an ability to confront the future as real. Indeed, it is "back to basics"—but this dialectical looking and listening builds on firmer ground than before, since cognitive skills acquired in the course of development are now fast advancing to completion. Sensorimotor skills are used not only in connection with an effectance motive, but also with true cognitive awareness of the need not only to cope in the present but also to establish one's place in the future. The adolescent has moved beyond the immediate, concrete experience to a conception of the present that also incorporates the future.

*   *   *

Various developmental periods have been defined and analyzed and, in the scientific tradition, continue to be debated. Theorists will differ and controversies linger to distinguish as well as to open up new points of view. Even as perspectives expand, these older differences permeate the adolescent literature. This new pragmatic, sequentially programmed view of the nature of the passage through adolescence encompasses the intuitive and the environmental; the biological, emotional, and cognitive domains; both the continuous-development and the discrete-state schools. Its reference to the overlap of childhood with adolescence and its emphasis on future orientation, lead to a connection that appears to offer a view of an integrative developmental pattern. Moreover, formation of a self-structure using all of the forces both within and without the individual, added to the socialization process oriented to a society outside his or her realm, suggest that adolescence is a crucible in which the later developmental periods not only seed, but also are crystallized and solidified to a greater extent than heretofore advanced. Thus, Dynamic Functional Interaction may hold the promise of a first step toward unifying theories of adolescent development in a perspective embracing developmental schools from several disciplines and diverse approaches.

Part II
Adolescence and the
Peer Group

3 Adolescence: Conceptions from the Literature

Adolescence is considered a period of radical change in the total individual, difficult to understand within any exclusive theoretical discipline. It encompasses behavioral change as well as observable physical growth and biological maturation from child to adult. Changes in one domain of growth have an impact on the other. Thus physical changes affect social and psychological behaviors just as social factors affect decisions and opportunities for change. Psychological factors in turn have physiological and social effects (Josselyn 1952). Adolescence may range from as early as nine, ten, or eleven up to the early twenties, with wide individual and cultural variations. It ends earlier in primitive societies (Benedict 1950). Representative views have been summarized here in order to frame a picture of the adolescent pertinent to the discussions in the chapters that follow.

Early Views

The antecedents of current theories of adolescence can be traced to developmental notions implicit in works of Plato and Aristotle, to theological conceptions of homuncular man, to John Locke's doctrine of environmental determinism, and to Rousseau's eighteenth-century naturalism. These antecedent notions may be seen falling within Ausubel and Sullivan's (1970) framework for broad classification of developmental theory, as follows:

1. *preformationist theories*, which are couched in theological conceptions of instant creation
2. *predeterministic approaches*, which set forth sequential unfolding stages of development
3. *tabula rasa theories*, which deemphasize genetic and biologic factors in favor of environmental determinants

The recent literature generally falls between derivations of the first two classifications, considering adolescence a specific stage characterized by storm and stress that is almost pathological in character, and derivations of the third category, deeming the vicissitudes of the period as little different from the general ebb and flow of any period in the developmental span.

G. Stanley Hall is considered the father of the field of adolescence and is credited with the advance from philosophical formulations to an embrace of the scientific method. As a consequence of the deep impression made on him by Darwin's principle that the evolution of biological life was continuous from a single-celled organism through numerous higher developmental stages to the complexity of the human mind and body, Hall began to study child and adolescent development from an evolutionary standpoint. His two-volume work *Adolescence* (1916) develops a psychological theory of recapitulation, asserting that characteristics of a certain age in the development of the individual correspond to historical stages in the development of the human species. Thus Hall finds maturity recapitulated in the beginning of modern civilization. Since Hall assumed that growth and development occurred through genetically determined physiological factors subject to internal maturational forces, it followed that development and behavior occurred inevitably and universally. Hall also posited a span of four stages, with emotional life during adolescence depicted as oscillating between contradictory trends. In terms of recapitulation theory, Hall related adolescence to the turbulent, transitional period during those last decades of the eighteenth century characterized as "Sturm und Drang."[1]

A position opposed to that of the "Sturm und Drang" of adolescent development was advanced a decade later by Leta Hollingsworth (1928), who thought little of Hall's conception of personality wrought by storm and stress during adolescence. Her thesis, suggesting imperceptible degrees of growth from childhood to adolescence and on into adulthood, rejected the notion of specific developmental stages. Thus she saw adolescent growth as reflecting all other points of continuity of growth, and the quality of the organism as a constant with no concomitant personality change. Disclaiming universal patterns, she saw observable stages of adolescence in the United States as specific to the culture.

The respective positions of Hall and Hollingsworth represent forerunners of the still current controversy. Whether adolescence is a period of storm and stress in which innate determinants stimulate more abrupt segmented adolescent experience, or part of a continuous developmental sequence of an earlier developmental pattern, continues to be debated despite the expansion of theoretical perspectives.

In the late 1920s and early 1930s the sister field of anthropology offered support to the position of environmental determinism with data from field studies. It is well known that the underlying assumption of cultural anthropology is the concept of cultural determinism and that cultural relativism is a further extension of this concept. In early writings, Margaret Mead (1928) and Ruth Benedict (1938) represented this theoretical perspective, questioning assumptions of universal patterns of development. Mead did not view pubescence as causally related to adolescence or adolescent turmoil. In fact, she held that adjustment became crucial at whatever point the society decided to stress a particular adjustment. Some societies regarded puberty as such a period. Depending on local societal mores the menstruating girl was regarded as either blessed or evil. Benedict offered the notion that from a cultural-anthropological viewpoint development can be a gradual, continuous process. It is the culture that provides either continuity or discontinuity. Discontinuity in socialization occurs when children or adolescents are required (1) to unlearn a form of behavior that had been previously reinforced or (2) to learn a form of behavior directly opposite to one for which they had earlier been rewarded or punished. Benedict contends that role-status conflicts are a component part of cultures such as ours; in other words, breeding grounds for discontinuity problems are built into U.S. culture. On the other hand, the Samoan culture would provide a contrasting example of cultural continuity. In such cultures youth are assigned a particular area of dominance and are given an opportunity to regard activities that are natural and pleasurable and to view birth and death. By contrast, "modern" U.S. culture asks a child trained in a nonresponsible, submissive, asexual role to reverse these patterns in adulthood in order to fulfill not only a responsible but also a dominant sexual role.

The findings of cultural relativists like Margaret Mead and Benedict held implications for the study of adolescence since the anxieties and/or insecurities seen as concomitant to inconsistencies created by cultural conditioning were pertinent to forces alive in adolescence. Unable to be ignored, these theories imposed on psychoanalytic thinkers the necessity to broaden their scope to include social factors in their view of the determinants of behavior. A complementary broadening of perspective has been increasingly evident in the past two decades by cultural anthropologists such as Mead (1958, 1962), who now allow broader theoretical positions, taking biogenetic factors into consideration.

The Continuum

Current theoretical postures generally range along a continuum from those that see adolescence as a period of storm and stress in which innate determinants stimulate an abrupt segmented experience, to those that view adolescence as just another developmental period in which developmental patterns are heavily dependent on environmental influences. Supporters of the "Sturm und Drang" position (primarily followers of psychoanalytic tradition) conceptualize adolescence as a period of turbulent, irrational behavior, elicited by the upsurge of both instinctual urges and the defense mechanisms necessary to contain them. It is considered a normal disruption essential to full passage to adulthood, although improper resolutions may hold developmental dangers. Some of these proponents even conceptualize a condition of extreme neurosis wherein the adolescent may be susceptible to pathological behavior patterns as a function of weakness of the ego.

Adherents of the alternative position who tend to deemphasize internal determinants, seem to hold a position generally consistent with that of cultural anthropologists. Adolescence is seen as merely another stage in the continuous development of child to adult. The tasks of adolescence are solved or not solved with no greater urgency than those of any other earlier or later period. Vicissitudes in adolescent behaviors have been attributed to such factors as the impact of increased physical strength and greater independence from the reinforcement contingencies that existed under the control of parents and/or of the adult group.

Theoretical views of adolescent affective development falling somewhere between these extremes are represented in adolescent literature by psychosocial (Erikson 1950, 1968) and interactionist (Ausubel 1954, 1977) perspectives. Although the controversy may serve to highlight the need for parsimony in theoretical constructs, current positions still reflect strong connections to seminal works and reflect the dilemma involved in conceptual synthesis—the danger of reducing the richness of existing theoretical conceptions.

Affective Orientations

Stage theorists, who identify the onset of adolescence in the pubertal awakening, postulate a turbulent course incorporating yet another separation and individuation necessary to eventual self-definition, culminating in an ability to unite with a second person and to find a functional role in society. Anna Freud, who proceeds from a psychoanalytic perspective of human functioning pioneered by her father, Sigmund Freud, is a prominent proponent of stage development.

The original version of Sigmund Freud's (1905) theory placed relatively little emphasis on pubescence and adolescence, concentrating instead on the oral, anal, phallic, and latency stages that precede adolescence. Adolescence was conceived of as the attainment of genital primacy and as the definitive completion of the process of nonincestuous object finding (a second opportunity to rework the oedipal conflict). Sigmund Freud held that pubescent development heralds the onset of adolescence with the reawakening of the sexuality that has been repressed and sublimated into the varied interests and pursuits of the latency period. This increased sexual tension, according to Freud, revives many incestuous objects of the earlier oedipal period; libidinous feelings are directed toward them, further escalating tensions.

This reawakened conflict must be resolved before transfer of libido to an appropriate love object can be effected. For Sigmund Freud, this transfer represents the major task of adolescence. The process of resolution is unconscious and may manifest itself in outwardly erratic, impulsive, and even hostile behavior on the part of a previously compliant and stable offspring. Behaviorally, the accomplishment of resolution is reflected in reduction of tension.

Sigmund Freud's acclaimed position that the first five years of childhood are the most formative ones for personality development provided the ground on which Anna Freud could defend her father's relative neglect of the adolescent. Anna Freud (1936, 1948) concentrated more precisely than did her father on the dynamics of adolescence. Within the psychoanalytic framework of biologic drives and societal precautions, her development of ego psychology and defense mechanisms placed great emphasis on the role of the reality-governed ego and the mechanisms of defense it employed against the impulses of the id and the protestations of the firm superego. In the adolescent, Anna Freud sees reawakened id impulses/drives, which had been repressed in latency, disturbing the equilibrium. In fact, she sees the assault from within as so strong that normal resistance to pathologic behavior is weakened, and the individual is in danger. Therefore, she sees adolescent equilibrium as unnatural and adolescent turmoil as normal. Three factors are involved in adolescent conflict: (1) the strength of the id impulse (physiologically determined during pubescence); (2) the capacity of the ego to handle ego instinctual forces effectively (dependent on the development of the superego in terms of flexibility or rigidity); and (3) the character and quality of the defense mechanisms at the disposal of the ego.

She identifies two defense mechanisms as active in pubescence. They are invoked to hold in check the anxiety signaled by the reawakening of oedipal fantasies and to reverse the libidinal impulses to act against the self, relieving guilt. For example, asceticism is a defense mechanism by means of which the adolescent wages total war against the pursuit of pleasure—going beyond mere denial of the sexual impulse into extremes in eating, sleeping, and dressing habits. The second of the two prominent defense mechanisms of adolescence is intellectualization—a change from concrete to abstract interests. The adolescent moves away from concrete satisfactions to abstractions, becoming involved in theorizing, philosophizing, exploring exotic philosophies, and so forth. The adolescent may exhibit rigidity and/or an uncompromising attitude in an effort to control the unacceptable drive. As a defense against the unconscious impulse, the outward behavior is the extreme opposite of the unconsciously desired behavior. Hence, this outwardly ascetic and/or intellectual behavior may be seen as based on the unconscious fear of giving in altogether if the rigidity is relaxed even a little.

Anna Freud sees the task of adolescence as that of reestablishing harmony between and within the systems of id, ego, and superego at the least psychological cost. The mode of resolution of the conflicts raging within the emotional systems markedly determines the adult personality. If the ego—the psychic reflection of reality—is overridden by the id, the personality will enter adult life uninhibited in gratification of instincts. On the other hand, if the ego is too severe, it may confine the id to a limited area and hence cripple the expression of instinctual tendencies in adult life. Such personalities may be badly incapacitated by a lack of the flexibility that a changing reality demands. A balance will avoid pathological development. Anna Freud derives her formulations of the normal by way of the pathological, as did her father. She views adolescence as a near-pathology that occurs normally in its chronologically specific period.

Peter Blos (1962), another proponent of the psychoanalytic perspective, also views adolescent turmoil as a component of normal progression toward adult development. Well known for his delineation of adolescence into five discrete stages—preadolescence, early adolescence, adolescence proper, late adolescence, and post adolescence—Blos sees adolescence as a second separation-individuation phase, another psychic restructuring wherein the child again sheds the object tie and becomes a member of the adult world. However, Blos postulates that a major difference now characterizes shedding the object. Since the three-year-old recognizes that the mother is no longer a part of the child (as was perceived in infancy), the child sheds the tie to the external object. Since the mother is accepted as being out in the world, the object is then internalized in order that the mother can be out of sight. In adolescence, however, the separation is from the *internalized* object.

With separation from the internalized object comes a withdrawal from formerly internalized structures. Hence, with separation the adolescent simultaneously experiences a withdrawal of ego support. Blos sees erratic behavior as a consequence of buffeting by quantitative increases in drive of an impoverished ego. In an adolescent weakened by the strength of new drives, outwardly erratic behavior is also a function of adaptive defense mechanisms that have come into play. Hence, Blos conceptualizes adolescence as an energy system involved in differentiation and then stabilization prior to the establishment of a new equilibrium. He developed a precise formulation of the ego development and drives of the adolescent in five stages: In preadolescence (stage 1) there is a withdrawal of cathexis from the parents, with the male internalizing the ego ideal and the female transferring libido and dependency to the "crush." The phenomenon of ego ideal occurs in early adolescence (stage 2). Adolescence proper (stage 3) has two themes: (1) revival of the oedipal conflict and (2) disengagement and identity. Late adolescence (stage 4) includes consolidation, emergence of self, and decision about life's goals. Blos' last stage (stage 5) is postadolescence, a transitional stage to adulthood, involving even more consolidation.

As the adolescent psychologically withdraws from the parents, a withdrawal of ego support is simultaneously experienced, making a substitute support necessary. This condition, earlier established in the psychoanalytic literature, lays the groundwork for the introduction by Blos of the concept of the ego ideal. He argues that in the process of establishing a new equilibrium, the adolescent allows a peer whom he views as just like himself and to whom he transfers libido to take over some of his own harsh superego functions. This new area of support—the ego ideal, the peer chosen to act in loco parentis—serves to tide the adolescent through the period of beginning withdrawal from his parents. Psychological maturity is achieved through a freeing of libidinal ties with parents. Blos argues that this is accomplished by way of immediate transfers to a series of peers and models.[2] Within his five-stage model, Blos details psychosexual aspects of adolescent development with corresponding behavior manifestations. Adolescence is conceptualized as a normal passage achieved through freeing libidinal ties with parents, but also as a turbulent period productive of either healthy sexual identity or serious malfunctioning, wherein maladaptations as a consequence of faulty progression through the aforementioned stages can occur. The adolescent moves to mature status through intermediate transfers to peers and models whereby sexual identification and heterosexual life are achieved.

The psychosocial theorists offer formulations that interlace societal factors with the psychoanalytic constructual base of id, ego, and superego. These theorists in a sense bridge the gap between adherents of the stage formulation of adolescence and those who subscribe to the tradition of cultural relevance that views the character of the specific society as a major determiner of the behavior exhibited. The esteem accorded to Erik Erikson (1950, 1968) has in great part been earned by his modification of the Freudian theory of psychosexual development to include perspectives from the field of cultural anthropology, whereby he modified the emphasis on libido to include societal factors and affiliations that affect smooth structured progression. Erikson's theory was in fact developed out of concern about a psychoanalytic framework distinct from its sociocultural bed. Insofar as the psychoanalytic method is essentially a historical method that interprets medical data as a function of past experience, Erikson considered his theory one of historical processes. He sees it as a study of the conflict between the mature and the infantile, the up-to-date and the archaic layers of the mind. Thus psychological evolution is studied through the analysis of the individual. Erikson's area of concentration is the study of the ego, and the central concept offered in his theory is that of ego identity. It appears that for Erikson the causes of distortion of the individual ego are less germane than is an analysis of the ego's roots in social disorganization.

Erikson contends that psychosocial development proceeds in steps representing crucial determiners of progress or regression. His psychosocial model of development assumes: (1) that there exists a predetermined steplike readiness to be cognizant of and to engage with a widening social radius, and (2) that society is organized in the service of encouraging the potential for interchange as well for piloting proper rate sequences and speeds of this readiness (1950). Erikson's developmental model comprises eight stages, each one of which presents its own conflicts or crises to be resolved by means of the successful resolution of a dominant task. Unsuccessful resolution of any stage distorts successive development. Each conflict that is successfully resolved builds a positive quality into the ego. Unsuccessful resolution means that the negative quality is built in and the developing ego is damaged.

Adolescence is the fifth of these eight stages, and the task is to discover and establish an identity. Erikson describes identity as the attainment of a holistic connection between what the person once was, what that person is now, and what he wishes to become. The psychosocial model places the process of identity formation in the unconscious structure of the individual but emphasizes that its resolution is rooted in and dependent on the society of immediate people and accepted values. In other words, identity does not develop in isolation. The task of ego identity appears to have a common element in all cultures. In order to achieve a strong, healthy ego development, the child must receive consistent recognition for his achievements, although the specific achievements will vary from culture to culture.

Erikson suggests that the adolescent struggle revolves around achieving a sense of continuity and sameness between what the individual was and what he or she is now. Role diffusion, though appropriate to initial attempts to establish ego identity, becomes maladaptive if not resolved. Erikson contends that the tangible manifestation of this resolution is in the ability to select a career and to know who one is sexually. Role diffusion may be manifested in an inability to make a career choice; or, if the problem is one of sexual identification, possibly in delinquency or outright psychotic episodes.

A major point in Erikson's discussion of identity is the self-reflective aspect of growth.[3] What the adolescent perceives himself to be in the eyes of others, compared with what he himself feels he is, Erikson considers the crucial component of a struggle to maintain a continuity between past and present. In psychological terms, identity formation employs a process of simultaneous reflection and observation of others in relation to a personally significant typology (1968). Erikson's formulation implies that the adolescent self-judgment contains a depository of what the adolescent perceives as others' judgments of him. Those judgments by others also are nested within the context of judgments of performances idiosyncratically important to them. According to the Eriksonian model, circularity between self and other appear to be inescapable. An awareness of prevailing values seems essential to the assessment of one's own performance, which is judged in relation to these same values. Thus Erikson argues that adolescent psychological needs demand close peer association in order to work through the conflicts of this stage.

Irene Josselyn (1952) sets the adolescent struggle conceptually within the psychoanalytic tradition. Since the adolescent is still a creature of his past, and inasmuch as earlier developmental conflicts have rarely been ideally resolved, behavior may reflect reactivation of earlier problems in addition to difficulties peculiar to adolescents. The more aggressive attack on life's problems, the striving for maturation, and the struggle for heterosexual adjustment become fused into the typical behavior of the adolescent as he struggles to find a pattern of behavior that will give substitute gratification for internally determined impulses (made more complex by new demands of a reality that presses for new patterns of behavior). Josselyn points out the effects of external changes in the adolescent, which then typify the new demands of reality. For example, the child whose rate of growth is markedly different from the average may find himself alienated from his chronological peers and may be drawn to those who are perceived physically to be more truly his contemporaries. However, these others are not readily accessible inasmuch as young people consider chronological age the real indicator of level of maturation. Josselyn suggests that defensive reactions to the rejections experienced may be manifested in fantasy or in acting-out behavior in order to relieve the resultant anxiety. Although Josselyn's view of the psychosocial nature of development within a framework of past patterns juxtaposed against the present needs and demands of society is similar to Erikson's, she adds the important component of a dimension of pressure to reach the nebulous but demanding goal that the adolescent sees for the future. The uncertainty of the pursuit of such self-direction stimulates tension, which is manifested as mounting disorganized energy that adults would like to see channeled toward constructive goals. The adolescent, however, has not yet determined his goals; hence the energy is expressed impulsively. Adults seem to want what adolescents cannot yet do.

In the psychodynamic tradition, Ruthellen Josselson (1980) categorizes adolescence as a second phase of individuation. She extends the adolescent task of freeing oneself from one's parents to include freeing oneself from dependence on the external environment, including parents and peers, as well as from submission to an archaic superego. Like others (Newman and Newman 1976), Josselson finds Erikson's rich description of the identity crisis applicable to late adolescence since she considers middle adolescence a period in which the adolescent works to become an individual but continues to remain a satellite of the parents. Late adolescence occurs when the satellite strives to find his own orbit and when the future takes on a new reality—when "Who am I?" gives way to "Who shall I become?" She suggests that ego development in adolescence focuses on the problem of internalization of values, controls, and self-esteem, and that since developmental tasks seem to be taken in order, adolescence may be defined by growth tasks rather than by chronology.

A review of the literature of quasi-longitudinal studies (James Marcia 1980) suggests that the safest generalization is that identity attainment increases incrementally from early to late adolescence. Through the earlier years, one may expect a predominance of temporary foreclosures and identity diffusions, many of which will begin crossing over into moratorium and identity-achievement status around age eighteen. By age twenty-one the highest proportion of adolescents will meet the criteria for identity achievers. Marcia calls for more research in identity formation in women and more attention to the design of cultural institutions within which identity is formed—particularly such contexts as colleges and high schools.

Commenting on the present status of adolescent theory, Adelson and Doehrman (1980) suggest that it is hard to imagine a satisfying theory of adolescence without the strongest contribution from psychodynamic theory, since no other approach can offer potentially a comparable depth and range of observation, nor is any as well suited to pull togther evidence drawn from other sources. On the other hand, they consider psychodynamic theory currently a fossilized doctrine, resisting innovation in method and unshakably parochial in outlook. They point out that until very recently reading psychodynamic literature on adolescence has meant reading about the male youngster. They call for a vastly increased pluralism and an openness to new research methods, diverse populations and competing ideas.

Normative Approach; Physical Components

The normative approach to adolescence of Arnold Gesell (1933) is also conceptualized within a biologically oriented framework of predetermined maturation. Gesell envisioned the total organism of the child as a growing action system, structurally and functionally, which comes into the world endowed with prodigious powers of growth. He posited a rhythmic pattern of growth achieved through processes of differentiation and integration of forty developmental levels from birth through the age of sixteen. Genetic factors control the direction and sequence of this maturation, and pubescence and adolescence are not distinguished. Gesell's description of the adolescent years reflects his theory of rhythmic patterns in development, wherein behavior oscillates between movements toward and away, diffused and then organized, extreme and then moderate—eventually manifesting progress. Adolescence is considered a period of crucial transition from childhood to adulthood in which abilities and attitudes are attributed to instinctual changes, a sequence in the mode of a ripening process rather than a period of "Sturm und Drang."

Although Gesell's theory of physical development and its psychological manifestations is theoretically in concert with Freud's formulation of maturational unfolding of predetermined characteristics, Gesell rejects the idea that unconscious motives direct. He is concerned with the observable. Development takes place in sequential patterns or cycles. In spiral fashion, there are plateaus and even periods in which the child may regress in order to consolidate his gains. Regression is not seen as pathological. Gesell conceptualized the up and down gradients as a growth-adjustment mechanism much like Piaget's more recent concept of equilibration—a self-regulatory mechanism that serves the establishment of equilibrium. Gesell's empirical study sought to bring into view the direction of development and the relative nature of age, maturity, and immaturity. This early work provided general descriptive guidelines of each passing year from ten to sixteen, stimulating more rigorous attention as well as offering clues for further exploration of the general outline and rhythm of psychological development.

The literature has also examined the impact of the physical component of development, such as the rate and timing of physical growth, adolescent body image (Schonfeld 1966), and perceptions and consequences of early or late maturation (Clausen 1975; Mussen and Jones 1957). Parental and peer environments are considered as influential variables in adolescent acceptance of or anxiety about body change. By both overt and covert means, parents and peers can and do communicate positive or negative evaluations of the adolescent's appearance. Petersen and Taylor (1980) include parents and peers among the variables that potentially influence adolescent ideation about biologic changes and their subjective meaning or affective significance, within a two-category model describing pubertal change in relation to psychological development. Pointing out that although puberty is often considered the beginning of adolescence (confirmed in terms of markers such as menarche), the end of adolescence is even less clear and often may have been completed long before most definitions would indicate. Petersen and Taylor provide a context for an organized scrutiny of relationships between biological change, modification of psychological systems in the individual, and the effects of variations in socialization and sociocultural factors on the process of modification. Within a focus on psychological and psychobiological adaptation to puberty, models of pubertal maturation and of psychological development are divided in two general categories: (1) direct-effects models, where psychological effects are directly connected to physiological sources, and (2) mediated-effects models, which connect psychological effects of puberty to mediation by chains of intervening variables (culturally influenced or socially controlled).

Within this second model of cognitive mediations of psychological adaptation to puberty, the inner representational world of the adolescent is pertinent. Biological developments received into an adolescent's ideational, attributional, or representational context may be imbued with various affective meanings. However, it is not the biological occurrence but the subjective stimulus value and the significance attributed to it that determines the effect on the adolescent. Interpretation of the meaning of the changes is based on situational cues derived from the immediate circumstances of the subject or from the subject's own behavior. Hence, Petersen and Taylor suggest that it is important to codify potential variables that influence the adolescent's ideation about his biological changes and their subjective meaning or affective significance. These variables include (1) childhood patterns of thought and feeling, (2) parental and peer attributions, and (3) publicly shared ideas about pubertal events or their symbolic significance.

An Interactionist Position

David Ausubel (1954), recognizing the combined forces of the biological and the social on the adolescent, adopted an interactionist position that attributes development to processes involved in the interaction between nature and development. Ausubel regards the adolescent transition period as one of thoroughgoing reorganizaton of the personality structure, deriving from a shift in the adolescent's biosocial status. Since Ausubel considers the essence of maturation to be the achievement of volitional independence and primary status, the task of the adolescent is thus to attain economic independence, learn a biological sex role, and achieve emancipation from the parents. Ausubel sees the parent as playing the role of the cultural representative, thus motivating the child's bid for extrinsic status.

Ausubel defines a series of ego reorganizations that starts in infancy. The newborn, in the dependent state, fantasizes himself as omnipotent and volitionally independent inasmuch as all demands are met on his command. However, these exaggerated feelings of power and independence change at age two or three as he recognizes his dependence. His ego recognizes itself through acceptance of his satellite role and his condition of derived status. Since it behooves him to be in his parents' good graces, he internalizes parental values. Learning becomes the product of identification with the person on whom he is dependent. When he leaves the home at school age, he continues to be dependent. Now status with his peers depends on performance—not on what he is, but on what he does. According to Ausubel, this preadolescent condition is one of volitional dependence: status is derived. Essentially, Ausubel depicts the road of maturation as emerging from omnipotent volitional independence to achievement of the equivalent of derived status previously experienced in a state of volitional independence.

Insofar as Ausubel finds urban culture not organized to provide the adolescent opportunity for external status, he proposes that the peer group serves this function. Here the adolescent can desatellize and leave the derived status of the parents in order to resatellize and achieve primary status. Levels of aspiration, a part of maturational progress, are based on cultural expectations. Adolescents are expected to mature at a certain rate; if not, they face the possible loss of status and of advantages otherwise accruing from successful maturation. Anxiety can be reduced only by suitable evidence of maturation, which in turn gives rise to appropriate levels of aspiration. If the culture induces low levels of aspiration, the adolescent is disinclined to seek out role-playing experience propitious for personality development. When the cultural unavailability of adult status is extreme, it retards personality maturation even more directly.

Societal Poles on the Continuum

The societal, rather than the biological, pole of the theoretical continuum is represented by those who subscribe to a view of adolescence as but one period falling within the spectrum of continuous developmental periods. Factors embedded within the cultural context and general societal climate are seen as forces more instrumental to the course of the adolescent period than are biological determiners. This group of theorists contends that adolescence is within a continuum of developmental periods and is not one of essential or characteristic difference. Rather, a continuity of social learning from childhood to maturity both in and out of the home is seen as the elicitor, shaper, and maintainer of behavior patterns evident in modified terms even much later in life (Bandura and Walters 1963). Positively reinforced behavior remains in the repertoire; negative reinforcement discourages maintenance. The process and vicissitudes of adolescent behavior are seen as externally, not internally, based.

Bandura's study of adolescent boys in middle-class families (1964) opposed widely held tenets of Sturm and Drang. His findings revealed that:

1. External controls had been lightened, inasmuch as boys had already internalized parents' values and standards of behaviors to a large degree.
2. Since boys adopted parental standards of conduct as their own, they did not regard parents as adversaries but as supportive guiding influences.

3. Emancipation from parents had been more or less completed, rather than initiated, at adolescence. Hence, development of independence seemed more of a conflict for parents than for the adolescent.
4. The peer group often served to reinforce the parental norms.

The last finding was similar to that of Elkin and Westley a decade earlier (1955).

Bandura considered the Sturm and Drang concept to be based on generalizations of deviant adolescent myths allowed by the mental-health professions and reinforced by the mass media (since the deviant adolescent is of greater functional value to the mass media than is the typical high-school student). Adolescent idiosyncratic fashions and interests are held to be no different than the fads of the latency-age child or, on an adult level, those of the slavish follower of Parisian couturiers. With respect to those adolescents whose behavior is characteristic of Sturm and Drang, Bandura argues that this defiant oppositional pattern was probably present all along but that physical size contained its expression until the adolescent years. With the achievement of a power reversal and a decrease of parental importance as a source of reward, adolescent acting out is subject to a minimum of sanction.

Theorists clustering near this opposite pole of the controversy are regarded as supporting a position in which adolescence is considered a continuation of development that began at birth and in which variations of developmental pattern are equally possible at any point. Societal factors are held to be prime determinants of behavior. For example, Daniel Offer (1969) took exception to the conception of turmoil and imbalance as a component of—or the essence of—adolescence. In order to offset the lack of systematic and/or longitudinal studies in research on normals by followers of the psychoanalytic model, he examined the relative influences of internal psychological and external environmental factors on the functioning of typical adolescents over a four-year period.

His findings generally refute the Sturm and Drang conception of adolescence. Stability rather than change is seen as the overriding characteristic in the psychological pattern of the reaction of these model adolescents. The ideal parent is seen as parallel to their own parents and in general 88 percent thought that they were disciplined fairly. Notable was the lack of report of any emotional or physical trauma. Although some rebellious behavior was manifested at ages twelve and thirteen, school and studying were the most important areas of conflict. Determination of vocational and educational goals presented the most difficult problems to resolve. Teacher influence was small. Criticism of the 1969 study stressed the unrepresentativeness of the sample and the lack of direct observation in a methodology that included interviewing, projective tests, and self-reports of perceptions. In Offer's later account (1974) of a ten-year longitudinal study of fifty-one of the seventy-three students who served as subjects when they were in high school, three alternative models of developmental paths through normal adolescence were offered as more typical than a singular Sturm and Drang model. Once again, the methodology utilized was psychiatric interviewing and self-report, self-image questionnaires for data collection. Cluster analysis was the method of analysis. All three groups were considered normal and well adjusted. The first route, characterized by continuous growth, is favored by a genetic and environmental influence of no traumatic experience. The second developmental route, surgent or "wavelike" growth with a cycle of progression and regression, is characterized by more rocky relationships with parents. This route belongs to a less confident individual of uneven genetic and environmental influence. Death and separation have been experienced. The third route is tumultuous and is the most similar to the adolescence conceptualized by the psychoanalytic posture. Here, backgrounds are less stable, characterized by overt problems such as mental hospitalizations and broken homes. Except for the tumultuous group, relationships between parents and adolescents are satisfactory. Dependence on peer group was strongest in the tumultuous group. Offer conceptualizes normality along a bell-shaped curve. It is seen as a transactional system that involves the integration of biosocial variables over time. He substitutes a continuum of shades of development for a black-white polarity.

The 1950s and 1960s

The adolescent literature of the late 1950s and 1960s also addressed the biologic or societal controversy from an indirect perspective through the contributions of those individuals who dealt with the stunning adolescent group phenomena of the era. We have earlier discussed how the literature is divided between conceptualizing rebellion as a defensive effort to handle threatening libidinal forces, as opposed to a manifestation of the continuity of earlier problems that can now be acted out with greater strength, or as a directly manifested response to a perceived social influence and/or condition. The literature of the late 1950s and 1960s was also concerned with sociological manifestations—the phenomena of protest movements and alienated behavior. Contributors to this literature—the alienation theorists—reflect varying positions with respect to the phenomenon of adolescent rebellion.

Richard Flacks (1967) contrasts conditions of the late 1950s and early 1960s with historical reminders from sociologists such as Veblen, Eisenstadt, and Coser. Students and young intellectuals in particular pursue change and/or opposition under two sets of conditions: (1) when the marketplace cannot offer jobs commensurate with their training and abilities, and (2) when the values that accompanied their development are no longer in harmony with what they consider to be their developing social reality. These were not the conditions that prevailed in the early 1960s, which witnessed the emergence of organized protest and activism. In fact, during the 1950s sociologists and social psychologists recounted the decline in political commitment and the rise in security-oriented conformity, particularly among the young. A variety of studies reported students as overwhelmingly unconcerned with value questions, highly complacent, status oriented, privatized, and uncommitted.

The phenomena of the protest movements have been attributed by alienation theorists of the 1950s and 1960s, generally concerned with sociological manifestations, to (1) the advanced technological structure of American society (Goodman 1956; Friedenberg 1963); (2) the interactional effects of societal structure and consequent familial patterning, as when the involvement of the father in his occupation leaves the raising of children to the mother, with the concomitant effects of estrangement of father and children and overinvolvement of mother (Keniston 1965); and (3) to a living out rather than a rebellion against parents values (Keniston 1967; Flacks 1967). Proponents of this general view ascribe overt adolescent behavioral response to component societal conditions. Varying combinations of parental postures were postulated—for example, the parents as "the good guys," either absenting themselves or being unwilling to take a position against which the adolescent might test out different values and new thinking. The absence of a place in a highly technological society for real contributions was held to contribute to the abdication by youth of the 1950s and 1960s of efforts toward finding meaning in a society that did not make room for them (Goodman 1956; Friedenberg 1963).

Alienation experienced both personally and from the greater society was suspect as a factor in the cessation of efforts by scores of adolescents to complete the necessary adolescent-stage tasks. Kenneth Keniston (1965) depicted life in modern society as divided into compartments for cognitive work and instrumental values quite separate from the rest of life. Since the former assumes primary importance, commitment to adult life in such a society is seen by youth as submission. Keniston offered a clinical portrait of a segment of adolescent youth who handle their adolescent conflicts by "turning in" rather than "turning out," distinguishing between "rebels with a cause" (activists) and "rebels without a cause" (the uncommitted). For the adolescent who handles conflicts by turning inward rather than acting out, the self is defined by perception, not action. Whatever conscious meaning life has for this select group is through immediacy, experience in the "cult of the present." A search for identity is abdicated in favor of a search for sentience. Adulthood asks too high a price—the relinquishment of fantasized and immediate satisfactions to an older society that dissociates and subordinates the expressive aspect of life. Keniston's analytic interpretation depicts adolescence as an interruption of normal growth. His thesis is that we have allowed technology to reign and that it has exacted a heavy human toll; that it has cultivated a new alienation defying the historical criteria of poverty, exclusion, sickness, oppression, and lack of choice or opportunity.

Although the literature just discussed suggests that discontinuities both within society and within individuals are the stimuli to the two faces of rebellion—activism and alienation—other formulations on adolescence regard protest as the manifestation of the adolescent desire for continuity with parents. Westby and Braungart (1966) contend that students were attempting to fulfill and renew the political traditions of their families and were not converts from or rebelling against the political perspectives of their families. Rather consistently, individuals involved in protest reported that their parents held views essentially similar to their own and accepted or supported their activities. Flacks (1967) suggested that activism may be related to a complex of values shared by students and their parents. His research also emphasizes that family socialization and other antecedent experiences can be determinants of student protest. Keniston's (1967) review of the literature on student protest concludes that activists are not repudiating or rebelling against explicit parental values and ideologies, but that there is some evidence that such students are living out their parents values in practice.[4] Paradoxically, cultural discontinuity and desire for continuity can both be seen as contributors to adolescent rebellion. Although the manifest rebellion must be considered within a framework larger than response to biological instincts alone, the decline of both protest and alienation implies that such behaviors are adolescent in character rather than a manifestation of character carried over into maturity.

The 1970s into the 1980s

Braungart (1980), unlike those earlier writers who support notions of generational conflict, suggests in his generational-unity theory that youth are not rebelling against society but, instead, are creating new forms of a consciousness partially resulting from generational and social-structural forces. In her review of the literature, Judith Gallatin (1980) concludes that given methodological limitations of field research and the mass of semidigested data, it is difficult to reach definitive conclusions about political socialization during adolescence. She does, however, tentatively cite a few trends: (1) adolescents have an overall grasp of political issues and concepts that seems to increase markedly between early and late adolescence; (2) parents do influence youngsters' ideals toward politics; and (3) most adolescents are interested, but few are active.

In a review of the literature that brings historical forces to the expressed values of modern day adolescents, Conger (1976) suggests that deeply personal values such as love, friendship, self-expression, and the importance of education have not been abdicated by today's youth, but that more traditional values have been juxtaposed alongside them. Resulting is a continuing call for self-fulfillment, sexual freedoms, equality, and so forth, but within a context of a more pragmatic approach to life. For those youth more advantaged economically, there seems to be a seeking of own goals and directions apart from what was in the prior decade a consistent confrontation of the ills of the system. According to Conger's review, these deeply personal values expressed by college youth in the 1960s have indeed survived. In the early 1970s they were generally in the same proportion between college and blue-collar youth. In other words, he suggests that since the 1960s there has been a diffusion of new values of the 1960s to noncollege youth. Many youth still express views that can be considered those of alienation to the system; fewer youth appear as identified with their own generation for more grandiose value purposes. But although youth of the 1970s appear more related to their own lives, they have not set aside the questions raised by the 1960s. These issues are embedded in their generally more sophisticated perspective.

Cognitive Dimensions

The field of cognitive development is distinguished by Jean Piaget's extensive investigations and his theory of the emergence of logical thought, within which we find an understanding of adolescent manifest behavior from a framework of cognitive capacities still under development. Prior to adolescence, intellectual activity was involved initially with sensorimotor equipment and later with the achievement of the ability to hold the concrete image in mind, to abstract the concrete image. The advent of adolescence, according to Piaget, heralds the development of an abrupt broadening of intellectual scope, with the ability to think in abstract terms and to hold in mind all the possible combinations in a system. The final achievement of formal operational thought enables the adolescent not only to conceptualize his own thought, but also to conceptualize the thought of others. In this initial period of the broadening process, however, there is a failure to distinguish between one's own acts and those of another. The adolescent, therefore, assumes that others are as obsessed with his behavior as he is. Piaget offers two mental constructions to explain the adolescent cognitive status. These constructions are manifested in behavior as the adolescent reacts to (1) an "imaginary audience" to whom he is as important as he is to himself, and (2) a "personal fable" of uniqueness and immortality, which gives rise to behavior reflecting his increasing sense of power and ability. On the one hand, the adolescent is limited by the sense of being in the limelight;

on the other hand, he experiences a new sense of freedom and power wherein reality is secondary to possibility. Absent is the framework of yesterday that bounded his previously more limited abilities. The adolescent's cognitive status is manifested behaviorally as the adolescent alternates between dreamer and innovator, recluse and socializer, between extreme self-involvement and outward egotism and altruism.

According to Piagetan theory, the adolescent is caught in this egocentrism. The cognitive task is to decenter and thereby complete the gradual move away from egocentrism that began in infancy. Decentering involves a process of continual refocusing of perspective and the acquisition of multiple perspectives. The final stage, which manifests itself in a clear perception of reality and the adolescent's place in it, involves enlarging the perspective toward objectivity and acceptance of the elements of reciprocity. Like the theorists of the affective domain of the previous discussion, Piaget sees the peer group as the available arena in which to work at this task.

Youth is transformed from idealistic dreamer to achiever as he slowly reconciles thought and experience. An adolescent world in which all is possible and in which he is willing to take on unlimited challenges is tempered only by the advance of time and the impact of consistent realities. In the process, affective innovations parallel intellectual transformations. Piaget theorizes that the presence of a life plan changes the emotional force in behavior and subordinates affective whim to adoption of social role. Thus, it is professional work or the pursuit of it that restores equilibrium. The scale of values acts as the affective organizer complementing the cognitive organizations necessary to undertake the work. Piaget concludes that affective and cognitive acquisitions must be regarded in tandem. To understand the intellectual functioning of the adolescent, it is necessary to place this functioning within the frame of reference of the total personality, just as understanding personality growth requires us to understand the transformation of thinking.

Keating's (1980) recent review of literature on adolescent cognitive thought raises some questions about whether adolescent thinking does in fact differ from that of children. Beyond the obvious, but important, performance descriptions, Keating questions the accuracy of the account of the change given by the Inhelder and Piagetan theoretical model.

Moral Development

Lawrence Kohlberg (1970) has observed the preoccupation of adolescents with formulating ideals for bringing order and value to their lives. He investigated moral development in the adolescent within a framework of moral judgment, not conduct. Building on stage notions of development, he formulated a typology of definitive and universal levels of development in moral thought, with two stages within each.[5] As in Piaget's (1965) formulation, each stage is a higher cognitive organization than the one before, taking into account everything in the preceding stage but with new distinctions and organizations. The stages represent an invariant developmental sequence. In the first stage the child interprets labels of good and bad in terms of physical consequences. The second level adds maintaining, supporting, and justifying the social order. The third level that the adolescent can reach, the postconventional, reveals an involvement in autonomous moral principles whose validity does not relate directly to the concrete groups or individuals who identify with those ideas. Congruent with Piaget's notion of the development of abstract thought, Kohlberg defined the third level as one in which the moral conceptualizations are not necessarily applied systems, but can exist independently and in juxtaposition to conflicting moral statements, abstract and ethical rather than concrete, with an awareness of the relativism of personal values and opinions. Kohlberg's formulation corresponds to Piaget's developmental scheme of logical structures and is consonant with the behavioral manifestations accompanying the adolescent's new cognitive world: an upsurge in feelings of power and a readiness to evaluate and compose new systems for society. The adolescent's newly acquired ability to think about thoughts permits him to pass beyond the world of reality to the world of possibility. Kohlberg reported data from cross-cultural research in Mexico, Taiwan, Yucatan, and Turkey that support the nature of the sequence, notwithstanding that rate of development is affected by varying social, cultural, and religious conditions.

Hoffman (1980) offers a theoretical overview of three approaches to moral development: (1) the psychoanalytic theory of rigid early superego; (2) the cognitive-disequilibrium theory, which assumes that young children are not moral and that they operate on a premise of reward and punishment; and (3) the empathy-based theory, whereby experience is limited to immediate situations. All three approaches view the morality of the child as limited. Hoffman suggests that adolescence brings hormonal changes that demand a more appropriate control system. Cognitive disequilibrium, expansive new thinking, and new experiences all pose new contradictions. Hence adolescents begin construction of their own, more viable moral system. Hoffman's conception of an empathy-based morality stresses the importance of the integration of the adolescent's capacity for empathic arousal with the newly emerging cognitive awareness of others as well as of themselves.

Feather (1980) points out that the number of studies linking value content to developmental stages is very limited and that more research is needed, dealing not only with abstract moral values but also with quite general personal and social goals. He recalls that Adelson (1975) has already pointed out that on the basis of research, it is naive to expect a pre- or young adolescent to answer questions about political institutions and ideology because the capacity to manage abstract concepts has not developed sufficiently. Hence, general questionnaires such as "A Value Survey" (Rokeach 1973) may be inappropriate for teenagers since abstract concepts assumed to exist can be formed only in a concrete or rudimentary manner or are not present at all.

A Relevant Theory of Motivation

In contrast to orthodox theories of motivation from which conceptions of adolescent upheaval stem, and which view adolescence as a period of reactivation of primary drives looking for satisfaction and defenses arising to contain them, a brief reference to Robert White's (1959) general cognitive motivational theory of competence effectance is pertinent. Although not addressed to adolescence, White's perceptions of motivation seem to be particularly relevant to that period. According to White, it would be antithetical to development for higher primates, whose learning is slow (Hebb 1949), to be left with just primary drives operant only between periods of satisfaction. White posits a more complex picture, including needs that remain after primary drives have been satisfied, a conception of motives without consummatory response. Neural centers occupy a prime position. Primary drives are augmented by a competence drive whose goal is effectance within a society. This represents what the neuromuscular system wants to do when otherwise unoccupied or when gently stimulated by the environment. Although primary drives yield consummatory response, effectance motivation that serves the competence drive does not. Satisfaction comes in the affective experience of competence. Seen in this way, the effectance drive augments the action of the primary drives. Significant to our concern is White's contention that effectance motivation singularly aims for feelings of efficacy, not for the learnings that are its consequences: it is affectively based. Motives for exploration, novelty, activity, and mastery are all placed within the concept, involved in an intrinsic need to deal with the environment to serve effective rather than consummatory needs. White's formulation contributes to an expansion of the motivational framework in adolescence to include neural factors along with tissue needs as lending a goal-oriented discriminating quality to behavior. Forces for competence effectance must be included among the components considered in understanding affective response to a new and seemingly capricious transitional environment.

Values and morality are influenced by historical influences and political events, which gives added cogency to Elder's (1980) criticism of the literature's paucity of historical perspectives. Raising the question of our ability to measure objectively without knowledge of historical and social influences, he frames the more challenging issue of the presumption of attempting to understand the psychosocial development of youth without knowlege of life course and historically episodic collective experience. Most longitudinal studies pay scant attention to social change. Elder's review of the literature suggests that the 1960s brought change in life-span conception that in turn has led to change in attitudes toward historical perspectives since then.

Consensus and Challenge

Adopting and further incorporating a historical and life-span perspective on adolescent development does juxtapose some universals next to a transitional period otherwise regarded as idosyncratic. The literature is indeed unequivocal in grouping adolescents as experiencing similar slow, incremental transitions to adulthood on physical, emotional, and cognitive dimensions. More accurately, there appears an ebb and tide for each adolescent so different from that of his coadolescents that the impact of the change is, paradoxically, experienced on a solitary level along with chronological age mates.

This abbreviated reference to the pertinent areas of focus in the rich adolescent literature suggests a continuing theoretical dialogue about the major causal influences in the adolescent developmental posture as well as about the tasks of the period. Although distinct theoretical divisions exist, the adolescent development literature generally depicts a transitional youth, buffeted by powerful developmental advances in physical, emotional, and cognitive capacities. No domain is separate from developments in the other domains. The task of adolescence has been set forth as integration of advances in the various domains into socialized behaviors that will meet adult roles and responsibilities. Physical, emotional, and cognitive forces, as well as characteristics of the immediate and greater social milieus are a continuing focus of the literature. Behavioral manifestations of compliance, protest, and/or alienation have been attributed to individual and/or societal causation. An interactionist perspective is now, strictly speaking, a basic assumption rather than a theoretical posture. The current task is to establish periods of impact; to determine the precise locations of primary impact; to identify and understand the processes at play; and, if necessary, to reorient theoretically.

Notes

1. "Sturm und Drang" was a movement by a group of young German writers who sought to free themselves from accepted standards through literary innovation. Followers of Rousseau, they inaugurated a new type of political thinking that judged society against the measure of personal life and inner need. They valued all theory only insofar as it corresponded with experience, with heightened consciousness of being vital beings. The distinctive characteristics of this movement are most often found in its poetry. Sturm und Drang is considered a harbinger of nineteenth-century romanticism and realism (Pascal 1967).

2. In his initial formulation, Blos (1962) described a different process for the female, who selects a "crush," usually of the same sex, whom she can love passionately.

3. This vital contribution has essentially not been developed further in the adolescent literature. It has been dealt with in the social-psychological literature and will be discussed in chapter 6.

4. Keniston hypothesized that activists seem to possess an unusual capacity for nurturant identification. He finds a similarity between the protest and aliented families. In the alienating family the mother-son relationship is characterized by maternal control and intrusiveness, whereas in the protest-prompting family the mother is a high individuating force in her son's life, pushing him to independence and autonomy. The student of alienation is determined to avoid the fate of his father; the protestor wants to live out the values the father has not worked hard enough to practice (1967).

5. Early studies of moral character in the United States were studies of honesty, service, self-control (Hartshorne and May 1928-1930), responsibility, friendliness, and moral courage (Havighurst and Taba 1949). An important but surprising finding was that character cannot be taught. Findings also disclosed that cheating is situational and not a function of character.

4 The Adolescent Peer Group: Prevailing Views

Adolescence has been described in earlier chapters as a period of transition; a time of acquisition of a new sense of physical, emotional, and intellectual capacities; and as a period of experimentation during which few former guides or guideposts retain relevance. The majority of theoretical formulations have suggested that a selected group of peers becomes important to the adolescent during this period. In the interests of juxtaposing multiple perspectives on the adolescent peer group, we have separated the theoretical notions on adolescent peer groups to be discussed in this chapter from the more inclusive formulations on adolescence addressed in the previous chapter. Although this separation may interrupt continuity of conceptual thought in some instances, it does serve to bring together a variety of notions on miscellaneous aspects of peer-group theory that are pertinent to the chapters that follow.

Affective Environmental Functions

Some theorists have suggested that in a sophisticated, age-segregated, technologically oriented Western culture, the peer group is of necessity the only arena in which important adolescent needs are met. Generally, theoretical formulations of the functions served by adolescent peer groups in the course of the developmental process seem to vary in their emphases between being viewed as serving (1) affective environmental functions, (2) interactional functions, and (3) end functions. Josselyn (1952), a theorist in the psychoanalytic tradition, emphasizes affective environmental functions. She proposes that the peer group represents an island apart, to which to flee when panic arises as a result of unresolved conflicts or when one is frightened by the need either to express or to repress an impulse. The peer group provides support. Josselyn sees the sudden inability to handle love and hostility toward the same love object—the parent—as reflected in the adolescent relationship with friends. At times the adolescent needs to be reassured of acceptance, and any behavior is accepted as if acceptance were the price paid to maintain security. At other times, restrictions imposed by the friendships give rise to feelings of loss of individuality. But fear of rejection stands next to anger at the demands. Josselyn suggests that the adolescent is more ready to adapt to the standard of the group than to those of parents since concession to peers does not mean surrender. There is the opportunity to agree while still maintaining independence. Direct concordance to parents would exact the exorbitant price of continued dependency. Therefore, what superficially appears as slavish allegiance to the standards of the membership group actually meets the adolescent's need for escape from a dependence that has become painful. Other thinkers whose formulations fall within an affective environmental function conceptualize the peer group variously as the only arena provided by an otherwise rejecting society (Friedenberg 1959; Goodman 1956; Bronfenbrenner 1970); as a way station on the path to maturity (Keniston 1965); as an atmosphere in which reversion to childhood ways would be acceptable (Gesell 1956); as a family substitute in which libido can be transferred in the process of sexual-identity resolution (analytic theorists); as an atmosphere for social play (Erikson 1950); as an arena for external control (Erikson 1950; Josselyn 1952); or as a haven away from external pressures (Newman and Newman 1976).

Although these theorists developed notions on the affective environmental function that the peer group serves as an arena away from home, still others emphasized the peer group's interactional function. They saw peer-group functioning as a setting in which to discover limits and powers and assess new value systems, as well as a setting in which to try out new roles.

Interactional Functions

Erik Erikson (1950, 1968) is representative of theorists who see complex Western society as having no place for the adolescent, in sharp contrast to simpler and/or more primitive societies wherein the physically mature adolescent is incorporated into adult society and offered a functional role. Erikson argues that a peer group is formed of necessity. The peer is charged with providing a substitute structure in which important needs can be played out, identity formation can begin to take place, and the danger of role diffusion can be skirted. Emotional support can be elicited from peers since a peer stand-in for the parent is in many ways asked to provide substitute functions as adolescents integrate newly experienced changes and struggle with apparent or real loss of identity. Eager to be affirmed by peers, they are ready to be confirmed by rituals, creeds, and programs, and are available to engage in role play.

Erikson argues that the peer group affords the necessary peers to serve various crucial needs:

1. They can use one another to protect themselves against apparent loss of identity.

2. They can fall in love with one another. Adolescents arrive at definition of own identity through a process of projection, reflection, and clarification (this explains why young love involves so much conversation).
3. They can form cliques that provide emotional support.

Defining one's identity is facilitated by projecting one's own diffused ego image onto another peer and seeing it reflected and gradually clarified. The adolescent receives feedback in the task from the judgments of others at this period of rapid change. Since judgments fluctuate with the alteration of contextual peer values, the currency of one's behavior affects one's judgment by other peers. Contiguity to adolescent peers is essential to keeping abreast of changing peer values and to the process of simultaneous reflection and observation by which the adolescent assesses and evaluates himself through his perceptions of how others judge him. Adolescent needs are seen juxtaposed against a modern technological society that Erikson finds so specialized as to obviate a place for the adolescent. This societal condition, together with adolescent psychological needs, contributes to the rationale for what is well known as Erikson's concept of the psychosocial moratorium and the creation of a forum of peers for the type of interchange with others and self-reflective contemplation that carry potential for eventual consolidation.

Reformulations of Erikson's conception of adolescence by Newman and Newman (1976) emhasize the power of social cues in the adolescent struggle. They have divided Erikson's adolescent stage into two discrete stages: one extending from the onset of puberty and ending with graduation from high school, and the other beginning at approximately eighteen years of age and continuing until age twenty-one or twenty-two. For the former stage, which they call early adolescence, they posit a psychosocial crisis of group identity versus alienation. The psychosocial crisis of the second stage is one of individual identity versus role diffusion. Since they view Freud as focusing on the entire period, Coleman and Piaget as describing the high-school period, and Erikson to be discussing the college-aged person, they consider that their second stage closely parallels Erikson's conceptualization of the entire period of adolescence—hence the need for a discrete early stage. In addition to pressure from within, external pressure to join the peer group is seen as emanating from three sources: the family, age-mates, and the school. Parents may try to encourage or discourage certain associations. Age-mates also expect the adolescent to make some kind of peer commitment that allows for neat cataloging in a group. Such an individual is apparently more easily dealt with than is the adolescent who does not affiliate, is less acceptable to the social system, and remains aloof and unidentified. The Newmans consider that the school itself is the final source of pressure for peer-group identification since its organization is such that categorization by peer group allows for smooth role assignments within the school as well as creating groups of students of more manageable sizes. This evidence of strong pressure from three influential sources indicates that the adolescent need for acceptance and approval from peers is not only internal.

Newman and Newman suggest that the central process that occurs in the peer group is peer pressure. The experience of this pressure provides the context for resolution of the adolescent crisis. A rise in tensions may be experienced on any one of a number of varying dimensions for which there are peer expectations of conformity. Although the peer group exerts pressures for conformity, it is generally seen as supportive and flexible toward eccentricities of group members, providing a haven as well as an atmosphere for trying out adult roles. If the costs become too emotionally potent, however, the adolescent may withdraw and not open himself up to necessary group pressures. Then he will not establish the sense of group identity that these authors see as central to the psychosocial growth of the stage. At a time when the adolescent is seriously engaged in a process of self-evaluation for which he needs peers, he may experience alienation from peers and some degree of self-depreciation. The Newmans contend that positive resolution of the conflict between group identity and alienation occurs when the adolescent perceives an existing group that seems to meet his social needs. The perceived sense of group belonging supports and facilitates psychological growth and serves as an integrating force for successful resolution of developmental tasks. Newman and Newman stress that resolution of this psychosocial crisis is not dependent on relationships between adult and adolescent but is heavily dependent on interaction of adolescent and peers. They emphasize the necessity for identifying a group of like others and then sustaining membership. Resolution of the stage of early adolescence is determined by the achievement of this sense of group identity. The second stage of adolescence witnesses the resolution of a sense of personal identity and autonomy from family.

David Ausubel's position (1954, 1977) is grounded in a conception of the close relationship between biology and society. He subscribes to a position of interactionism that attributes development to processes involving an interaction between nature and environment. Ausubel conceptualizes adolescence as a thoroughgoing reorganization of the personality structure due to a shift in the adolescent's biosocial status. He contends that maturation is the achievement of primary status and volitional independence and is clearly incompatible with being a satellite of one's parents. Therefore, the task of the adolescent—achievement of volitional independence and primary status—is related to attainment of economic independence, learning the biological sex role, and thereby achieving emancipation from parents. Like Erikson, Ausubel stresses adolescent tasks in an urban culture not organized to provide the opportunity for external status for the adolescent. Both authors offer the peer group as a place wherein adolescent tasks can be worked out, or at least begun. Ausubel, however, suggests that in order to resatellize, the adolescent must desatellize, notwithstanding warnings of limitations that are inherent in the process of desatellization through resatellization: (1) lowering of standards (since peer-group standards become substituted for adult standards), and (2) restraint of the exploratory learning orientation because of the need to conform to the peer group.

Not all adolescents mature and achieve primary status and volitional independence. Ausubel describes two types of nonsatellizers: (1) the overvalued child who has no opportunity to exercise his own volitional independence and may suffer from a loss of self-esteem because of this very limitation, and (2) the rejected child, who, by contrast, is usually overdominated and obliged to adhere to stringent standards of behavior. The nonsatellizer's self-esteem becomes wholly a creature of environmental vicissitudes that can either deny or gratify the exalted ego aspirations on which he has staked his value as a human being. Although the satellizer's extrinsic self-esteem may be damaged by status deprivation during adolescence, Ausubel contends that this injury tends to be peripheral because of a residual core of intrinsic self-acceptance. In addition, the satellizer experiences the ego support and "we" feeling that is derived from the act of dependent identification with and self-subordination to group interests.

Peer-group interactions are viewed by the aforementioned theorists as a path to rejecting earlier means of value transmission through parents and culture onto one's own ego system. With a slightly different perspective on its interactional function, the peer group is considerd a source for intellectual decentering since it provides a real opportunity to experience genuine feedback on emerging concepts and actions (Piaget and Inhelder 1958). The process of decentering, as Piaget and Inhelder suggest, involves continual refocusing of perspective and the acquisition of multiple perspectives. This occurs both in thought processes and in social relationships. It takes place for the adolescent in the peer group as he tests his thinking against the responses of acknowledged real fellow travelers. The strength of the peer group for the adolescent is that it functions as a real audience, in contrast to the "imaginary audience" that characterizes adolescent thought. Hence an interim reality is projected. Manifest behavior may reflect acquisitions of either the affective or the cognitive domain or the interaction of the two, since Piaget and Inhelder suggest that no separation from the relative impacts of affective and cognitive acquisitions is possible in assessing outward behavior. Actions accompanied by slow reconciliation of thought and experience eventually transform youth from idealistic dreamers to achievers. The peer group offers initial opportunities for this transformation.

End Functions

Theorists have also focused on the end functions served by membership in a peer group. It has been presented as a place offered to work out self-definition (Friedenberg 1959); as the setting in which to work through the adolescent developmental task of identity in love and in work (Erikson 1968; Blos 1962); as the arena within which one becomes free from the bondage of egocentric thought (Piaget and Inhelder 1958); and as a subsociety that can serve the needs of a transition period with interests and responsibility far removed from real responsibility. This last focus was the outcome of seminal work by James Coleman (1961) on what he came to term the *adolescent society*. Coleman investigated adolescent-peer-group influence in shaping attitudes and interests. His theme is that industrial society spawned a peculiar phenomenon most evident in the United States but emerging also in other Western societies—adolescent subcultures with values and activities quite distinct from those of adult society. Industrialization and rapid change put parents out of touch with the times, rendering their parenting skills obsolete. On the one hand, the period of necessary training for assumption of adult roles had been extended; on the other, traditional systems of child rearing are no longer deemed appropriate. Coleman's observation that industrial society had made the high school a social system of adolescents stimulated investigation into status systems extant in ten midwestern high schools. Analysis of survey data collected by Coleman yielded a picture of contemporary adolescent society in which adolescent values dominated the status ladder and parental concern was secondary. Teacher influence was negligible. Although contributions to superordinate goals determined male status, individual female aspirations were toward social success. Social success for females took the form of activities leader in schools with students of higher economic status, and of good looks at lower socioeconomic levels. For boys, athletic ability was the primary value, regardless of socioeconomic level. Scholastic achievement was secondary. Attributes or talents that were functional to immediate peer preoccupations were valued, whereas future-related behavior of little immediate group value was not. The need to be "in" was found to be far more taxing to the adolescent than the academic strain parents are worried about. Coleman concluded that the pertinent factor in determining status derived from service to the adolescent community. In fact, he recommended a revision of high school activities so that scholastic achievement might assume a service function, as in interschool competition. Criticism of Coleman's findings centered primarily around research techniques that seemed to maximize chances for adult-adolescent differences and for an impression that the only important influence on adolescents came from peers. Douvan and Adelson's (1966) survey of adolescents lent support to this skepticism. Yet although Coleman's methodology was subject to attack and some of his findings questioned, he pioneered an area that stimulated later empirical study on adolescent peer groups and on the relative influence of parents as opposed to peers. Research of the 1960s on dimensions of parent-peer influence covered such topic areas as religious ideologies (Putney and Middleton 1960); social behaviors such as drinking and smoking (Bealer, Willets, and Maida 1964); selections of friends (Epperson 1964); and advice seeking (Bandura 1964; Elkin and Westley 1955).

In the discussion of his study undertaken in the previous decade on a specific instance of parent-peer cross-pressure, Rosen (1955) highlighted attention to a contaminating variable that may be present and influential in data collected on the relative proportions of parent and peer influence. Although he acknowledged what Coleman later was criticized for not recognizing—that adolescents may have referents other than parents—Rosen nevertheless restricted his study specifically to parents and peers. Since his sample was small and ethnic and his subject esoteric, his results are not easily generalizable. He offered an important observation, however; when a significant relationship exists between the attitudes of the adolescent and those of his family, the relationship is more marked when attitudes of the peer group cohere with those of the family. His data were also consistent when attitudes of peers differed from those of family. The attitude of the adolescent was more closely related to the norm of peers than to that of parents. Rosen cautioned that even in a situation in which parents and peers do not conflict, the importance of peer-group attitudes must be recognized as contributory.[1] (Coleman's influence continued into the 1970s, when research on peer-parent influence focused on areas such as marijuana use).

The emergence in the 1960s of the youth culture, an extended peer-group form, was examined from a number of perspectives. William Burlinghame (1970) organized impressive studies of the youth culture within four complementary theoretical formulations:

1. The first type, theories of changing social fabric, detail the effects of technological progress, industrialization, and transition from a rural to an urban society in which the means of production are no longer visible, and in which the adolescent is left to feel useless on the labor market.

2. Second, theories of threshold and market attribute the emergence of an adolescent youth culture to the product of sheer numbers of adolescents and to high-powered advertising and marketing practices.

3. Theories of an age-level manifestation of the deterioration of adult values maintain that there is no place for idealistic youth who strive for effectance, that the societal bureaucracy thwarts youth and in a dehumanizing manner denies them opportunity and threatens their identity.

Hence, youth are seen as turning to their own youth culture for values and meaning.

4. Psychosocial or ego process theories see the youth culture subsocieties as way stations en route to maturity, where ego synthesis and self-direction can be secured and protection received from both external and internal assault, where identity crystallizes as peer interchange provides feedback to secure each individual's identity and to separate him from his parents.

Burlinghame elaborates on four organizing criteria of youth culture: (1) chronological youth, (2) valuing of social interchange with peers and aspirations for status within the group, (3) readiness to accept group values, and (4) willingness to project some degree of criticism of the older generation. Burlinghame's attitude scale on several aspects of youth culture, administered to thousands of adolescents in diverse settings revealed that (1) the peak of adherence to the youth culture for girls occurs in middle or late junior high, for boys through the tenth grade; (2) for boys, membership in a youth culture means opportunities for risk, action, and danger; (3) to girls it represents an opportunity for social esteem. Social esteem from contemporaries along with supportive family relationships and achievement was found to be one of three factors within the life space contributing to self-esteem. Burlinghame's findings that the less available these gratifications are, the more the culture of age-mates becomes attractive, is generally consistent with conclusions reached earlier by Sherif and Sherif (1964) and later by Gisella Konopka (1966) and Daniel Offer (1969).

Dimensions of Power

The theorists already discussed have focused major attention on functions served by the peer group for the developing adolescent. Fritz Redl (1974) looked at behavior that is a manifestation of the adolescent's response to affiliating with a group. Redl focuses on the power of the peer group. He considers strong adolescent group alliances to be acts of reverse discrimination in response to mass categorization of their developmental stage as "teenage." Hence, as a group, they reject anyone over thirty. Behavior that in an earlier time approximated actions ascribed to delinquent adolescents is now considered normal adolescent behavior. Redl offers three phenomena he considers to be acted out with almost religious blindness: (1) role battle with adults, (2) the phenomena of the childhood imaginary group, and (3) the choreography of the dare. He makes the point that none of the three find their genesis in rebellion but, rather, derive from the experienced weight of the perception of the group focus and from the suction power of the peer-group code. Furthermore, manifestations of an increase of raw aggression, involving rudeness or crudeness and possibly entirely out of harmony with the personality of the adolescent, is not at all independent of the group psychological fallout effect. Hence, the power of the group may also be present in what outwardly appears to be a one-to-one relationship with the adult; this is the "group under the couch" phenomenon. A phenomenon Redl refers to as the "group code value cassette" allows frequent behavior changes since adolescent group codes or values easily supplant one another.

The peer-group code that Redl finds to have major impact on adolescent behaviors can be conceptually linked to generic formulations in David McClelland's (1965) theory of societally based cues as bases for motivation. Redl describes individual behavior that changes easily with a change in adolescent group codes or values. McClelland proposes that all motives are learned and are not experienced as either pleasures or discomforts until linked to societal cues. Hence, the more an individual or society values a motive, the more likely it is to develop. Over time, clusters of expectancies or associations grow up around affective experiences. The strength of a motive is measured by counting the number of associations belonging in this cluster. Motives and strengths of motives do change and usually are likely to occur in an interpersonal setting. A new motive may surface and persist if it is considered a sign of and/or instrumental to membership in a desired reference group.

Whereas Redl (1974) emphasizes rapid value changes in a peer group, Ausubel (1954) refers to lower standards in the peer group than in the adult group. Both positions are congruent with McClelland's (1965) attribution of reduction and/or increase in specific motives to social perceptions. For example, if peers perceive the motive for competence in one another, the result is positive reinforcement to the individually held motive for competence. If the motive is not perceived, reinforcement does not occur, and the motive structure will eventually change. Once identified with a desired reference group, members motivate and reward each other for related thoughts and acts through constant mutual stimulation and reinforcement. New mutually held networks are strengthened as members constantly provide each other with cues to rearrange the associative network. This process reduces the continuity and connections with older, stronger networks. Application of McClelland's formula to peer-group relationships sheds light on Redl's notion of the peer-group value cassette wherein group codes or values easily supplant one another. They might better be viewed as "tryouts" rather than as individually owned or established values. The length of time such values operate in the group, within McClelland's formulation, is mitigated by social cues.

Formulations of peer-group and/or adolescent societies incorporate this notion of societally based cues as a basis for peer-group behavior. For example, as mentioned earlier, James Coleman's (1961) pioneer study of adolescent-peer-group influence .in shaping attitudes, interests, and behavior introduced the view that industrial society had spawned a peculiar phenomenon, an adolescent subculture with values and activities quite distinct from those of adult society. Formulations dealing with peer groups vary, however, with respect to the motivating causes behind affiliation. Their postures range from theories of escape from libidinal impulses to those implicitly incorporating the competence-effectance needs and the need for a "tryout arena."

Behaviors of both individuals and groups stimulated as a function of these gatherings have been explained by some as a simple response to social cues and by others as manifestations of conformity needs and a striving for acceptability. Some formulations persist in limiting the dynamics of the peer group to those of response to the altered relationship between parents and peers. Coleman (1980) suggests that what becomes clear from his review of the literature is that friendship does indeed provide support during adolescence but that it is also associated with tensions and anxiety, especially among girls. Coleman reached the general impression that the peer group appears to exercise less influence on teenagers than adults believe and that the common notion of outright conflict between parents and peers is simply not substantiated by the evidence. Furthermore, he suggests that the peer group be seen in more realistic terms as (1) a source of influence more often congruent with, rather than contrary to, parental values, and (2) a support and reference group playing a major part in situations wherein the family proves inadequate.

Consensual Notions

Representative views from the literature of the adolescent peer group have been presented. Within this variation of emphases, there is general agreement that peer-group society serves transitional needs of the adolescent and provides a framework within which the adolescent can move toward independent functioning, away from the protective and sometimes intrusive environment of childhood. The peer gathering is seen as offering a forum for support, reality feedback, tryout of new roles and skills, and group identification. Although the intrapsychic interactions are not spelled out, some specifics of behaviors are described, and developmental functions are broadly defined.

The formulation to be offered in forthcoming chapters *departs* from the existing literature to suggest that the peer group is the primary forum during adolescence in which development is stimulated and actualized. The peer group and the interactions taking place therein are seen not as convenient or even casual, but as essential. A theory of specific dynamics of peer-group interactions is offered, detailing their sequential activity as well as their role in development. First, however, we will turn to a brief discussion of reference-group theory in order to *place the adolescent peer group within a general framework of relevance.*

Reference-Group Theory

Reference-group theory and research may best be seen as directed toward an understanding of the processes by which people refer themselves to groups, highlighting the social interaction of most individuals with a diversity of persons who make somewhat contradictory demands. It takes into account that one can be influenced by a group without becoming a member of it. We have seen that the adolescent, in a period of physical growth and cognitive and emotional expansion, feels dislocated, buffeted from without and within, lacking a framework and a place in society. The literature provides that the adolescent joins a peer group for a variety of reasons and uses his peers in his own process of development in relation to the task at hand and the presence of unique and distinct influences. Hence, some discussion of reference-group theory is indeed basic to conceptualizing the topography of the adolescent's psychological field and its pertinence to peer interactions.

Hyman and Newcomb were among the pioneers of reference-group theory. Hyman (1942) first explored the concept in investigating questions of self-ranking in terms of comparison with other figures, whereas Newcomb's Bennington study (1948) explored the effects of varying influences in determining the extent to which female students allied themselves with the prevailing college political attitudes. Merton and Rossi brought the ideas and concepts of reference-group theory to prominence in their simplification of two types of reference groups: *membership groups* and *nonmembership groups,* dependent on whether the person is a member of the group (as cited in Hyman and Singer 1968).

Harold Kelley's (1952) later distinction between two categories of reference groups placed conceptions such as Hyman's within the framework of *comparative reference groups,* and conceptions such as Newcomb's within the framework of *normative reference groups.* Kelley describes the two relationships between a person and a group as he defines two corresponding functions of reference groups. A normative function involves setting and enforcing standards and evaluates members based on the degree to which they conform. The second function is comparative—serving as a standard or comparison point against which the person can evaluate himself and others. These two functions may at any time be served by the same group, either the membership or the nonmembership group. Furthermore, one cannot identify another's reference group by observation of the interaction alone. Positive and negative reference groups, as well as reference individuals and reference groups, are also conceptually distinct. Positive reference groups are those to which the member aspires for acceptance, whereas negative groups are those by which he does not want to be treated as a member (Newcomb 1948). The reference group may also be a single person who serves as an ideal or model. When more than one of his roles is related to, the other is a *reference individual* (Merton 1957).

Individuals often have multiple reference groups to which they refer in the process of forming a total picture of self with respect to their own abilities and/or in the process of assembling a total attitudinal constellation. Various reference groups are used, each for a particular point of comparison (Turner 1955). Turner's hypothesis is that only those groups that are relevant to a particular aspect of self-appraisal will be taken as points of comparison. If a group's standing is so high or so low that it is not meaningful, it will not be used as a comparative reference group. In the search for reference groups the individual will keep in mind those groups that can enhance his self-regard or protect his ego (Hyman and Singer 1968; Thibaut and Kelley 1959).

How individuals use each group and which groups they select are issues that reference group theory addresses. In his discussion on the consciousness of self, William James held that the person has as many social selves as there are distinct groups of persons about whose opinions he cares. Furthermore, he generally shows a different side of himself to each of the different groups (in Hyman and Singer 1968). Merton (1957) discusses a condition of "anticipatory socialization" wherein the individual begins to socialize to the norms of the group before experiencing its influence. Litwack's (1960) discussion of social mobility posits multiple references for the group in his "stepping-stone reference orientation," whereby integration in one group is considered a prerequisite for integration into a second group. It thus becomes possible for the individual to view both current membership group and future membership group as reference groups without endangering his integration into the current group and without preventing his joining a different future group. There are costs, however. Prevailing attitudes in the groups may be similar and hence mutually supporting and strengthening; they may also be divisive and conflict producing (Hartley 1968; Rosen 1955).

Of particular pertinence to the adolescent condition of seeking self-insight and identity is that the specific reference group or groups may influence individual behavior by defining the actor's self-conception or identity, specifying appropriate roles or norms, and exercising appropriate sanctions. In order to know which roles or behaviors are appropriate for him, the individual identifies himself in relation to other people or to a position in a social structure. Self-definition occurs in relation to the groups to which he belongs or aspires (Clark 1972).[2] The implications of Jones and Gerard's (1967) concepts of reflected appraisal and effect dependence are appropriate here. Both concepts deal with the affective dimension of the self-image, which results from the individual's perceptions of group reaction. In fact, if group response is congruent on an aspect of self, that aspect of self becomes more resistant to change than any prior perception of group response since conformity to the expectation of the group will aid in securing a position of desirable status and self-identity (Backman, Secord, and Pierce 1963).

Most relevant to an examination of the processes involved in the adolescent task of self-direction are notions that detail the strength of the influence of reference groups in the determination and selection of goals according to objects valued in the reference group, and in standard setting. Standards are set partly through the process of comparing oneself with others but, more often, are based on individuals and groups close at hand than on reference to public figures and groups. Evidence that others like oneself hold the same ambitions is available as a source of courage for necessary risk taking (Turner 1964).

Adolescent Peer Group as Reference Group

The foregoing brief departure into discussion of reference-group theory becomes meaningful as we see that the adolescent peer group can be conceptualized as a reference group. It can be either a membership or nonmembership group; it can function as a negative or a positive reference group; it can provide a normative or comparative function or both. It may or may not be the primary reference group; it exists in relation to other groups or figures with varying degrees of strength. Its selection is a product of individual needs, the social situation, social demands, and the normative orientation as a product of a history of secondary reinforcements.

In adolescence the peer group is functional far beyond being a mere situational effect of society utilized in personal passage between stages. It is a functional entity into which the adolescent needs initiation. The peer group, as reviewed here, meets all the criteria of a reference group, although it is not the only relevant reference group during adolescence.[3] Thus recognition of the reference property of the peer group as a powerful determinant in adolescent progression adds a significant dimension for both the individual and the peer group itself. The conception of the adolescent peer group as a reference group in no way opposes or conflicts with the theoretical conceptions heretofore enumerated; rather, this new dimension expands current contextual views of the peer group.

In light of the adolescent condition of change in several domains simultaneously, the peer group comes to loom as more significant than in earlier developmental periods. That its importance survives throughout the entire period of adolescence suggests a structural position not adequately defined by the individual theorists or by any combination of analyses offered. Such a central emphasis is suggested in the new view of the peer group proposed by Dynamic Functional Interaction and set forth in the following chapter.

Notes

1. This condition was directly addressed in the Adolescent Reference Group Index (ARGI) as part of the Philadelphia Study, in which the measuring instrument was designed to measure the relative degree of influence of varying reference groups on discrete issues. See note 3.

2. Selection of reference groups that represent the "next step up," as found in studies of college students and industrial workers by Turner (1964) and Patchen (1961) may be characteristic of societies with high rates of upward mobility and therefore cannot be broadly generalized. They may, however, be pertinent to the adolescent search for competence.

3. Insofar as the reference-group literature did not contain a reference-group measure for adolescents that reflected the conception of the peer group as one of a number of reference groups, the Adolescent Reference Group Index (ARGI) was developed. The relative influence of discrete categories of peers relative to other prominent reference groups, including parents, was examined. The ARGI was administered to high-school boys who participated in the Philadelphia Study. The conceptual model on which the ARGI was developed extended the potential sources of influence on adolescents to include a broad range of reference groups. Results of the study lent support to the existence of an adolescent reference field rather than to the peer-parent dichotomy that had been reflected in the literature previously. Within this broadened frame of reference, which includes a breakdown of the global peer group, it was also possible to discriminate areas of distinct peer influence rather than a more abstract notion of a global peer presence. Although the continuing primacy of parent and family was underlined, the peer group ranked highest on seven of ten issues. The data supported the premise that the peer group is more than a haven or escape for a adolescent whose mind, body, and views of society are changing. The data lend support to a conceptualization of the peer group as an influential, active body to which immediately pertinent issues are selectively brought. Involvement with peers is not selected because of a paucity of other available sources for relationship but because it is seen as the arena into which to bring relevant concerns. The data imply that adolescents move with directed precision toward that reference group or figure considered to

be most relevant, to have most information, and/or to offer views perceived as most pertinent to the issue in question. The findings revealed a discriminating adolescent selectively seeking influence from the source determined to be functional to his goal (Seltzer 1975, 1980).

5

The Peer Group as a Social Institution: A New Perspective

A New Social Institution

The central developmental role ascribed to the peer experience offers a new perspective on the impact of peer affiliations. The adolescent peer group might well be counted along with the family, the school, and the church among the social institutions of Western society. Social institutions have been examined within the context of social, political, and human needs. Their effectiveness is judged from the point of view of the individual in society, of the institution itself, and of group needs. Any institution is a structural element of a culture or society that cannot be understood without reference to the general society and its other institutions.

Generally, institutions begin in order to satisfy some purpose or need. When individuals congregate in institutional postures, an automatic set of structures and operations is assumed to be put into play and specified actions and interactions are expected to occur (Leslie 1979). Social groups such as the family in which specific roles and role responsibilities have been delineated, have been subject to some rigorous analysis (Parsons 1955). In fact, the debate is still current as to whether a family exists when a couple comes together, or only after natural or adopted offspring enter the picture (Rossi, Kagan, and Harevon 1978).

Although each institution contains an internal structure—one might say a "life of its own"—if institutions were not living, changing, active participants in the culture, they would not serve individual needs and would cease to be viable. The peer group meets critera for a viable institution. As will be demonstrated in following chapters, it functions as a vital structural frame for the adolescent period, generating its own interacting forces. The group changes in its unique force and focus as the adolescent progresses through it. It serves the individual's adjusted needs in a flexible manner.

Studies of the peer group heretofore have not proceeded from an institutional perspective, and the rigorous examination of forces within other institutions has not been extended to an analysis of peer groups. However, the literature does provide an examination of the structure of peer groups, delineating leaders, followers, cliques, subcliques, and larger groupings, as well as a consideration of why peers congregate. Just as matehood and marriage have been examined and attributed to serving the functions of mating and procreation, so the literature reviews reasons for peer-group formation, including separation from parents, tryout of new functions, the need for a sounding board for new ideas, and so forth. However, a conception of the peer group as a social institution that serves specific purposes and must meet definite objectives before the individual is ready to leave the institution has not been advanced. The emphasis placed by Dynamic Functional Interaction on the developmental functions actualized by interacting in a peer group serves to make any description of adolescence that lacks this central structural institution appear hollow.

The absence of this perspective on the peer group may be connected with the customary delineations of social institutions as being based in an assignment of prescribed roles and planned functions, whereas the peer group appears to spring up spontaneously. Historically, however, this is not supportable. In the case of the family, for example, were not its planned functions initially also an outgrowth of a naturally occurring organization grounded in the satisfaction of physical, emotional, and social needs? So, too, the origin of other social institutions may appear structured after the fact, when in truth natural forces may have coalesced to gestate the structure. The theory of Dynamic Function Interaction advances a similar motivational model for the adolescent peer group. Peer congregation and full involvement in the adolescent peer group meets needs that are a necessary part of preparation for adulthood. The fact that the adolescent peer group has not been a subject of rigorous investigation stands in contradiction to its importance.

We have seen in earlier chapters that significant theories have addressed the how and why of the adolescent peer group. Those that dovetail with and/or grow out of a rich psychoanalytic tradition have identified the internally based struggle to cut loose the parent-child bonds. Some of these formulations have identified the peer as the object of choice for support as the adolescent cuts loose old ties and transfers them to a more chronologically appropriate age-mate. Psychosocial formulations advance the notion of the peer group as a place in which adolescents can work on aspects of self-discovery and identity formation. Alternate theoretical approaches posit casual action of environmental determinants rather than internal ones, ranging in derivation from the phenomenon of the Western market system and its advertising techniques to the need to create a subsociety for role play prior to occupying a productive role in a complex culture that demands specialized skills. Still other theorists attribute the strength of adolescent involvement in a youth culture or peer-group association directly to the relative strength of other primary relationships.

These formulations certainly offer insights and shed light on aspects of observable adolescent behavior. But although these theoretical formulations closely examine the adolescent tasks of psychological separation and individuation, as well as the relationship to other adolescent peers, they generally posit the movement toward peers as originating in a negatively stimulated move away from adults. They neither address the need for the "group" aspect of membership in a peer group nor contemplate the sheer numbers involved.

Let us recall from what point the peer-group member arrives. Adolescence is conceptualized not only as a span of years but also as a developmental condition whose determinants are a blend of physical, emotional, and cognitive changes unique to the age. These profound changes, biologically stimulated and manifested in expansive emotional and intellectual energies that themselves swell and constrict as the tide of development uniquely ebbs and flows, give rise to the adolescent condition and its vicissitudes. The condition is unique, however, because at this moment in time (unlike the moments of change in the developmental process of infancy and childhood), along the most basic of dimensions, the adolescent is at sea. Previous boundaries and guideposts no longer are functional. The period is unique in its lack of any framework. In earlier developmental periods, expansion and growth exist within a context of familiar motion and exercise. The adolescent condition is different, however. The adolescent is possessed of new physical and intellectual capabilities that are both mystical and mystifying. He finds himself in a no-man's-land between childhood and adulthood. The allure of the adult world calls and is strong even as the safety of childhood is close and still beckons. Yet neither fits; the one is outgrown, the other not yet encompassable. There is a pervasive sense that this passage demands the integration of both voyager and ground, independently and yet simultaneously. The loneliness, confusion, challenge, and fear—perhaps, more correctly, anxiety—are compounded by these conflicting imperatives.

Contrary to current theory, we suggest that the motive for congregation is not escape and does not signify that the adolescent has no place in the adult world. Rather, there is a need for a group experience to be transacted in preparation for adult life. Thus adolescent congregation, far from being an activity of flight, is in fact an activity of preparation. The peer groups are by no means transitory. The adolescent groups we observe are socially based in our complex Western culture. They stand as protestants to an adult population that has heard but not comprehended their cry of *understand our congregation.* They speak of needs to be served. The need is to congregate.

As the one-room school house and, later the elementary school, middle school, junior high, high school, and college have been incrementally accepted as preparatory to full functioning as an educated adult in a complicated society, so the school has achieved recognition as a bona fide social institution. In this context the adolescent peer group must be seen as another setting—an institution—designed for a developmental experience preparatory to adult functioning. Peers and the peer group serve profound perparatory needs. Seeing this phenomenon only as a vehicle for separation from parents provides a limited perspective. It is an institution that requires passage.

Dynamic Functional Interaction approaches peer congregation as a natural and inevitable occurrence—in fact, as a positive movement. The proclivity of youth to congregate is easily observed and perhaps even puzzling in its apparent strength. The genesis of this new form is consistent with the beginnings of other social institutions. In the history of currently vibrant social institutions, it is evident that social forces seem to institutionalize only after naturally evolving responses to expressed needs are recognized and become valued. In the adolescent peer group, the phenomenon of the evolution of a new institution is being enacted before our eyes. Yet its significance is so far neither recognized nor acknowledged, perhaps because of its very inevitability and naturalness. This naturally occurring social institution, the adolescent peer group, answering distinct developmental needs as do the family, the school, and the church has emerged within the context of a changing social system. Of course, societal conditions and demands contribute heavily to the formation of social institutions. The prevalence and nature of peer groups and the apparent satisfactions they provide demand recognition of the more universal role played by the peer group.

A fascinating contrast to the concern over the movement away to the adolescent peer-group association is provided by leave taking of parents by youth when they choose to marry or mate. This transition is unquestioned since the need to mate has been recognized by society in its institutionalization of the family as a path through which mating and procreation are accepted (Bernard 1964). This move away from parents is regarded as a developmental epoch naturally stimulated and societally approved as a smooth developmental progression. If we reformulate the developmental progression lines from childhood to maturity to mating, into a conception of an essential passage from *child-through-peer-group membership to mating and maturity,* then movement toward peers can be seen as a natural developmental step, not maladaptive and not rejecting of or competitive with other institutions. A conception of peer-group membership as neutral or inconsequential only serves to bypass this essential developmental epoch.

The peer group, though informally evolved, is indeed a functional developmental and educational institution geared to the requirements of transition from youth to adult status. Involvement in the dynamic functions of a peer group is perceived within this formulation as necessarily traversed and experienced in the developmental phase just prior to appropriate social functioning at the succeeding levels of adulthood and, ultimately, family formation. It follows that we regard a youth who is denied peer-group experience as being deprived of a developmental need and a social right—just as is one denied of family or schooling. Evidence of the central structural role of peer-group membership is apparent when it is absent and when we ask what happens.

Why Movement to Peers?

Western adolescents, unlike pubescent youth in primitive societies, live in too complex a society to see simple models of future life. In a simpler society, youth feel new powers, they are soon in a position to experience the functional value of their abilities as they are assigned immediate societally valid roles (Spindler 1974). Hence the phenomenon of the adolescent peer group, now common in Western societies, does not flourish. By contrast, the adolescent in a complex society is devoid of simple pictures of functional skills and, accordingly, is at a handicap in directing his energies.

It is instructive to recall the infant, removed from the known world of a womb, whose anxiety is relieved in cleaving almost instinctively to the mother, aware that security and satisfaction of growth needs lie therein. The infant is thus rooted to the source of nurturance. Dynamic Functional Interaction has set forth as a parallel the idea that entry into adolescence brings a second sense of a lack of framework, that the adolescent condition and its accompanying anxiety stimulate a second rooting orientation. This time, however, orientation is toward peers—not *peer,* but *peers.* This rooting orientation differs from that of infancy, in which needs were nourished by the adult's drawing the child near. The adolescent's impulse is not for satisfaction and protection, but for independence, freedom to investigate, and expansion. Reduction of tension now comes by way of knowledge of utilitarian skills and abilities that afford early independence. Knowledge of the degree of their skill in relation to that of parents or family members is insufficient and no longer relevant. Pragmatically, adolescents understand the contours of the world in which they will live. They know that neither their real nor their psychological world will be inhabited or dominated primarily by parents, but rather will be the domain of their own peers. Therefore, former guides and guideposts no longer suffice.

The social institution of the family, established for procreation and nurturance, has fulfilled its primary function by the onset of adolescence. A new school in which relevant and functional talents and skills can be identified and evaluated is needed. The functional value of talents and skills is assessed in relation to societal needs; more concretely, and more immediately available, is the necessary self-evaluation in relation to fellow travelers in the society. Thus, just as the infant instinctively cleaves to the mother for nurturance, so the adolescent seeks the relevant others—the peers—for the relevant developmental tasks. The proliferation and power of adolescent groups can be understood through this lens. The peer group magnetically attracts large numbers; its influence is strong. All adolescents need to be members. The group's cohesive character underscores the power of the adolescent peer group to serve developmental concerns. Understanding its functional nature opens the way to understanding its numbers, its power, and the universality of the need to be a member.

Although the formal social institutions sanctioned and established by the society serve the functions for which they were originally structured (for example, high school and college for formal education and licensing), adolescents have in fact structurally added their own informal schools. The new interim society that the adolescent seeks is not intended for moratorium but, rather for active preparatory work. What society has not understood, adolescents have taken into their own hands. Although parenting generations of teachers and scholars have witnessed the strength of the call of peer to peers, they have not heard its message. Some, sensing their own inability to comprehend, have personalized the movement as rejection. Others may have projected anger onto the peer group and still others onto society by way of criticism of the complexity that necessitates functional sophistication on the part of adolescents.

Yet the adolescent seems willing to be sophisticated, and in fact he is. He chooses to assess his own system of weights and measures in his own way. He is surprisingly logical, and his prescriptions are simpler and more direct than theories recognize. Fads, formulas, laughter, and raucousness belie the serious function of adolescent peer groupings. Our formulation sees in these group formations, heretofore misunderstood as action against society, action in service of society—that is, to the societal structure in which they consider they will be an integral part. To be sure, the older generation of adults, as well as younger children, are components of their world, but their relevant cotravelers will always be their peers.

The adolescent community appears to have recognized the breadth and depth of its needs as calling for more than a "program". Newly possessed of enormous energies and of a cognitive view of the world as "full of possibility," they have decided not to wait. They have acted, directly, and with the means at hand—each other. In rudimentary fashion they have themselves established a (formally unrecognized) societal institution—the adolescent peer group—to serve necessary functions of social development. Adolescents have thus fashioned a complex school, an arena in which to discover and to test out their own strengths and weaknesses in relation to the persons they view as inhabitants of the world they too will occupy. Peer congregations can be conceptualized as schools with distinct functions—a course of study and a self-recognized graduation. In such schools there are those who do not enroll and there are dropouts. For some who do enroll, their tenure is short. Some complete the course successfully, and others do not. Some find the process particularly painful, and some find the benefits marginal.

The adolescent peer group is presented within our formulation as a naturally evolved prototype of what adolescents are calling out for—a societally recognized structure, organized to receive the adolescent from the time the family structure no longer totally suffices to the achievement of autonomous adulthood. Until now, the message of their congregation has not been understood. Furthermore, their assemblies have been suspect and even regarded as a rejection of traditional institutions. Rather, they make a plea for recognition as one such institution. The peer group is neither a casual gathering nor only a congress of individuals seeking support and shelter from the pressures of an adult world. It is a purposeful, goal-directed assembly of adolescent peers whose congregation functionally serves essential developmental ends.

The following chapters attempt to explain why adolescent peers choose to congregate with one another, what happens when they do, and when and why they eventually leave the peer group. These chapters address the forces that motivate adolescents to congregate, delineate the forces that actively engage their continued membership, and analyze the developmental forces that stimulate readiness to leave the informal institution of peer-group membership in order to seek entrance into the formal and/or informal social institutions that eventually become developmentally appropriate.

**Part III
The Developmental
Significance of the
Adolescent Peer Arena:
A Theory of Dynamic
Functional Interaction**

6 Forces for Affiliation

Views from the developmental literature offered in an earlier chapter have described adolescence as an example par excellence of emotional and cognitive upheaval. A transitional, if not marginal, position between two worlds is depicted. Childhood lies behind and the adult world is ahead. Western society has been described as having a split-level structure, with the adult sphere separate from those of the not yet adults, and with little opportunity available to the adolescent to act on his newly felt potential. The literature has generally identified the peer group as the society to which the adolescent turns for lack of any other.

Relevant Social-Psychological Literature

Our conception suggests that the focus of attention has been misdirected. A consideration of social-psychological theory and empirical data blended with conceptual notions of the precarious developmental condition of the adolescent suggest potent forces that encourage affiliation with peers. These discrete forces are viewed in this conceptualization as acting in tandem on the adolescent, constituting a powerful motive toward affiliation with those who are also experiencing the impact of the adolescent condition and with whom affiliation would augment the individual's own capacity to meet his adolescent growth needs. Dynamic Functional Interaction offers as its major premise that a period of peer-group involvement is necessary for successful adolescent passage. Those forces that combine to stimulate adolescent affiliation with a peer group are the subject of this chapter.

Cartwright and Zander (1968) have delineated four properties of attraction to a group. They suggest that, in general, such attraction will depend on the perceived balance of desirable and undesirable consequences and that attraction is determined by four interacting sets of variables:

1. *motive base of attraction*, consisting of needs for affiliation and values that can be mediated by the group, such as recognition, money, and security
2. *incentive properties*, such as goals, programs, and characteristics of other members
3. *expectancy*, a subjective perception of beneficial or detrimental consequences

4. *comparison level*, a conception of the level of outcome forthcoming from membership

Earlier, in describing the condition of the adolescent as one of instability, insecurity, and lack of framework, it was suggested that the behavioral condition is akin to a state of anxiety experienced by an individual. In fact, Anna Freud and followers of the psychoanalytic tradition have described this state as near-psychosis (1948).

Within the field of social psychology, the behavior of individuals experiencing anxiety has also been investigated. In a highly original research program, Stanley Schachter (1959) studied the effects of experimentally induced states of anxiety on the desire to be with other people—the desire to affiliate with others. Schachter's findings supported his hypothesis that a state of anxiety leads to the arousal of affiliative tendencies. The motive to affiliate was found to be directly related to (1) need for anxiety reduction and (2) need for self-evaluation. Participants were uncertain about whether the anxiety they were experiencing was appropriate or not. They wanted to evaluate their anxiety response, and social evaluation was the available means. Schachter also found that subjects under conditions of high anxiety not only preferred to wait with others awaiting the same experience but also preferred being alone to being with others who were not participants. Schachter argues that the reduction of anxiety brought about by the presence of others derives in part from the fact that each member of the group involved in the same experience helps the others define the nature of the emotional upset and locate the appropriate responses to it.

These experiments can be applied to studies of the adolescent experience since the descriptions of the participants are all generally applicable to the state of adolescence: anxiety, a state of anticipation, a need to validate emotional upset and one's responses, a need to communicate and to determine how others are managing. Furthermore, a high degree of uncertainty and concern about the future is characteristic of the adolescent condition.

In other original experimentation not specifically designed to study adolescence, social psychologists have explored questions further that also appear to have direct relevance for application to adolescent development. A follow-up study of Schachter's experiment by Darley and Aronson (1966) investigated which of two responses in the Schachter experiment was the more important determinant of affiliation. Their findings revealed it to be the evaluation of the appropriateness of emotional response. Radloff (1966), intrigued by the Darley and Aronson findings, questioned whether the same need might be present for individuals who were uncertain but needed reassurance about the validity of their opinions, rather than their emotions. His experiments demonstrated that the needs for evaluation of opinions are also important determinants of affiliation with a group.

Certainly, leaving childhood and entering the expanded world of adolescence prompts the individual to seek validation of both newly felt emotions and newly formed opinions, the former resulting from biological puberty and the latter a function of cognitive growth. Hence, the conditions investigated in the experiments mentioned earlier that were found to stimulate the motive to affiliate (anxiety, uncertainty about the correctness of one's opinions and one's emotions) are active within the adolescent and converge to motivate him strongly toward affiliation with a group of like others. In the United States, inasmuch as age-mates are similarly programmed, it is the adolescent peer who qualifies for the "same state" category Schachter finds to be crucial to the motive to affiliate.

Once the components that converge into the forces for affiliation are established, the next question is that of which processes become activated upon congregation to support the aforementioned conditions. Again, formulations developed within the general field of social psychology, though not stimulated by questions about adolescents or restricted to adolescent behaviors, are pertinent to the current area of interest. In his theory of informal social communication, Leon Festinger (1950) dealt with the question of what individuals do in a position in which no objective standard is available by which to evaluate the validity of opinions or attitudes—a condition that characterizes adolescents.[1] Festinger reasoned at the time that where there is a high degree of dependence on physical reality to validate one's belief or opinion (for example, the table is 4 feet wide, and a ruler is used for this measurement), the dependence on other people for one's certainty about such opinions or beliefs is very low. In other words, it does not matter much what others think, if an objective measure exists. At the other end of the continuum, however, where dependence on physical reality to validate an opinion or action is low or absent (for example, is the table worth what I paid?), the validity of one's belief depends to a large degree on whether or not other people share one's opinion. If other people believe the same thing, the opinion appears to be valid; otherwise it does not. Festinger established that people communicate to establish a social reality in the absence of a physical reality. He extended these formulations on opinions to include the appraisal and evaluation of abilities (1954) and found that the same drive for self-evaluation energizes each.

The connection between Festinger's pioneering work and the highly creative work of Schachter, Darley and Aronson, Radloff, and others is apparent. Festinger's theories carried implications for understanding the stimulus to group formation and membership. To the extent that self-validation can be carried out by affiliation and self-evaluation can be accomplished by means of comparison with like others, the needs to seek out similar others and to affiliate are activated. For the adolescent, therefore, there are two strong incentives to affiliate: (1) a condition of uncertainty and (2) the visible availability of other similarly programmed age-mates. The opportunity exists through affiliation with the group to evaluate one's own abilities and opinons in relation to those of relevant others.

The investigations of Jones and Regan (1974), again, though not conceptualized for the study of adolescent behavior, help us achieve further understanding and particularization. Jones and Regan investigated situational determinants of a desire to affiliate for purposes of social comparison. They reasoned that the desire to evaluate an ability should be stronger in situations in which decisions involving the specific ability evaluation would lead to actions utilizing the ability than in cases in which direct utility is not anticipated. Results revealed that people are more desirous of information about their ability levels when they anticipate making a decision about an action based on the ability than when the decision has already been made. Certainly, the adolescent is at a chronological point at which he will be making important decisions. In fact, the adolescent condition is characterized by a generalized anticipatory state and future orientation. Furthermore, since during adolescence it is not only a single ability that needs evaluation, but in fact the adolescent must discover, investigate, and evaluate a spectrum of abilities, the conditions that Jones and Regan describe are present in the adolescent to a marked degree. He must decide which of his attributes are truly talents. He must assess and categorize a spectrum of strengths and weaknesses preparatory to decision making about his life directions.

Jones and Regan also found that the desire for comparison with similar others is strongest when those others have already used the ability in situations relevant to the decisions in question. This extended the criteria for selection of a comparison person by shifting the emphasis from "How much ability do I have?" to "What happens to people with capacities like mine?" This second finding stunningly addresses the adolescent's anticipatory status and motive to affiliate. In this instance, the peer, in an age-segregated society, is perceived as the cotraveler not only in the adolescent's present, but also in his future. The peer group potentially offers some snapshots of "What happens to people like me?" Thus, a group of peers carries relevance for present and future—both urgent tenses for the adolescent. Since a large number of areas need to be experimented with, certain peers will have already experienced these specific trials with a resulting mixture of some errors, some failures, and some successes. Each member has his own unique priorities and rhythm. What one has already experienced, the other may yet try. Affiliation with like others thus offers feedback from a pertinent, relevant other. Hence the adolescent appears to more than meet both of Jones and Regan's criteria inasmuch as he is in (1) a state of unparalleled future anticipation and (2) a condition in which the abrupt appearance and burgeoning of abilities and talents necessitate evaluations of their utility in the marketplace.

Two criteria for productive affiliation are met by the adolescent peer: (1) Schachter's "like other in the same condition" and (2) Jones and Regan's "relevant other" where the comparisons can yield information and evaluation not only of today's performances and responses, but also of their future functional value. Therefore, since the forces for affiliation are strong and since peers meet the descriptors of the desired "other," some light is shed on the gathering of adolescents into peer groups. It appears to be a behavioral manifestation of the desire to satisfy growth needs that are perceived to be best met through interaction with relevant others.

The next logical question might be why it needs to be a group of many peers. Why are a few peers not sufficient? Once more, experimentation in social psychology offers insight into why numbers of others attract the adolescent to affiliate. Radloff (1966) examined the reasons for the necessity of comparison with a number of others, rather than only a few. He considered when such comparison left feelings of insufficiency and question. Subjects evaluated their performance on a variable-speed pursuit rotor over a series of trials by comparing themselves with others. Findings indicated that self-evaluation is most accurate for people within the range of average ability. This accuracy was due to the fact that there are usually a *number of people* in the average range of similar ability to compare oneself with. Furthermore, they are available over a continuous period of time. For individuals at the two ends of the continuum, however, self-evaluations were less stable. Not enough people were represented in these extreme groups to provide any sense of stability of the evaluation. In other words, for comparison and evaluation, the presence of a few others is unsatisfying, and that of a larger number of others is necessary for what is experienced as a valid comparison. Association with another individual, or even a few individuals, does not suffice. Translated to the adolescent condition, Radloff's findings offer insight into the attraction base of adolescent peer groups.

Further evidence supporting a motive for affiliation with a group is drawn from yet another social-psychological investigation. Wheeler, Kelley, and Shaver (1969) pondered the question of the directional turn of the need to evaluate oneself. They asked whether it was greater in relation to the individual who represented the highest achievement or in relation to the lowest achiever. In the former situation, they conceptualized the actions to be self-evaluational, whereas the latter response would be considered self-enhancing. In essence, was the evaluational need prominent, or was the need for ego enhancement greater? The results of their unique experiments were fascinating. They found that although the subjects were primarily concerned with those better off—indicating that the evaluational need was greater than that of ego enhancement—it was even more important to them to determine the boundaries of the performance. They wanted to know the *range of performance* so that they could then assess and anchor themselves in relation to where they fell on the continuum of performance. A group of just a few peers does not provide enough people to establish a range. In groups of age-mates, adolescents can gather together in sufficient numbers for there to be a range of like others with whom to compare oneself. In adolescent terms, this means affiliation not with *some peers*, but with a *peer group*.

Affiliation Readiness

Aspects of the social-psychological literature discussed earlier expand our understanding of why individuals affiliate and offer data on the forces for affiliation with others. In considering the condition of the adolescent as described in the developmental literature, it becomes increasingly apparent that the adolescent condition is one in which a number of forces for affiliation operate simultaneously.

At any given moment in time, the adolescent could experience one or more of a number of unique conditions—anxiety; anticipation; future orientation; uncertainty about appropriateness of behavior, feelings, and opinions; desires for self-seeking evaluation and validation—any one of which causes individuals to seek the opportunity for self-evaluation and validation available through affiliation with a group. Certainly, a conjoint condition intensifies the motive to affiliate.

The responses of sixty-six adolescent males who participated in the Philadelphia Study (Seltzer 1975) of interactions of adolescent males are pertinent. Since the large, urban, eastern-seaboard high school drew its population from the entire city rather than from one neighborhood, these senior-class students represented a variety of racial and ethnic groups. As part of the study, they responded to a questionnaire designed to tap adolescent cognitive awareness of adolescent affiliative needs. They were asked to agree or to disagree. There was a high percentage of adolescent agreement on the following issues:

Percentage Agreement

93.9   There is nothing so comforting as a good group of friends.

93.9   Conversing with friends makes me realize that I am not the only one who is uncertain.

95.5   If I'm feeling unsure of an opinion or decision it really helps to talk to friends about it and see what they think.

79.5   Knowing how a variety of friends are progressing helps me judge my own progress.

These findings reveal a considerable degree of cognitive awareness of the satisfactions to be gained from affiliating with peers—emotional support and information about status and the correctness or incorrectness of one's own position. It may be that adolescent affiliation carries a stronger cognitive component than heretofore recognized, what we call *affiliation readiness*.

Another formulation from the field of social psychology, Leon Festinger's theory of cognitive dissonance (1957) can be meaningfully applied as we attempt to understand adolescent motivation for affiliation with peers. Festinger argues that in a condition in which cognitive dissonance is experienced, the strength of the pressure to reduce the dissonance is a function of the magnitude of the dissonance. Given the condition of the adolescent as discussed in the literature, wherein the familiar world of childhood activity and habit is now incongruent with biological, cognitive, and emotional advances, the pressure would be strong. The adult world beckons, but the adolescent is not yet ready. Childhood, however, is too far behind. It is difficult and painful to assess the requirements of future roles and responsibilities, perhaps as personified by parents or other models, and, concurrently, to confront one's own current skills. Affiliation with a group of like others confronting similar conditions of past, present, and unresolved future may appear an attractive haven in which dissonance will be reduced, or perhaps even escaped.

Thibaut and Kelley's (1955) work on the psychology of groups also offers a perspective pertinent to affiliative choice. They argue that one reason individuals are attracted toward membership in a specific group is the perception of the "costs and rewards" connected with it. An individual will be attracted to a group in proportion to how favorably he perceives the outcomes he is likely to derive from membership. In other words, the group he will join will be the one he expects to get the most from. If this reasoning is applied to the adolescent, it is clear that affiliation with younger individuals would reduce the anxiety of comparison levels because the skill of the adolescent would generally be relatively more advanced. Ego enhancement might occur to some degree, but the necessary self-evaluational data with respect to future-oriented motives would not be available. Conversely, affiliation with adults might yield the latter, but the comparisons made might greatly increase disillusionment and possibly raise the anxiety level because of the perceived differential in skills and abilities. Since the newly developed cognitive status of the adolescent permits him to assess the more abstract concepts of relative loss and relative gain (Piaget and Inhelder 1958) affiliation with adolescents appears to offer the best balance. Thus, the cost-and-reward premise of Thibaut and Kelley, applied to the adolescent, suggests a deliberate cognitive dimension to the affiliative choice. The following responses to three questions asked in the Philadelphia Study (Seltzer 1975) emphasize the relevance in adolescence of the Festinger premise of actions toward reduction of dissonance, as well as the Thibaut and Kelley concept of costs and rewards.

Percentage Agreement

84.4   It is a relief to be with friends away from pressures and expectations of the adult generation.

82.2   Older friends, relatives, and parents have a lot of skills and accomplishments I do not have.

75.8   I prefer to be with others who are in the same stage of life as I.

Whereas earlier formulations generally regard affiliation in peer groups as migration to an available forum on a negative motivational base, these findings combine to lay the basis for a revisionist approach. Dynamic Functional Interaction views the migration not as going *from* but as going *to*. Obvious physical development has forced the adolescent to a perception of a changing self. Cognitive growth has challenged the formerly secure boundaries of the world of concrete thought. Possessing an increasing ability to engage in abstract thinking, the adolescent may experience the shock of his own expanding powers, not only physically, but also cognitively. Emotional changes that accompany puberty place the adolescent in a moment of exquisite sensitivity to self, to an expanding world, and to its members. But this heightened awareness brings with it concerns about his role, function, and place in the adult society. The adolescent, sensitive to his condition and possessing an intuitive sense of his immediate developmental needs, therefore manifests an *affiliation readiness*. Adolescent peers share this condition and these concerns. As a unique congregation of like others sharing like conditions, they naturally cleave together.

In order to broaden the scope of reference on the forces that motivate the adolescent to move to membership with a group of peers, beyond the rich views currently expressed in the developmental literature, the first portion of the theory of Dynamic Functional Interaction—forces for affiliation—introduces a social-psychological interactional perspective to adolescent affiliation with peers. This conception evolved out of blending adolescent theory on the developmental condition of the adolescent with social-process dimensions of social-psychological theory. Within this model affiliation with adolescent peers is viewed to be functionally stimulated and functionally oriented since forces emanating from the developmental condition of the adolescent gather together with social-psychological forces that operate simultaneously to stimulate the affiliative motive. Taking interactional forces into account, then, suggests a perspective on adolescent movement to affiliate with peers as a positive, growth-producing activity.

The second section of this three-part theory—the interactions in the arena itself—incorporates a similar blend of a social-psychological approach to adolescent development with the interpretation of the developmental component in adolescent interactions with peers.

Note

1. The theory of social comparison (Festinger 1954) was an outgrowth of this first theory of social communication. The theory of social comparison held that in order to evaluate his opinions and abilities, an individual selects a similar person with whom to compare himself.

7

The Arena Proper: Introductory Overview

The adolescent, fresh from the safe, firm reference world of his elders, from the security of knowing that a child is not part of a vast adult world, comes upon a world in turmoil. His socialization has come through school and through play in controlled groups compatible with childhood growth. The literature has established that the adolescent is in a state of change in three developmental domains: cognitive, emotional, and physical. These changes, as well as the prolonged state of change itself, stimulate the adolescent to question the stable references of childhood by virtue of changes within himself that are not yet understood. The literature suggests that adolescents are future oriented and are in an intermediate state, having left childhood and being propelled into the future. It further establishes that the adolescent seeks acceptance, verification, confirmation, and eventually identity.

Less clear in the literature is the irrelevance of elders and the family and the vacuum left by the lack of desire to seek answers from parents—in short, the need to be with peers in a peer group. Frameworklessness is a void, a place without stable reference points in which shifting forces now support, now attack. Unknowns abound. Such a void or turmoil surrounds and permeates the awareness of the adolescent. Somehow, the adolescent must emerge from this environment knowing who he is, what he wants to be, how he is to be perceived, who he wants to be with, why he has certain feelings about things. Out of this anarchic state, he must ask, "Why, where, who, what?"

To ask these questions some basic premises must be established. No longer can the adolescent look to those references pertinent to his childhood stage; yet the adult world is too far away. Hence, he is stuck in this urgently private state of erratic anxieties, pressing questions, and strange feelings. Communication seems possible only with another person at a similar stage. Even then, where does one begin to establish useful language for communication?

Mathematicians can apply game theory to a problem of many variables and several unknowns. This involves establishing approximations in order to test whether unknowns might be within such arbitrary limits, or whether characteristics of unknowns might be established by inductive reasoning or processes of elimination. The process is then repeated and refined to bracket the most knowns and reduce variance. This approximation, trial-and-error, test-and-refine procedure eventually systematizes the search in ever more definitive categories until satisfactory information or definiteness is established. Thus a mathematics is established to deal with certain combinations of variables and some related unknowns. *Zero* and *infinity* are theoretical formulations that set the starting and ending limits within which humans have devised precise systems of measurement and other problem-solving techniques, as well as symbolization of a variety of values. Practical systems have evolved using these two theoretical poles of reference—zero and infinity. In similarly pragmatic fashion, the peer group can be seen as providing elements for developing a mathematics, a system, a practical method of approaching the adolescent world of variables and unknowns. The "zero" of childhood and the "infinity" of adulthood exist for all in the peer group, as do the variable emotional levels, physical changes, and cognitive emergings.

What happens inside the arena, inside this incubating womb of dynamic forces interlacing and crossing over? What makes the adolescent remain in this atmosphere that brings anxiety and pain as well as satisfactions? How does he cope within? How did he get to this group of peers? The self-consciously changing adolescent organism naturally seeks someone in similar circumstances with whom to establish emotional contact and test the erratic intrusion of cogenerative changes and physical alterations he does not control. Stages of contact must be sought: he must start someplace. Similar others in the same position may be open to contact and experimentation. Hence, the congregate group of peers is the place in which to assure contact and communication; to receive feedback on self-expression that is empirical and subjective, with no judgmental component; and to correct, refine, risk, experiment, confirm, and grow—all without judgment from above.

The arena (the various aggregate groups of peers in which the adolescent is a member) is likened to a reactor column in a giant chemical plant. The reactor vessel is a tank into which are piped various chemicals that are subjected to regulated heat and pressure in order to break up and separate elements that will re-form as new molecules or compounds. With a kind of intuitive calculus within this arena reactor vessel, the variables of emotion, cognition, and physical change, as well as the rate of change, permit arbitrary choices to congeal and then to be broken and re-formed differently. New molecules crystallize and attach to different clusters to suit the reaction of the moment. Likewise, situations may atomize moments in time out of their usual forward direction for later reinstatement in the proper order of development. This is the process of assessment, selection, rejection, approval, and refinement that is designed to reduce variables or, more precisely, to attack unknowns.

This is the "mathematics" of a system for coping with a lack of context in the midst of dizzying changes. To accomplish this, computers amass information and select pertinent facts in accordance with desired programs.

Each adolescent does, in fact, function as an enormously sensitive "computer," noting facts about other adolescents—their complexions, dress, hairstyles, manner of speech, fingernails, athletic prowess, school grades, intellectual interests, social standing, food preferences, and so forth. From these facts he quickly rejects some and selects others for more intense exploration. New facts are fed into the computer and selected or rejected; they can be stored and later retrieved for use on the next target available within the reactor arena.

The computerlike cataloging and selection functions are very rapid, as well as extremely sensitive and adjustable. Reaction and action feed others' computers as well as one's own, always in the service of evaluation, refinement, and movement forward to more knowns and fewer variables. In the frameworklessness caused by a bombardment of changes and dizzying unknowns about the self, the adolescent reaches out to become his own person, to become the individual he fantasizes adults to be, to escape the nurturance of incubating parents, to establish self-definition. With his intuitive computer he progresses through stages, by means of pragmatic systems of tests, selections, and evaluations, toward resolution. As the self begins to acquire a structure, these rapid-fire changes abate and supersensitive antennae are no longer needed for information. Likewise, the cyclotron atmosphere of the arena is no longer necessary for self-definition. The computer, the reactor, the cyclotron—these sophisticated mechanics particularize, isolate, and arrange the basic elements of nature. The mechanics of the adolescent are equally complex and equally subtle. Indeed, the allusion to modern scientific methods here suggests the new science as a metaphor for the intuitive adolescent deep-structure processes.

The thrust of this chapter and those that follow is precisely that the peer group is functional, that interactions are dynamic, that immense simplicity and coherence attaches to the entire path of adolescent development when viewed through a lens of dynamic functional interaction. Dynamic Functional Interaction examines the processes, actions, and interfacing effects of the group and the individual in the group within the context of the arena, where the mathematics of development are being worked out as the individual progresses from entry to departure.

8

The Primary Peer Group: Forces for Action

The adolescent period is described as one of physiologic changes of such an order that they dominate the individual's new state. New cognitive and emotional powers assert themselves biologically. In this three-pronged offensive of physical, cognitive, and emotional realities, social forces compete for equal time. Indeed, Dynamic Functional Interaction suggests that by the very fact that these various fundamental changes intersect, the resulting upheaval places social experience into prominence. Social forces either act in service of further upheaval or can be called on to facilitiate integration and direction.

The Uniqueness of the Peer-Arena Membership

Earlier chapters have identified some adolescent forces for affiliation with peers: the physical, emotional, and cognitive changes stirring within the adolescent; the troubling feelings of breaking away from the secure nurturance of childhood. Their reality is one of frameworklessness that has a sudden impact on a heretofore safe childhood. This gives an urgency to future understandings and identification and a desperation to the desire to be with others in the same condition. Thus the child enters adolescence programmed to look forward but unsure of what to expect. The condition of frameworklessness cannot be overemphasized. It is an overriding condition unique to adolescence, born out of and combining with changing physical, emotional, and cognitive states. The adolescent is driven to affiliation with similar others, but the frameworklessness itself is the base from which he must operate individually. This base is a crucial factor in determining which processes come forth to function for his needs.

It is this combination of unique conditions that manifests itself in an urge toward action in an arena of similar others: the adolescent peer group. The adolescent brings with him energies and urgencies that he cannot handle but intuitively directs toward the service of the immediate adolescent task of self-identity and self-direction. Individual developmental processes, though idiosyncratic in their timing and impact, have by this point produced a common condition of frameworklessness for each individual peer. Thus a uniquely experienced development has fostered a common status. The adolescent peer group is unique among groups in that each member is characterized by the identical adolescent condition. Each comes with a preprogrammed status.

Specifically, peer members are alike in nine basic characteristics:

1. They are all near the same chronological age.
2. They are at similar levels in the educational sphere.
3. Generally up to this point they have been similarly programmed by society.
4. All are in transition between childhood and adulthood.
5. The developmental condition of each of the members is similar—cognitively unstructured, emotionally changing, physically unsteady. Each has only recently experienced the beginnings of both biological and cognitive change, stimulants to the characteristic flux of emotions.
6. All are increasingly aware that the changes have incrementally altered their previous position as children. Yet there is also the constant reminder that they are not adults.
7. Confounding the dilemma, although each peer is aware of his own varying degrees of change, differences are apparent everywhere. An individual may experience instability in areas that heretofore were reliably firm. For example, relationships that have spanned a period of time are not necessarily stable; rejection may be experienced. A former acquaintance of the same sex may have changed along the same dimensions as one's best friend—which, in turn, may reflect a different developmental domain than that of the subject. Or the more precocious sexual development of a friend, who now shows interest in the opposite sex, may present an interference to continuing contact. Substitute friendships more often than not do not follow as a matter of course, and certainly not with the same depth for some time.
8. Hence, the adolescent must cope not only with apparent rejection, but also with "aloneness."
9. Cognitive growth may have wrought change in academic performance. Talents may be appearing in age-mates that were not previously present, as a function of the cognitive and biological changes occurring in varying degrees at different moments in time. Past certainties may be gone. Indeed, the future is full of uncertainties: a changing body, a changing scene. Formerly familiar peers appear quite different—changed from their past selves, yet still quite different from one another. No one area is stable.

Daily tasks are still required but now lie within a broader context of awareness that the process of decision making must begin. A firm identity must be established, as well as a direction to follow in life. Yet the adolescent is certain of very little; his present and future both seem unstable. A condition of change and frameworklessness usually stimulates a need for present identity; but the task of identifying "what I will be" appears of such dimension as to create a critical period of sorts and to reduce the urgency of finding one's current identity. Future orientation introduces the recognition that physical development and change will soon end, as will all the remaining vestiges of childhood. The adolescent confronts questions of the future for the first time with the stunning impact that the discovery of identity includes establishing self-direction. The concept of adolescent identity thus differs from the concept of identity at other points in the life span.

By virtue of the generally concurrent experience by each member of changes in three basic areas of growth (physical, cognitive, and emotional), the adolescent peer group is identified as unique. It can be argued that developmental milestones in the three domains were experienced simultaneously prior to adolescence. The experience was immediately relevant, however, and carried no future implications. Thus a second unique characteristic of the adolescent group is its conjoint character of future orientation. The end goal of the definition of "who am I" necessitates that the simplest exchanges and experiences be functional to this end. Immediate tasks are now bound up with future-oriented concerns. Even though specific individual outcomes may differ in content, the end goals of the group members are identical. (For example, one adolescent considers himself to have artistic talent and looks into the field of architecture, whereas another adolescent with new physical strength discovers mechanical ability and speculates on the appropriateness of a construction career. Each has speculated on a different type of vocation—but each must select some vocation.) The necessity to reach this latter end goal is the third identity of the adolescent peer group.

In sum,

1. The state of instability and change is experienced in tandem.
2. The process used to seek identity and direction is engaged in concurrently.
3. The goals of achieving identity and direction are parallel.

Although the content of the achievements or activities may differ, the similarity of the condition, of the process, and of the end goal defines this congregation of adolescent peers as "unique" in their similarity.

The affective condition and stance of the adolescent also conform to common descriptors. His instability, beautifully depicted by Kurt Lewin (1951) as that of a marginal man between two worlds is manifested behaviorally in extreme vacillations in mood. Each needs support; yet they share a posture of resisting dependency on elders. Considerable effort and energy are dedicated to maintaining an independent stance, and dependence is seen as necessary to abandon en route to independence. The demands of this process dictate that the familiar guideposts become obsolete. Former vantage points lose their potency and/or their meaning. Flight from elders allows for freedom from directives as well as escape from the results of many comparisons and expectations and therefore may be experienced as freedom. In exchange for this freedom, however, adolescents give up a framework within which to assess their progress or retrogression. Adolescents are rendered impotent to evaluate the meaning, worth, and currency of their thought and behaviors in relation to the world they prepare to enter. The paradox, unfortunately, is that in order to discern cognitively what is valid and what is invalid, to ascertain what will facilitate the achievement of their goals and what will divert their efforts, they need the information that the authority figure has offered.

Ironically, then, this new freedom robs the adolescent. Alone, insecure, and lacking a framework, the searching adolescent craves relief from dissonance. The members of the peer group therefore also share parallel experiences of separation from those who were once close to them. Reduction of stress must be achieved both on an emotional-supportive and a cognitive-informational level. Each without the other is insufficient to meet the two sides of the question. But the quest is made difficult by its primary descriptor—the necessity to be independent of adults. The challenge is to find support without endangering the venture toward independent functioning. Hence, the *fourth dimension of similarity* of the membership that defines the peer group as a unique assembly of like individuals is the felt need to be with others who may understand and even offer support, but who will not extract or elicit dependence. In actuality, the condition of the group members does not allow the group to be casual. The condition of adolescence is one permeated by need. Past resources are no longer suitable. Surface behaviors are deceptive; the weightiness of the need does not dictate lightness of spirit.

The adolescent peer group should be seen as a group of individuals with identical, not shared, tasks—a group of individuals with individual agendas. There is no superordinate goal whose achievement yields a common good and that requires cooperation and dependence on one another. Neither are the goals shared. Each seeks a parallel, but individual, end goal of self-identity. The tools to reach the goal are not books or teachers, as in the educational institution. In this informally organized new social institution, the adolescent peer group, the tools are the members' perceptions of one another.

In essence the peer group is defined by its unique character as an assembly of youth in an identical condition characterized by urgencies and imperatives. When they congregate, there evolves a field of forces and actions that services each of the members and also services all the members.

This motion of forces and actions—the juxtaposition of group and adolescent, the imperatives surrounding the group, the changing drives and levels of its members, their interactions and limitations, the sheer need of congregation itself—all combine to describe not merely a peer group but rather a peer "field-of-force" group. It is this peer field-of-force group and the action it brings over a span of time (a span of changing) that is the *arena*. The arena is replete with stresses, compulsions, inquiry, and action brought by its players. Within the arena surface actions can mask responses as well as apply to serious work. Dissonance and consonance alternate, attitudes are assumed and dropped, friends are life and death matters—but only for the moment. Basically, the present-oriented activity is consciously in service of the future, a world that is remote but inevitable. In fast and furious activity, within these forces, both conflicting and parallel, the future is being hammered out. The members of other groups at any point in the life cycle share both the identity of stage and its physical developmental manifestations and the direction of their psychological task. This is an elite, exclusive group, experiencing identical conditions, facing identical tasks. Their developmental needs are such that they do not find the dissimilar relevant or desirable. Indeed, the peer group is unique in its uniqueness.

It has been established that an adolescent seeks affiliation with like others and needs many peers with whom to functionally interact. Now peers combine to pursue their separate but parallel tasks, and group forces evolve to stimulate the assembly. An arena emerges of the forces each adolescent brings with him, the combined forces of many adolescents, and the group forces of assembly. To understand what the adolescent is undergoing, why he responds and moves forward, how he changes, we must look at the adolescent through the lens afforded by the arena. The arena is where peers congregate for action. It is this action that we must investigate.

The Unique Peer-Arena Function

Although the change from child to adult has been extensively examined, the specific process of this change is less well developed. There has been little investigation of the processes of social development. Indeed, clues may spring from areas of research other than development. In the field of attitudes and value formation, the work of Milton Rokeach (1973) carries implications for adolescent development. Particularly relevant to the present conception of the developmental-growth functions of peer-group interactions is Rokeach's investigation of how attitudes and values can be taught. He concludes that when stable self-conceptions do not exist in the cognitive structure, traditional educative approaches cannot be utilized. Kohlberg (1964) and Turiel (1966) have reached similar conclusions on the teaching of moral development. In fact, Rokeach contends that educative techniques are most effective when they pose contradictions to a stable self-conception. In the definition of adolescence, presented here, the absence of stable self-conceptions is a central characteristic. In fact, the major adolescent task, achievement of identity, involves the acquisition of a stable set of self-conceptions. It follows that traditional educative techniques would not be functional to the developing adolescent. Yet attitudes and values make up a basic part of a mature socialized personality and provide essential foundations for major decisions in life. If adolescence is indeed a preparatory period for adulthood, Rokeach's findings raise important questions about whether an individual without elements of self can attain the set of attitudes and values that are a component part of social maturity. A further question could be raised by observers of adolescent behaviors who witness a changing array of supposedly "firm" attitudes and values, often inconsistent or even contradictory, as to just how these were arrived at. Dynamic Functional Interaction proposes that attitudes, values, and goals can be and are developed by adolescents specifically within that period of peer-group membership, functionally utilizing interactions with peers. In the course of their acquisition, self-identity evolves and self-direction is formulated. Integrated closure of the three domains of development—biological, cognitive, and emotional—is outwardly observable in mature verbal and nonverbal social expression. Hence, Dynamic Functional Interaction holds that the true end function of peer-group membership goes far beyond the widely acclaimed support function. The peer group offers a dynamic interactional arena for exercising a nontraditional means to social growth and development.

Looking behavior and the tactile manipulations of play provide the route through which the child learns and develops, but for the adolescent, discussion replaces play. Adolescents can use the peer group as a nontraditional educational arena in which to learn about themselves by interacting with one another—to identify, assess, and evaluate who they are and/or what they want to be. The educational materials are the other group members. The method is to use their own cognitive information-getting skills and to deal with their own affective responses. Therefore, the path often may be rigorous and even painful. Determination and perseverance are required.

A number of functions generated spontaneously upon congregation appear in sequence to energize the dynamic-functional-interaction system. Computerlike actions spell acceptance or rejection of memory storage for later recall. Adolescents act consecutively and/or simultaneously. They arrive at identity through this process of weighing the functional use and merit of qualities they see in others and through fitting these to themselves. The adolescent goes through a process of inquiry into the functions and values of each quality, eventually assembling those he feels are of merit. Together, these will create a functional self-structure.

In sum, the adolescent enters the peer group with a cognitive tabula rasa ready to be filled with conclusions gained through participation in a nontraditional set of sequential, interrelated processes. Latent readiness exists, a product of growth in the three developmental domains that combine to define the entering adolescent condition. Peer congregation stimulates the actualization of the Adolescent Dialectic (AD). The AD, the paradoxical product of a felt need for protection against a lack of framework and a life-giving force for growth, stimulates a step-by-step sequence of functions, dynamically activated by the field-of-force process, which act in pursuit of the completion of adolescent tasks. This individual program of functions is the Individual Adolescent Dialectic (IAD). (Each function will be elaborated in the following chapters within their respective context.) Without participation in the assembly, the functions of the AD that can now unfold would lie dormant within each individual. By the conclusion of his period of functional interaction, the adolescent has built an integrated self-structure—and enters maturity.

The adolescent congregation is described as unique because of the identical components of their members' present condition: the necessity to find an interim framework, an identity, and a future direction. Coming together as a group, they sense each other to be similar others and therefore assume each other to be capable of supplying the emotional support and understanding that they dare not take from their elders, lest they give way to the dependence they are fighting so hard to be rid of. Although adolescents have left the world of childhood and are on their way to being adults, the gulf between must be filled. The adolescent's condition is that of one in search, not in possession—a tabula rasa condition. His task is to assemble a self-structure. This sense of self—referred to as an *identity*—will serve as guidepost to establishing a future direction.

The literature describes an adolescent as an individual full of energies, possessing a sense of who he was and a sense that he needs to be someone, but with no direction for filling the gulf. The adolescent comes together with his peers for a variety of reasons, a primary one of which may be for the comfort of associating with a similar other who might also have information about the future. Furthermore, physical, cognitive, and emotional developmental achievements herald a sensitive period of readiness for social development and progression into adolescence. This period does not involve the past nurturer. The child is now in a position to leave family nurturance behind and to enter a community of age-mates. Affiliation with an adolescent peer group occurs at a point of developmental readiness. Then, as a product of this congregation, latent energies are stimulated.

A Spontaneous Group Characteristic

Dynamic Functional Interaction holds that upon assembly all interaction becomes functional. The group characteristic of functional interaction

arises to serve the developmental needs that initially energized the affiliation. The group functionally services the adolescent condition to satisfy
those needs stimulated by change in the various developmental domains of
physical, intellectual, and emotional growth. It functions toward the integration of the mystifying behavioral counterparts of changes that, in
themselves, may elicit additional dissonance. Although this group
characteristic of functional interaction arises automatically and is energized
upon congregation, it in turn energizes. This group phenomenon nourishes
the satisfaction of individual adolescent needs. In this manner the group
characteristic of functional interaction is aliment and hence magnetic.

Dynamic Functional Interaction is engaged in and experienced almost
immediately by the adolescent and is continuously reexperienced in the
course of the group's interactions. The adolescent is drawn to participation
by a "deep-structure imperative." Dynamic, pulsating fields of energy are
injected into an active reenergizing system. Forces and fields of forces interact to create dynamics that are functional, both in service of the individual group member and in service of the group itself in a systemic
reciprocal reaction or interaction, each necessary to and contributing to the
other. The activity appears undirected but in actuality is pertinent to the individual searches for self-definition, evaluation, and direction. This
energizing interaction does not circulate freely in spiral fashion without end
but, upon hitting a target, jets off to gather goal-oriented data and then
returns to the major system. For most adolescents an intuitive awareness of
the other is active, reciprocity in using each other is open, and common use
of the group and group forces is seen as functional and conscious. This
functional use of one another is a functional reciprocity that also contributes significantly to the circularity later discussed in conforming
behavior.

An Adolescent-Kinetic energy (Ado K) effect is inferred from the motion of interaction. The energy the adolescent brings is integral to the early
status of entry. The group characteristic of dynamic functional interation is
the product of the interacting adolescents in their individual fields of motion. They create fields of tension as they move between the affective desire
to remain childish and the cognitive knowledge that they must mature and
assume adult responsibilities. Each adolescent in motion contributes to the
dialectical field of force. The collective fields of energy give birth to a contextual group force. The rapidity of each individual field of motion contributes to the field of force. This same field of force in turn increases the
motion of each adolescent. The collision of individual motions gives rise to
the group characteristic of dynamic functional interaction as a product of
the forces coming out of the individual dialectics.

Surface-Level Actions and
Deep-Structure Imperatives

Upon congregation, within the always present group dialectic of dynamic functional interaction, the interaction operates on two levels—one a surface level and the other a deep structural level. On the conscious level it is interaction that is deliberately interactive and socially motivated. But the adolescent is attached on a deep structural level as well. On the deep-structure level the interaction is also simultaneously preconscious—searching and analyzing. Synthesizing antennae are targeted along a variety of discrete areas. Once connections are consummated, information is consigned to a memory storage system of discrete qualities. This deep-level inquiry is a spontaneous action of strength—an *adolescent imperative.*

Recognition of this deep-structure, subliminal imperative can shed light on the apparent urgency adolescents feel to congregate with one another—the need to go to the dance, the importance of Jane's party, and so forth. Often the intensity of the apparent need is incomprehensible to a nonadolescent and may fly in face of what appears objectively to be a far more desirable alternative. Nor is this imperative necessarily understood by the adolescent who experiences it. The deep-structure adolescent imperative elicits the behavior, not the expressed surface rationale, which they may think causal. Although adolescents are concerned with surface-level interactions for social benefits, good times, and perhaps hedonistic experiences, the strong dynamic imperative to be with peers stems from the deep-level information-getting component. The adolescent needs the result of his looking and listening, needs to incorporate it by self-reflection and assessment at the moment of experience (or perhaps to store it for later review and more careful assessment). Deep-structure imperatives may be used to explain attraction not only of immediate friends or events, but also of other types of choices. Understanding the concept of the deep-structure imperative is helpful in adopting new means of understanding adolescents—perhaps listening less to words and looking less for a logical understanding of adolescent desires and behaviors. What seems indicated instead is reeducation in dealing with stage and developmental needs and recognition of the adolescent deep-structure imperative as a far more powerful dynamic than rational, objective circumstance or argument.

Members extend sensitive antennae to gather the necessary information in an attempt to bring some sense of progress to a marginal and aimless position. They need a framework to replace the one of childhood that they have just given up. It must serve both a present and future. Hence, they seek to establish an interim framework through information exchange with peers. The adolescent sees this group and his relative place in it as prototypic of his present and future world and strives to create interim worlds with peers now as the other tenants. But he also needs some sense of rank in this interim world. He must gain some sense of the range of abilities and opinions that surround them—and of his own relative rank. Once again, adolescents use one another to arrive at who they themselves are. They communicate with one another directly and indirectly. As Leon Festinger has suggested in his theory of informal social communication (1950), individuals communicate in order to establish a social reality. Adolescents no longer have a stable social reality. They engage in information exchange, trying to establish new parameters for themselves, which are at the same time those that are common to their now recognized fellow travelers through life. They assess themselves by virtue of their status in relation to another adolescent peer. This process, akin to the social comparison, introduced by Festinger (1954), that is present at all stages of life, in adolescence entails instant multiassessments that are intense and almost constant.

The experience of the physical changes and emotional counterparts of development stimulates tensions. Each adolescent brings his own set of tensions; hence congregation of adolescents is a collection of these tensions, which are manifested in varying forms of energy release. One is the necessity to engage many characteristics simultaneously. The whole adolescent self is involved. This differs from the intermittent self-questioning that takes place throughout adult life. In adolescence, the entire self is questioned both holistically and componentially. Self-interrogative processes in adolescence are rarely at rest. The presence of self-interrogative processes does not merely reflect aspects of the state, but actually defines the state. Complementing this whirl of self-questioning is the whirl of self-interrogative processes simultaneously operative in other peers. The combination of individuals sharing this unique condition and a unique position in the developmental ladder stimulates the appearance of the group characteristic of dynamic functional interaction—with its component processes—and reinforces its operation. Where peers are assembled, this becomes an ongoing characteristic.

The adolescent is not refining himself: he is establishing self, as are others in his peer group. The forces that motivated the adolescent to affiliate also activate the specific functions and processes of the interactions that promote development. Each has arrived without a structure of self; each must establish a self. Their keen state of readiness for developmental work stimulates distinctly functional interaction. This adolescent imperative is translated upon congregation into a spontaneous functional use of one another.

The Unique Dynamics of the Peer Arena

The individual adolescent, programmed for readiness by developmental achievements, can engage the Individual Adolescent Dialectic (IAD) in early adolescence, here regarded as a critical or sensitive period. The exchange of energies by adolescents, each of whom is ready to exercise his IAD, is necessary to stimulate its individual expression. In other words, the IAD cannot be actualized unless the adolescent is a member of a group of like others whose congregation activates an effect similar to the process and effect in an electromagnetic field. Thus a peer group provides the context in which the necessary development can take place.

During the period of membership, a series of specific functions becomes activated. They are functions of the preprogrammed Adolescent Dialectic (AD), now ready for expression. Each new function evolves out of an earlier one. Members are not all engaging the same functions at the same time; yet they may do so. But they are all engaged in at least one of the functions. Each proceeds at an individual pace in his development. Engagement of the functions serves developmental progress; enlarged scope and comprehension, in depth, incrementally follow. But the path does not follow the structure of traditional education. Development is a direct product of a nontraditional means—dynamic functional interaction with age peers.

Adolescence brings with it as an operative mechanism the Adolescent Kinetic (Ado K). Adolescent Kinetic needs a lot of raw material (inventory of elements) to become activated; metaphorically, it evolves out of the momentum of many movements. Therefore, many individual peers—a peer group, not a few peers—are necessary. When such a peer group exists, Adolescent Kinetic is energized in each member. When many Ado Ks are acting (whirling) at the same time, the peer group becomes an arena. Since congregation itself activates the functional dynamics, a peer group becomes an arena instantaneously as the field of forces is triggered by each member's Individual Adolescent Dialectic.

The subprocesses of the AD occur only in interactions. They do not operate to meet the adolescent imperative unless the interactions can be of a volume equal to the energy potential of the Adolescent Kinetic (Ado K). Hence, numbers of peers are crucial; many are necessary if there is to be the raw material on which to work to provide a cross-current field of forces that stem from each member.

Each member arrives in a unique condition of frameworklessness and change. The adolescent peer group is unique among groups because each member is characterized by this unique condition. Hence, each brings a preprogrammed IAD. By virtue of the preprogrammed IAD, with its energetic operative force, the Adolescent Kinetic, being present in each member, the field force of energy is potently dynamic and charges and recharges (as if it were an electrical component of) the field-of-force activity. Hence, the arena is spawned, consisting of an energy component (process) and a large raw-material component (content)—the varying characteristics, attitudes, and so forth of its members.

The first of the preprogrammed functions of the AD is the Initial Relative Assessor (IRA), which can be seen as prototypic of the subsequently unfolding dynamic process. The IRA, an early scanning device, yields an initial self-rank or rating to the individual in relation to the rest of the group. The later dynamics mechanistically act together to assess, evaluate, reassess, and reevaluate elements in similar or dissimilar others (abilities, attitudes or opinions) of individuals and/or of the stance of the group as a whole, one's own comfort or discomfort, and so forth. This early scanning device activates the computerlike actions of the Adolescent Kinetic, (Ado K) which controls the speed and scope of the processes of the AD. Generated spontaneously upon congregation, the IRA acts on elements in consecutive and/or simultaneous sequence. With intensitivity and sensitivity, the examined elements are rejected, accepted, or referred to memory storage for later recall. The AD, with its subsequently unfolding functions and its action-energy element, the Adolescent Kinetic process makes up the components of the preprogrammed, latent adolescent peer group characteristic of dynamic functional interaction. The combined force field of the individuals spontaneously activates the dynamic functional interaction upon congregation.

The Adolescent Dialectic (AD) is the umbrella under which subsequent functions fit. The IRA becomes active immediately. Its motion is a series of transactions moving back and forth between the self and another individual and/or the group. Ten substeps occur in sequential order:

1. general observation of other group members; general assessment
2. selection of specific characteristic for examination
3. risk of inquiry
4. incorporation of visual information/verbal response/reply
5. assessment of response/reply
6. evaluation of self
7. incorporation into self-image either in part or whole
8. readjustments of self-image
9. initial rank

For example, an adolescent girl, conscious of her own physical changes, enters a group. She may observe a number of varying physical characteristics in other group members:

1. A quick scanning may lead her to conclude that most girls and she generally appear similar.
2. She chooses to focus on breast development.
3. She focuses her glances on the clothing and precise figures of selected individuals.
4. She asks herself how she compares on this characteristic and finds that she is less developed than the high-status figures.
5. She decides that on the whole she is more physically like the majority of the group than not.
6. However, she is disappointed not to be like the high-status girls; she feels inferior in physical beauty.
7. In some ways, however, she recalls that she and the high-status girls are alike; for example, intellectually they are on a par, and they seem to dress similarly. Generally, she appears not too dissimilar from them.
8. She concludes that although her breast development is on a par with that of most of the other girls in the group, she is not as well developed as the high-status girls she admires.
9. Her physical development displeases her despite the fact that it is not out of concert with that of the majority of the group. This is one area she is not comfortable with. She ranks herself in the upper 70- to 80-percent status range.

She now has her IRA rank (IRA/R) on one characteristic. The process has been completed within a period of 30 seconds to 2 minutes. The same initial process will be engaged on other selected characteristics in order to arrive at other IRA rankings.

The condition of the adolescent is one in which concerns about the self are numerous and most areas are in flux—each stimulating questions that call for a reply. Hence, soon after the assessment of breast development can come the assessment of other characteristics such as hairstyle, skin tone, shapeliness, teeth—all examples of characteristics in the area of physical appearance alone. Intellectuality, social skills, and so forth also need evaluation, assessment, verification, rank, and utility quotient. The intuitive pressure of the scope of this projected activity is strongly felt.

Attributes that are important to the adolescent will be examined more deliberately in interactional processes later in the peer-group sequence. The fact that the IRA acts globally at first and is not aimed at specific priority characteristics is a manifestation of the adolescent condition of generalized lack of orientation—frameworklessness. Guideposts with which to judge relevance or irrelevance are absent. Feedback from the group will soon yield some guideposts in the form of group norms, reference points, and values. Establishment of an initial framework—one of the motivations for joining the peer group—begins to bear fruit.

The foregoing transactions with self and others begin, and to a considerable extent operate, on a latent rather than a deliberate manifest level. Hence, since the IRA arises spontaneously and is not deliberately invoked, and since it stems from latent-level operative dynamics, the adolescent may or may not be aware of the genesis of his good or unhappy affect. Nevertheless, he is left to deal with the objective results of the IRA function as well as with the affective response. The IRA yields a general estimate on a number of characteristics and attributes. Some occupy a high priority; other results mean less, and their aftermath is of a more casual concern. A composite ballpark rank, the Initial Relative Assessment Rank (IRA/R), is yielded.

In either case, the IRA is embedded in latent-level functioning. Group-assembly action elicits its spontaneous action. It is not available on a manifest level. The surface content of an exchange may be socially light and casual or intellectually heavy and serious. The discussion content may appear to stimulate the affect; but in fact it is the silent functional assessment that is the serious component. In sum, the adolescent imperative is present and in constant motion. Hence, when a group of adolescents gathers, the latent activity of each IAD is stimulated. Individual latent activity also occurs, in parallel fashion. Motion energizes a group effect and maintains the group characteristics, which is functional in nature. This activity transcends the observable simple rationale for assembly.

The Unique Parallel Processes in the Arena

Manifest behavior masks, and its content confuses. The serious activity in which the adolescent engages is at the level of deep structure. Even when the participants appear at rest, functional and dynamic interaction serving growth is active. The interaction is not exchange. It is transactive, not intrusive or personalized. It is the self-reflective component that affords the impact. The responses of others at this point in development are significant only as a means of self-assessment and definition. Peer relationships in the early stages of peer-group interaction serve as a means, not an end. The dialectic cycle may begin at any point. The motion then proceeds in a circular fashion.

The necessary raw materials by which to begin to weave one's own identity patterns are available through peer-group membership. In the peer group lies the potential for answers. An intuitive sense reigns of the peer group as the arena for essential work. A sense of a common, unstated imperative reinforces the impulse to service this deep-structure need. As each adolescent subliminally perceives that imperative being enacted by other members of the group, his own imperative motive is reinforced.

Again, in gestalt fashion, a motivational component arises as characteristic of the group assembly. McClelland's (1965) notion of societal cues is pertinent. He contends that the more value an individual or society gives to a motive, the more it is likely to develop. Changes in motives are not likely to occur in interpersonal settings, but new motives may surface and persist if considered a sign of and/or instrumental to membership in a desired group. Once identified as associated with a desired reference group, members motivate and reward each other for related thoughts and acts through constant mutual stimulation and reinforcement. Applying the McClelland findings to adolescents, it may be that the use of the group through its first function, the IRA, immediately increases the relevance of the adolescent-peer-group members to one another and hence decreases the relevance of other reference groups.

It is essential to understand that this commonly experienced group motive is not a superordinate one. The group behavior differs from what Deutsch (1949) suggests is promotively interdependent action wherein each positive step is a positive step for all. Here a similar, not a common, goal is involved. The dynamic action is the same, but it is individually experienced for individual purposes. Neither is it a shared motive. The preoccupation of each group member is with himself and his own process of growth and development. Other members may be experienced as self-involved or preoccupied. In the initial stages, however, preoccupation is not experienced by the other adolescent group member as rejection. Rather, the stance is not only accepted but also augments the adolescent need. It creates the desirable transactive milieu, since exchange is not desired. The adolescent needs the physical presence of others but does not really want involvement. The condition resembles that of the parallel-play period of early childhood. At this point of development, the condition of the egocentricity of adolescence of which Piaget and Inhelder (1958) speak prevails. The adolescent is egocentrically enclustered in his own process. He works out questions and answers from his own cocoon, emerging for the necessary nourishment that interaction yields. Although he is physically present, his psychological movement is in and out. True exchange demands more. These transactions are interactions, not exchanges.

The Unique Hold of the Peer Arena

The unfolding of a series of functions in which the adolescent will be involved as a peer-group member in his passage through adolescence has been outlined. An earlier chapter referred to the condition of the adolescent who joined the peer group that he perceived as an arena for support. In view of the stress experienced in this period, sustaining the will to remain in adolescence and not to engage in various forms of withdrawal is not a simple task. Dynamic Functional Interaction sets forth the peer group as a major factor in assisting the adolescent to remain in adolescence; membership is integral to the maintenance of a current state of development. This potent function of the peer group has not been clearly identified by the literature. The peer group is an informally evolved institution that serves the vital function of keeping the adolescent in adolescence. Membership in the peer group functions to avert regression or restriction of the personality, as a defense against an inability to handle the condition and tasks of adolescence, by providing a support system of like others in a like condition and by engaging the adolescent in processes that promote development.

Specifically, what encourages the adolescent to remain in the group? The bombardment of stimuli from generational elders and from within lead the adolescent to join a group of peers. But what is the nature of the experience that encourages the adolescent to stay? The literature to date has for the most part emphasized the support system of the peer group as the active function that maintains the tempestuous adolescent in the peer group. In considering the question, "why," it is well to remember the condition of the individual adolescent when he joins. The adolescent, bereft of former guideposts, is experiencing new internal and external stimuli and is generally in a state of insecurity and anxiety. This latter condition is difficult to withstand at any point in a lifetime. Schachter's study (1959) clearly demonstrates the power of this condition to stimulate the motive to affiliate. The consonant experience of similar others experiencing like discontinuities and uncertainties serves to sustain adolescent anxiety at a level at which defenses may not be called into action, particularly defenses that foreclose the adolescent experience. Some simple examples may serve to clarify. An adolescent boy may grow as much as six inches in one year. Irritating questions may be quietly expressed or unexpressed. Will I ever stop? Is this an unnatural rate of growth? Is there something wrong with me? Did I grow right? What will happen now? Has anyone else had a similar experience? What has happened to him? Is there anyone who is having this same experience? Since physical growth is observable, comments may be available from parents, siblings, and other adults. Yet a chronological peer who mirrors that same position not only offers objective areas of similarity but also provides the opportunity to observe responses to him from others. Responses to his counterpart among a group of peers are of immediate relevance. Cognitive and emotional changes, also in flux, require the operation of more complex inspection mechanisms. Over a course of membership, sensitive antennae develop to tune into the subtleties also available within the boundaries of peer-group interaction.

But although support may be a primary factor in affiliation, Dynamic Functional Interaction suggests that this important ingredient is not enough to sustain membership over a period of months or perhaps years. In fact, Dynamic Functional Interaction holds that it is the functional nature of the group interaction that reinforces continuing membership in the peer group. In the foregoing, not only support but also new information is yielded. The sense that in the peer group the adolescent is actively doing something about moving out of insecurity and instability maintains him in membership. The dimension of being understood and supported is enough initially to lure the adolescent into membership, but the functional value of the membership is what sustains him in it.

The reasons for remaining in the peer group are at times as paradoxical and confusing as the developmental stage of the members. Interactions in the peer group can stimulate an exchange of information that may be experienced as nonsupport or even as criticism. Hence, either reductions or increases of anxiety are experienced from the interactions. Yet however painful, feedback from peers moves the adolescent closer to the goal of self-definition. Doing something about one's own state may not be painless, but the pain of no progress may be even more intense. The adolescent is willing to continue to remain in the group out of a sense that progress is being made. In fact, it is when lack of progress in the solution of his adolescent tasks is experienced that the adolescent is more likely to leave the peer group. The reexperience of frameworklessness and despair may result.

The duality of support and information getting that peer-group affiliation yields keeps the adolescent a member of the peer group. As information about self and others builds up, overall tension is reduced as the adolescent experiences positive reinforcement that he is progressing toward self-definition and goal setting. Responses from the sixty-six male high-school seniors who participated in the Philadelphia Study will be of interest. The intent of this part of the study was to tap the degree of conscious awareness of the significance that peer age-mates held for each other in adolescence. In response to a questionnaire, the subject selected either "agree strongly" (AS), "agree" (A), "agree somewhat" (a), "disagree somewhat" (d), "disagree" (D), or "disagree strongly" (DS). The percentage of agreements and disagreements were as follows:

	AS	A	a	d	D	DS
In settling an uncertainty, it is helpful to see how a friend has handled it.	15.2	50.0	28.8	6.1	0	0
Conversing with a friend makes me realize that I am not the only one who is uncertain.	35.4	27.7	30.8	4.6	1.5	0

	AS	A	a	d	D	DS
Sensing how my friends feel about me is an important factor in how I feel about myself.	16.7	33.3	36.4	7.6	4.5	1.5
The more I talk with people at the same stage of life as I, the more I am satisfied that they are concerned about the same matters as I.	3.0	22.7	39.4	21.2	12.1	1.5
When I am unsure, it makes me uncomfortable if my friends disagree with me.	3.0	24.2	28.8	21.2	18.2	4.5
If I'm feeling unsure of an opinion or decision, it really helps to talk to friends about it and see what they think.	19.7	47.0	28.8	3.0	1.5	0
Agreement from friends makes me feel more certain of my opinions.	9.0	45.0	33.0	9.1	3.0	0
Knowing how a variety of friends are progressing helps me judge my own progress.	6.2	30.8	41.5	9.2	9.2	0

In sum, an active cognitive dimension exists in complementary fashion to the support dimensions of the group. These two differing but non-antagonistic gauges transform an assembly of individuals into a group that offers relevant substitutes for earlier sources of satisfaction. Satisfaction is now experienced in great part as movement toward the goal of adolescent task resolution. Hence, this new affiliation is experienced as functional. Earlier notions of the peer group as an island apart to gain support present only a limited view. Support in and of itself is not sufficiently powerful to warrant the extent of allegiance to peers despite the dissonance that arises. The developmental progress that takes place within peer-group interactions, although it may be slow, is what maintains the adolescent in equilibrium. Experiencing progress diffuses the overwhelming anxiety of a state of transition and indefiniteness and strengthens the adolescent's conviction to complete adolescent tasks. The motive to continue membership in the peer group is progressively reinforced. At this entry level, the adolescent does not want to leave the group, which he subliminally perceives as the only functional, relevant arena available for important developmental work. The satisfaction yielded in involvement with a group of peers is the means by which the adolescent can establish the equilibrium necessary to continue to function in his transitional status and to experience fully the stress accompanying movement through the period of adolescent development. The subliminally experienced sense of progress acts to modify the pain accompanying the self-assessment and evaluation process that the adolescent did not consciously anticipate as a component of the peer-group experience. It was a latent readiness for action of the IAD that he brought with him to membership—not an active, manifest intent. The consequences of active membership in the peer group reinforce the desire to remain a member. The adolescent, now aware of what he will lose through withdrawal, is not free to leave.

9

The Primary Peer Group: Functions and Processes

The Individual Adolescent Dialectic (IAD) program follows a straightforward path to make do with what is at hand: to use peers, to use the peer group, to test oneself and measure others (both similar and dissimilar), to try out attitudes and values, to keep future imperatives in mind as every present moment is used for its functional potential, to be open to group signals while conforming to peer appearances.

A systematic pattern evolves quickly in distinct functions and tasks that multiply in complexity and volume as the adolescent absorbs more and more data and greater awareness of possibilities and influences. It then eventually begins to ebb as some elements stabilize and slower refinement processes begin to displace the rapid kinetic-powered data collection. Although this straightforward path, a systemic pattern that is schematically logical and efficient, is easily generalized, the parts of each activity involve emotional investments and cognitive risks that belie casual appearances. Dissonance and anxiety are ever threatening. Change and movement are constant in a dialectic of tension and instability. Yet the adolescent is steadfastly task oriented, and the motivating dynamic makes every move functional.

A series of dynamic functions is activated that unfolds in service of the acquisition of elements of self. When these select elements become integrated, an adolescent self-structure is the result. As the cycle of actions connected with each dynamic function is completed, the succeeding dynamic function is activated. The adolescent begins the journey using widely scattered and unintegrated identifications with the attributes of peers in an effort to overcome the dissonance of the aimless, frameworkless state.

The Adolescent Dialectic

The preprogrammed functions of the AD in each individual are stimulated through the group congregation. The first function of the AD discussed in the previous chapter becomes operative and offers the adolescent an initial perception of rank: the Initial Relative Assessment Rank (IRA/R). This early scanning device is powered by the Adolescent Kinetic (Ado K), the process that controls the speed and scope of the processes of the AD. A borrowed stability is established temporarily through stand-in elements from peers through the Element Substituting Action (ESA) function. Its action is followed by the Assessment-Evaluation-Reassessment-Reevaluator ($AERR^n$), a function operative in conjunction with the Element Substituting Action (ESA) that provides the raw materials for the $AERR^n$ to act on. Later in development the ESA is replaced by the Specific Element Selection (SES), which also operates in tandem with $AERR^n$, now specific in focus acting as the Selective Element Refinement (SER).

All the aforementioned processes and functions are involved in the assessment and evaluation of characteristics and abilities seen in fellow peers that form the raw material from which the adolescent selects and goes on to measure the suitability of a characteristic to be incorporated in his own self-structure. The seriousness or casualness with which the adolescent regards the specific attribute alters the urgency with which he applies the Adolescent Kinetic. Ado K serves a computer function, as whirling, interacting, in-and-out perceptions jet back and forth, processing data for further review or storage. Many different attributes can be assessed almost simultaneously, if desired. They are assessed in relation to the individual's own response, the response of a specific peer or peers, the perceived group response, the conjoint individual and group response, and the group standard. As the process of development proceeds, the kinetic energy of the Adolescent Kinetic eventually reduces in intensity and scope, since as resolutions are made, less inventory is necessary.

The eventually selected self-elements are products of elimination from vast quantitative data and qualitative testing in the Primary Arena. They are stabilized one at a time, within smaller and slower-moving groups that serve as reduced arenas. As the self-structure builds, fewer relationships replace the heady volume of peer-group interactions. Dynamically active forces of the fields of interactions in the arena between Individual Adolescent Dialectics (IADs) work functionally and incrementally toward the establishment of self-structure and self-direction.

The Arena assumes a central importance not only as a congregation of forces of individual ADs and its own group-effect forces, but also as the crucible for interactions and for the incubation of each adolescent's kinetic energy. Fast and furious, conscious and preconscious, complex and multilevel interactions can be managed only by a powerful and exceedingly active intuitive energy. The Ado K functions in the arena in which inventory of others serves as a transmitter of signals to its sensitive antenna, even as it carries its own signals into the field of crisscrossing forces that is the force field of the arena. Within this field, heady interactions increase the energy levels in a cascading effect to fuel the Adolescent Kinetic (as an expanding electromagnetic field increases the electric potential). The Adolescent Kinetic thus handles an ever increasing load or demand as various sources and various needs call.

The functions of AD, interrelated within the adolescent and within the peer group, are serious, global, discrete, integrative, penetrating, subjective, and objective. They serve thoughts, beliefs, directions, and definitions. Functions act both separately and simultaneously. They cross the functions of other peers and intersect within the peer field of force (PFF). That these various functions operate instantaneously in service of each other (through the Adolescent Kinetic) is integral to understanding their separate roles in bringing the adolescent from frameworklessness to self-structure. Each of the functions (IRA, ESA, AERR^n, SES, SER) occurring within the interactions of sequential peer groups, by virtue of their progressive contributions to each other and toward the goal of self-structure, is dynamically deliberate in character. Operation of the energy mechanic of the Adolescent Kinetic, carrying the computer processes of each, sets forth the task as a process under the pressure of the future and goal determination that creates the dynamics of each.

The Adolescent Kinetic action is unique in scope, speed, and volume; elastic in capacity; and intricate in sensitivity. It is the operative mechanism to be regarded as the electricity that powers the functions programmed for the adolescent. These functions are activated only in interaction. The uniqueness of the peer group as a congregation of individuals in a unique condition of developmental identity is integral to the functional action that occurs—a product of these unique states in conjoint relation. Dynamic Functional Interaction encompasses the complete span of these functions, processes, and interactions from entry to graduation toward an integrated self-structure. This formulation further suggests that those psychological events that are programmed for social experience, by virtue of the adolescent's innate condition and his circumstances, can be dynamically actualized *only* within an arena of peers. Failure to participate fully in this dynamic interaction will delay and impede psychosocial growth and construction of the stable self-structure needed for adulthood.

This chapter defines interactional events in the arena of the primary peer-group period and sets forth the context, the dynamics of the interactions, and the developmental tasks they serve.

Peer-Arena Membership in the Service of Equilibrium

The dynamic action of the IRA, the first primary-peer-group function, gives the adolescent initial information about his relative rank vis-à-vis his peers. This information would be insufficient to sustain the allegiance and length of membership characteristic of peer-group affiliations. However, it is a first taste of forthcoming operative intrapsychic dynamic functions and processes intrinsic to adolescent-peer-group interactions that will yield an incremental experience of progress in development, serving to encourage the adolescent to continue the tasks of self-discovery and self-integration.

Gathered together, energized by one another, adolescents find the group itself to be nourishment; it feeds, it holds promise, it is magnetic. But it is the sense of progress in meeting the challenges of the task that maintains adolescents in this developmental stage.

Specifically, I have discussed two general means by which support and reduction of tension are offered within two dimensions in the peer-group arena:

1. through a cognitively conscious, close association with like others experiencing similar disorientations
2. through using the interaction opportunities within the peer group to
   begin to find necessary answers to open-ended questions about oneself.

However, this double-barreled process may also temporarily add stress.

A tension-modulation action system may be conceptualized. As the peer-group progression sequence is successfully completed, stress connected with lack of self-definition and direction will be reduced. However, at any point in the process the stress factor may be intense since not all interactions yield a positive balance. Some produce quite the reverse. Nonverbal stress reactions as a response to the occurrence of social comparison processes in adolescent peer groups already have been reported in the literature (Seltzer 1978, 1980).

The amount and degree of stress potentially experienced in connection with a disappointing self-appraisal can be appreciated when we consider that the Adolescent Kinetic processes are geared to many simultaneous comparative acts in connection with the all-embracing questions of self-definition. Urgency is the prevailing underlying tension. There is the strong need to answer queries about the self as well as other pressures cascading from within and without. The peer group is the informal, publicly unacknowledged arena in which raw material is available and progress can be pursued. The potential for increased calm lies embedded in an intuitive awareness in the adolescent that hard, painful work mediates a successful end. Adolescents are persistent in their determination to be with their peers. Yet behavioral manifestations of togetherness, lightheartedness, and joviality belie the adolescent functional imperative and the serious nature of adolescent peer congregations.

An earlier chapter traced the forces underpinning the motive for emotional support as instrumental to peer-group affiliation and suggested that the duration of peer-group membership is not determined only by the emotional support provided. A cognitive component of the adolescent condition also motivates adolescent membership.

The cognitive status of the child turned adolescent is that of frameworklessness; former guideposts are challenged by new powers of thinking and

experiencing. Although the development of logical new structures anti-
quates old ways of thought, new stable modes are not yet established.
Cognitive elements are unstable; an integrated self has not yet been formed.
In fact, daily cognitions bounce against a series of different selves. A sense
of stable reality is the important determinant of cognitive stability.
However, for the adolescent who is experiencing a world in flux and
change, this primary determinant against which knowledges and/or cognitions are checked is itself changing, transitional and unreliable. In fact, past
cognitive knowledges and/or elemental certainties have faced a barrage of
challenges. Furthermore, for the adolescent former reference groups in relation to whom assessments and evaluations, consistencies and inconsistencies
of existence have been catalogued, now seem antiquated if not totally irrelevant. Lack of a stable reality—conceptualized as a lack of stable elements—
motivates the adolescent to join a group of peers, perceived as projecting a
similar instability, in hopes that this congregation itself will be a buffer
against the uncomfortable frameworkless state.

Prior to the onset of this stage of development, most adolescents live
within a world structured by their parents. They have been graphically conceptualized (Ausubel, Montemayor, Svajian 1977) as satellites of parents.
The parental elements, understood in childish terms, constitute the reality
of the cognitive self in childhood. With the impact of puberty, these satellite
knowledges and elements in their reality are increasingly experienced as inappropriate to new needs. The adult set of realities that framed childish
elements and knowledges incrementally weakens as new cognitions daily im-
press the now tractable soft ground. With elements of the cognitive field no
longer stable, many even eliminated totally, and new elements having an impact, cognitively based dissonance is experienced.

Adolescence and Dissonance

Distinctions between conditions of dissonance and consonance, as set forth
by Leon Festinger (1957) in his theory of cognitive dissonance, are pertinent. Some discussion of aspects of his theory is in order before the introduction of the element-substituting action function in adolescent-peer-
group interactions, which finds its genesis in some of Festinger's basic
tenets. The term *dissonance* derives from inconsistency, but with a more
neutral base. Festinger proposed that dissonance is the existence of nonfit-
ting relations among cognitions. If fact, he framed an elegant theory on the
basis of the simple notion that the simultaneous existence of cognitions that
do not fit leads to efforts to decrease the dissonance and achieve consonance. This conception is quite appropriate to the adolescent position.
Festinger holds, further, that the removal of dissonance, in its own right, is

a motivating factor. As we have seen adolescent affiliation with peers is in great part motivated by this factor.

Festinger chooses to refer to consonance and dissonance as relations existing between elements. If two elements are dissonant, the magnitude of the dissonance will be a function of the importance of each of the elements. He goes on to argue that since knowledges cluster as they interrelate, it follows that the total amount of consonance or dissonance that exists between two clusters of cognitive elements is a function of the weighted proportion of all the relevant clusters of consonance and dissonance between the two dissonant clusters. Elements refer to cognitions—for example, what the person knows about self, behavior, and surroundings. Such information can also be called *knowledges;* knowledges can include opinions, beliefs, values, attitudes, and feelings. Their single most important determinant is reality. By and large, they map reality, which may be physical, social, or psychological. Thereby, Festinger's elements of cognition correspond with what a person actually does and/or feels, and/or with what actually does exist in the environment. What the individual has been told or encountered experientially, or what other individuals think or do, all may constitute reality. Reality impinges by exerting pressure to bring the appropriate cognitive elements into correspondence with that reality.

Festinger demonstrated that the magnitude of the dissonance increases as the importance or value of the elements increases. Accordingly, the strength of the pressure to reduce the dissonance varies with the importance of each of the elements. This pressure acts in the manner of a drive, need, or tension: it seeks reduction. In general, dissonance can be reduced or even removed by changing one or more elements. Festinger suggests that in the goal to achieve consonance and to reduce dissonance, it is easier to change a behavioral element (generally an element under one's own control) than to change an environmental element that is less apt to be under one's own control. Certainly, changing an element of the social environment is easier than affecting the physical environment. An element in the social environment can be changed by gaining the agreement and support of other people. When new cognitive elements are acquired through information exchange, these new elements may serve to reduce or reconcile dissonant elements. The reverse is also possible. If the necessary change must be on the behavioral level, Festinger contends that the change may involve loss or pain, especially when behavior may be otherwise satisfying except for the dissonant area. Change of the dissonant behavioral element could be under the voluntary control of the individual. On the other hand, he may not know how to change, or there may be no options available in the presently existing behavioral repertoire. Also, resistance to change may exist. An important source of resistance to changing either behavioral or environmental elements, but more germane to the latter, is the extent to which the existing element is consonant with a large number of other elements. The resistance level of the element to change may be seen as the extent to which changing it would replace those consonances by dissonance. As an example, in seeking support in the form of new information, a person will deliberately expose himself only to new sources of information he feels to be supportive to change and will avoid discussion supporting the dissonant elements. (Festinger 1957).

Festinger's theoretical propositions appear to lie within an assumption of the presence of a stable set of knowledges or elements in the cognitive structure—the relationships of which can be affected by a change in a belief, a value, and so forth. But the adolescent condition is defined by its lack of stability. Few, if any, stable knowledges or cognitions exist, and certainly not a set. Hence, the adolescent transitional period is particularly stressed since the stable set of elements does not yet exist against which new knowledges and/or elements may interface to reduce dissonance. The adolescent task goes beyond replacing some dissonant elements. In the adolescent condition, whole clusters of childish elements are dissonant with a new biological, cognitive, and emotional reality. The adolescent is a collection of changes that yield dissonance. In his transitional status he finds no firm reality that will act as an anchor to resolve or eliminate the dissonance. Since he is without a cluster of elements, manipulation and change in order to remove the specific dissonance and reestablish stability are pertinent. The adolescent must construct a cognitive structure whose elements represent his knowledges.

Festinger's model for dissonance reduction (when changing even one element often removes the dissonance) assumes the presence of elements. Adolescence, however, is a condition in which clusters of old elements have become obsolete and are eliminated. A stable reality formed out of new elements must be developed. Dynamic Functional Interaction conceptualizes the adolescent as lacking a set of stable elements necessary to hold opinions, values, beliefs, and attitudes, and introduces a conception of a peer arena aggregate as the forum in which major adolescent developmental progress occurs by way of the assembly and integration of cognitive elements—an essential and major task of the adolescent period. In essence, the assembly of cognitive elements is seen as a process requiring cognitive and emotional effort, trial, investment, and reward. Also involved is the corollary task of determining the valence of the elements in the general adult marketplace. This task, which is performed in both present and future dimensions, simultaneously measuring comfort and fit, is unique to the adolescent functions in both scope and degree of intensity.

Element Substituting Action (ESA)

The construction of a new set of self-elements is necessary, but the process takes time. During the intervening period, most potently at first, the adolescent lives with frameworklessness and may feel impotent. This sense of cognitive emptiness activates the second sequential function of the AD in the peer group: the Element Substituting Action (ESA). ESA affords an immediate path for dissonance reduction, as well as operating as an ongoing mechanism for assembling the adolescent's own self-elements. Most urgently, ESA serves the immediate replacement of gaps left by the rejection and/or obsolence of satellite elements. On the heels of the actions of the Initial Relative Assessment (IRA), the function of ESA inaugurates its dynamic operation as a life-preserving force to the adolescent, who, in the state of transition, has just forsaken older elements of cognitive self-structure borrowed from parents and elders. The dynamic function of ESA introduces a powerful phenomenon of friends to operate as stand-ins, as pseudoelements, in the cognitive structure. Friends come to represent the knowledges they verbally claim. The knowledges or elements (belief, value, opinion) to which the friend attests and the person of the friend merge into one ideational identity. Possession of the friend means possession of the element. Through this process of double identification, the element (be it an attitude, an opinion, or at times even a skill) becomes part of the cognitive structure—a pseudoelement—achieved through identity in the conceptualization of friend as element. Shortly following entry, the adolescent engages the spontaneous action of the peer group; first, the IRA/R offers a tentative rank, and then the adolescent begins to borrow the necessary elements to balance his initial perceptions. ESA is activated in service of assembling cognitive elements. In this way a temporary pseudoself is under assembly.

It may be helpful to sketch the action of Element Substituting Action (ESA), which proceeds as follows: the adolescent selects out a particular individual and those characteristics of the other that the adolescent desires become his own through a partialized identification. The friend figure is ideationally substituted in the cognitive structure for the element. Subsequently, his proximity as friend serves to effect a psychological image of possession of the desired element he represents. The mental process may be conceived as follows: "If Jamie is a talented debater [element of choice], then, since Jamie is my friend, he is like myself. Therefore, I too have a talent for debating." The logic and clarity of cognition are invaded by the strength of the painful effect of frameworklessness and the need for an anchor. By way of another example, it may be helpful to trace the progression of the substituting action of one element in an adolescent beginning the transition to adulthood: "Do I believe in God?" Before the onset of adolescence, the adolescent's religious beliefs have been satellite to cognitive structural elements of parents and other adults, perhaps teachers. Now he exists with weakened former elements, if not in complete frameworklessness. In the peer group this adolescent is exposed to a variety of positions on religion. ESA is invoked. Through its action, friend Jon's attitude on religion is borrowed and becomes a pseudoelement in the adolescent's cognitive structure. Initial attraction may have been based on Jon's unequivocal position or because Jon ranked high on the initial scanning (IRA). The final decision about the element to be utilized as "stand-in" depends on proximity and is a blend of attraction to the element (skill, belief, value) and the status value of the friend. Bandura's formulations on modeling are pertinent (1964). Jon models the element, and the adolescent assumes it as his "own."

In essence, an unconscious process of identification take place wherein the quality is taken for one's own as a function of the emotional investment in the individual as friend. In this manner the friend he perceives as possessing the quality (element) comes to represent the pseudoelement of his own cognitive structure. Such peer pseudoelements stand in for environmental elements in the cognitive structure as different friends come to represent elements of self. Bruce represents aggression; Roy represents music; Franc represents humanism; Aeryn represents artistic talent; Jon represents religion.

Immediate relief is gained as friends become the environmental elements that have meaning as stand in in the cognitive structure to represent the knowledge that make up the cognitive elements. In the cognitive structure, an assemblage of knowledges models an assemblage of friends. Elements of the cognitive structure, which in childhood were borrowed adult elements, now are constituted by peer stand ins. (*Stand-in* elements differ from *borrowed* elements, in that borrowed elements are globally accepted and assumed wholesale, whereas stand-in elements are selected on both cognitive and affective bases. Both the element and the person modeling the element must be perceived as consonant, possibly even similar. The stand-in element then becomes subject to another dynamic function, soon to be elaborated, for verification. A borrowed element is accepted, not questioned, hence its ease of rejection when the maturing organism enters adolesence.) The peer group provides the necessary inventory of stand-ins from whom to select—the raw materials being friends who then are chosen to serve substitute functions until the adolescent can assemble a permanent set of self-elements.

Large numbers of adolescent friendships are essential to providing sufficient raw material from which the adolescent can draw in quest of the characteristics and values he will claim as his own. In this beginning phase, a volume of peers is functional to fruitful actualization of Element Substituting Action (ESA); a few peers amount only to pleasant company. Friendship deprivation in adolescence may be as devastating to developmental progression as are sensory and emotional deprivation at other crucial periods of development. Friends serve one another in a functional manner. During adolescence, the crucial contribution of friends is to lend to the adolescent in the present what he himself does not have available—elements of self. The adolescent needs not only to function but also to appear to function well. Yet he has not had time to assemble all his self-elements. Over time, with the action of the two simultaneous ESA and $AERR^n$ dialectics, elements of the self-structure will develop, and clustering of his own elements for self-structure will occur. Reciprocity quickly characterizes the spirit of peer-group relationships as friends serve one another in a functional manner. It is an affective spirit grounded in a subliminal sense of reciprocity wherein one can not only *borrow from* the other, but can also *borrow* the other, while being available to be borrowed by the other as well.

Element Substituting Action (ESA) should be recognized as one process among others. ESA is invoked not for present assessment but in the service of immediate self-stabilization to fill the void left by the expulsion of earlier sets of borrowed elements. The emphasis varies as the adolescent progresses through development, but invocation of ESA is directly necessary to the daily task of functioning. Thus membership in a peer group immediately offers exposure to a group of adolescents who verbalize positions on issues and demonstrate varied behaviors. The transitional adolescent can quickly assemble a set of beginning cognitive elements—cognitive instruments. The immediate crisis of not knowing is averted. As long as he is exposed to peers who can supply elements to be borrowed, the presence of a cognitive structure can be represented. For example: Bob's overt stance and posture are seen to represent his current store of elements, within which Jon's attitude toward religion stands adjacent to Peter's attitude toward school, which in turn stands adjacent to Robert's conception of good teaching. The latter combine to produce a cluster of educational elements. Robert's view of cheating and Rich's views of political motivation may cluster with Steve's view of opportunity to become the values associated with the borrower's success value cluster. The sense of frameworklessness dissipates and greater comfort is experienced. The adolescent is able to manifest a carefree stance in place of his previously unsettling disconnected posture. Friends serve as anchors, temporal though these anchors may be.

Ironically, what may appear as a stable element in a friend, and then borrowed, also may have been borrowed by the friend. This implicit circularity affords conceptual insight into the overt sameness of views adolescents exhibit in mass opinions that are often defended vociferously. The notion offered here of cognitive identifications can move the conceptions of adolescent mass expression beyond commonly accepted attributions of similarity of behaviors to peer-conformity needs. Similarity of overt behaviors in adolescence does reflect the action of the dynamic stabilizing function of the ESA.

By contrast to manifestations of similarity and sameness, this substitution process of tryout is apparent in the chameleonlike posture often associated with adolescence. Adolescent beliefs are often inconsistent with behaviors. A staunch supporter of one position can switch within an hour to a contrary position expressed with equal fervor. These postures overtly reflect a psychological growth period in which the only relevance is the raw material peers provide for a series of adoptions and tryouts, not a logic of connections. Integration is sought as an end goal. Therefore, externally they manifest the currently operative discontinuities. The words and behaviors of the adolescent in the primary peer group (in early adolescence) may reflect a radical departure from the formerly consistent, predictable child.

Peer-Arena Membership in the
Service of Clarity

The length of the period over which the Element Substituting Action (ESA) is actively used to adopt friends as stand-ins for self-elements—figuratively, a free library from which to adopt characteristics, abilities, attitudes, and values as one's own—varies idiosyncratically but generally ends with the movement of the adolescent from the primary to the secondary peer group. During the period of the primary peer group, the adolescent owns the elements in a preconscious mode. Depending on the specific moment in the developmental period, varying numbers of pseudoelements temporarily stand in for the still undeveloped elements of one's own. Initially, these pseudoelements exist for two purposes: (1) to fill the necessary open spaces for still undeveloped elements, thus affording a temporary stability, and (2) for tryout as potential elements for permanent adoption. If the element feels congruent and is functional for the adolescent, he attempts to structure his own similar element. Numbers of pseudoelements vary with the number of "own elements" existing side by side with the pseudoelement. Through ESA a new, if temporary, adolescent stability is reached.

Assessment-Evaluation-Reassessment-
Reevaluation (AERR^n)

But just how is a more dependable self-owned structure of elements achieved? How does the adolescent translate temporary stability into something permanent? For this precise purpose, the third operative component of the Adolescent Dialectic, the Assessment-Evaluator-Reassessment-Reevaluation (AERR^n) is activated. The primary peer group can be likened to a plasma in which an adolescent cell contacts hundreds of other cells, combining, separating, recombining, and separating again. The adolescent is evolving his own private plasma with the elements from these contacts, which for a time are made part of his own cell. ESA is a function directing the acts of selection and combination. The function Assessment-Evaluation-Reassessment-Reevaluation (AERR^n), to be introduced here within this analogy, determines the degrees of retention and rejection. The adolescent will build his own plasma out of the primary peer plasma and will reflect its group manifestations most directly at the beginning of the process. Eventually, he evolves his own elements.

Assessment-Evaluation-Reassessment-Reevaluation (AERR^n), operating in tandem with Element Substituting Action (ESA), serves the definitional quest. AERR^n assesses and evaluates abilities and talents within the contextual goal of self-definition. It acts in service of response to the questions: Which talent or combination of talents do I have? What am I? The AERR^n dynamic function (employing its Adolescent Kinetic processes within the peer-arena of force) assesses and evaluates toward a programmatic profile of talents, opportunities, competitors, rank, and potential employing as many reinvocations as is necessary.

Membership in the peer group offers proximity to those numbers necessary for sufficient inventory to (1) supply the ESA with a choice of temporary stand-ins for self, (2) engage the Assessment-Evaluation-Reassessment Reevaluation (AERR^n) in testing out for pseudo-self-element tryout and possible adoption, (3) incrementally increase the stock of one's own elements. Many simultaneous processes occur, and the affective response may echo a blending of affect or even rapid changes in affect; for example, in assessing one's math ability, one selects a target individual for "element focus." The AERR^n may yield the information that the target person is as good as or possibly better than the inquiring subject. The yield is similarity—perhaps superiority—of the other. Since the result is surprising, more refined evaluations become necessary. Unless the initial results are definitive, AERR^n will need to continue its action over time until a reliable yield judgment is achieved. Initial AERR^n yields a ball-park figure (similar to IRA/R). Determination of a valid skill level in relation to relative status requires first, second, and third refined AERR^n motions—perhaps even more. Hence AERR^n must be conceptualized as an indeterminate repeated function or open power of magnitude.

AERR^n in the Service of Present and Future

The first function of the Adolescent Dialectic (AD), the IRA (scanning motion) afforded a route to an initial overall rank, IRA/R, in relation to objectively observable characteristics. The function AERR^n differs. It actualizes an in-depth examination that encompasses not only "what characteristics do I have?" but also "which *shall* I have?" The tryout period of characteristics, when the element is borrowed, invokes the present but in reality spans both present and future. The former implies a concern with self-assessment; the future aspect concerns self-establishment and establishment of goals. AERR^n offers the self-assessment functions in the service of present-oriented assessment of attributes and skills. However, one's perspective on the relative skills of other peers ultimately exists within a framework of future potential: "Where will these skills take me in life? Do they need further development? Should they be dropped? Are they adequate as they are?"

The question of "How far am I from the goal?" does not imply that *the* goal has been decided on or that comparisons of one's actions with those of others are focused on an already determined goal. Primary-peer-group membership usually occurs at an early period when deciding what the goals should be is part of the developmental posture. Once the goal has been decided on, the adolescent has progressed considerably along the developmental path. More characteristic of this developmental period is the coopting of the AERR^n function in repeated back-and-forth measurement of an element of the self in relation to estimating its potential and feasibility (its "fit" in achieving any number of goals). Although the identification of a set goal or goals frequently indicates that the end of adolescence is near, at any given moment the early adolescent may be enveloped in what he considers a goal, perhaps even *the* goal, without necessarily being aware of the tenuous nature of that goal. In cognitive terms his world has newly become one of possibility.

The primary peer arena and its AD functions operate functionally as a reality forum whereby fantasy is punctuated with reality. The reality that is brought to bear is that of relative merit, blossoming out of contact with heterogeneous peers through engagement of AERR^n within the primary-peer-arena aggregate. Initial confidence in the appropriateness of a goal may be shaken only after the AERR^n function yields information on an element or elements (characteristics, abilities, and so forth) connected with the attainment of that goal. Positive or negative resolutions next take on added dimensions in response to the group's posture with respect to other peers who are perceived as striving for the same goal or who have already mastered it. The goal may be dropped forever or may return in another cycle within a different context after other elements of self-discovery have been resolved.

Self-establishment moves with the ebb and flow of a process. Initial field forces operate at a high pitch and velocity. Tensions between the pull of childhood freedoms and adult roles make up the dialectic of dynamic functional interaction within the peer arena. Within this dialectic AERR^n contributes both intentionally and spontaneously, invoked perhaps to quiet an uncomfortable self-perception or simply to choose between a choice of options supplied by ESA. By seeking evidence of similarity with some or superiority to others, or in trying to bring a basis of reality to fantasized levels of aspirational goals, $AERR^n$ gathers evidence for resolution. With intensity and speed, the Adolescent Kinetic energizes the $AERR^n$, either alone or in conjuction with ESA, to assess, evaluate, reassess, and reevaluate a variety of elements simultaneously along individually selected and group-reflected criteria.

Specifically, $AERR^n$ serves two functions: information giving and objective evaluation. Do I have the skill or not? Do I possess the positive or the negative attribute? The information yielded carries an affective component. A good feeling is experienced if the skill or attribute is seen as positive. If the attribute is generally seen as negative, then possessing it is anxiety producing, whereas not possessing the trait would be experienced as positive and self-enhancing.[1] Once the attribute is determined to be present, $AERR^n$ supplies information about how the subject adolescent ranks in relation to his peers on the quality or ability in question. The latter process involves a series of rapid computerlike comparative actions, as with the IRA/R. The adolescent yields an estimate of self-rank relative to the perceived rank of selected others with whom he has decided to compare his performance along the selected criteria.

Patterns and Processes of the $AERR^n$

Targets of the assessment process include self, other, and self in relation to other. The value placed on the other is the estimate of the perceived combined assessment verdict of the group as reflected in the status accorded the other either holistically or partially according to specified elements. Assessment of an "other" or of the reflected group perception of an "other" sets in motion the same set of Adolescent Kinetic processes as if the question was about the self. Specifically, the choice of target is at first accidental, as was seen in the discussion of adolescent entry into the peer group when IRA is activated. Later, at the period of the $AERR^n$, it becomes more deliberate. Within a peer group there is usually a peer who represents the positive instance of a particular quality—the characteristic par excellence—or, contrariwise, one who stands for the negative instance. Both these individuals serve to define parameters along a continuum from zero to infinity. Because of the velocity of the Adolescent Kinetic, results can be immediate on the different forms of information exchange (watching, doing, talking) that occur in the interactions.

Generally, the $AERR^n$ function is operative in this sequence: the relative status positions of selected other members of the peer group along a variety of indexes is quickly assessed. The adolescent then decides to make a more precise determination of his own status relative to that of another peer on an ability on which the peer is perceived by him as similar, better, or worse than himself. In the Philadelphia Study (Seltzer 1975) sixty-six boys were asked to assess the academic standing of fellow peers as "high," "medium," or "low." Although they had never been asked to do this before, the information was obviously readily accessible and the subjects offered no resistance to the request. Thus by ascertaining his own performance level relative to that of a target peer, he begins a series of acts on one or a number of elements in an assessment process that incrementally refines and defines various dimensions of the self. Each successive act, focused on the same attribute or skill regardless of the target, yields a more precise assessment of the specific trait or decision for a reassessment or reevaluation within the same or broader context. Over time, a series of $AERR^n$ activities affords the adolescent some notion of his relative standing. $AERR^n$ may be engaged along a variety of models: (1) same characteristic with all levels of peers; (2) different characteristics with the same level of peers; and (3) a combination of (1) and (2).

What emerges is a beginning sketch along a variety of axes. For example, an individual may discover a lack of talent at football or an equivalence with those generally considered unathletic. This conclusion implies that four transactions of $AERR^n$ have occurred in short order, almost simultaneously: (1) with an individual perceived as good at the skill on to another perceived at a lower level, "A,"; (2) evaluation, "E"; (3) reevaluation of skills relative to other group members, "R,"; (4) reassessment, followed by a judgment that similarity is with the lesser performers, "R." Because of the speed of the Adolescent Kinetic, $AERR^n$ operations may occur simultaneously. For operational explanation purposes, the elements of $AERR^n$ have been described sequentially (A-E-R-R). In actuality, at any one time in the total $AERR^n$ process, any configuration of combinations is possible—AEER, AE, AER, ER, ERR, RR. The $AERR^n$ function proceeds as many times as necessary. Thus AERR to the nth power signifies open and repeated reinvocation and combined implementations as often as the variety of focus elements dictates.

Adolescents use two postures to carry on the functional process, a positive direct interrogation and a nonpositive indirect approach; these may be utilized in combination or sequentially. Either model will eventually yield data on a series of different attributes and opinions to be assessed within a range of performances by fellow peers. Questions that may be included within the two approaches are offered by way of example.

Positive Direct Approach

1. What are the areas of my abilities/attributes/talents?
2. Which constellations of attributes are attractive?

3. Am I content with the picture I get of a self with these valuations?
4. Who is my competition? What other qualities does my competition have?
5. Do I wish to pursue the other qualities?
6. Where will their pursuit get me?
7. If I do not, what will I pursue?

Nonpositive Indirect Approach

1. What are the distinct areas of my nonabilities/nonattributes/non-talents?
2. Who are the individuals who possess the talents I do not have?
3. Is the competition too severe?
4. Am I close enough to be really good enough?
5. What are their other talents? Do I need those too?

Conclusionary Interrogatives

1. How much work do I have to put in to get to the position of the positive instance (the highest degree or form)?
2. What are my choices in connection with these varieties of talents?
3. Would I want to travel through life with those who are represented by these attributes?

During this process, the adolescent can be likened to an individual who travels in his own orbit alongside the orbits of his peers. But the focal center of each individual orbit is made up of different combinations. Orbit 1: Jon evaluates his own arithmetic ability through comparing with Peter (an upward arithmetic-status figure), with Joe (a downward figure), and with Ron (who appears to be similar in ability). Orbit 2: At the same time, Ron is comparing his own arithmetic skills with Jon (a similar figure), with Stan (an upward figure), and with Richard (a downward figure). Orbit 3: Stan is evaluating his writing ability with Richard, who may be an upward figure in writing but who carries a connotation of a downward figure in all other aspects. In the case of orbit 3, Stan's evaluation of his own skill will most likely be affected by the results of interrelated comparisons: (1) comparison of the specific ability of writing, where Richard is high, and (2) comparison of his own performance on the ability in the context of the subject's total ability ranking (for example, Richard is a good writer, but not highly regarded in general). The fact that Stan is as good a writer as Richard does not elevate his total estimate of self but restricts the elevation to the writing and whatever effect this may have on the total self-image. Hence, being better in math than Peter, who has a positive ranking on all skills, might be more satisfactory than being better than Paul, who is a math genius but not perceived as able in other areas. In other words, each individual's self-rank is assembled as a product of a combination of factors: own performance, own performance relative to the performance of the comparison target, value attached by the peer group to that posture.

The criteria or the weight accorded to specific attributes may vary idiosyncratically with changing peer values or profile of peer-group members. Each conclusion is embedded in the current values of the peer group, conceptualized within this formulation as the social-reality counterpart to the absence of an objective physical standard by which to measure. Personal status rises or falls in relation to current peer value structure. Hence, individual conclusions regarding the trait are reached by data on three factors: (1) status accorded by the group to the adolescent who manifests the trait, (2) one's own performance on that trait, and (3) comparisons of the former two sets of data. The same process occurs with a combination of traits. Adolescents eagerly incorporate the data from $AERR^n$ processes as relevant since they are the product of an intense series of comparative acts with fellow peers and thus is perceived as a clue to the future status of these same traits.

As the period of primary-peer-group membership proceeds and task efforts intensify, additional steps are inaugurated for a more satisfying closure on an attribute. These vary among: (1) further refinement, (2) acceptance at current level, (3) elimination from repertoire, and (4) reevaluation of its functional value in conjunction with other traits already known. Examples of these four steps would be: (1) commitment to improve the level of one's flute playing by taking advanced-level lessons; (2) deciding that one's current level of skill is adequate relative to one's other traits; (3) experiencing disillusionment that leads to cessation of flute playing altogether; (4) assessing one's skill as part of one's general status in the orchestra. If the decision toward further refinement is made, two additional steps follow: (1) expanding targets for further implementation of the $AERR^n$ function and/or (2) engagement of $AERR^n$ on additional traits in conjunction with those already evaluated, so as to gain a broader perspective on its currency or importance. In the example of the flute, (1) would imply a decision to continue assessment and evaluation in relation to other flute players for an additional range of talent, whereas pursuit of point (2) connotes a recognition that associated attributes—such as general musical knowledge, ear for orchestral arrangement, or concertizing potential—are major components of the type of present- and future-oriented focus necessary to adolescents in preparation for adult functioning. Length of the resolution process would be dependent on the total number of target "others" or target characteristics selected, all of which are assessed and evaluated within a blend of group assessment, response, and standards by means of the components of the AERR^n function.

In sum, AERR^n is operative as a continuous and continuing characteristic function of dynamic peer-group interaction. Its action takes various forms: perceptual, auditory, verbal, nonverbal, olfactory—looking, listening, talking, acting, smelling. It follows a sequential path: (1) observation and listening; (2) isolation of an attribute for review; (3) selection of target peer; (4) assessment of attribute in other; (5) juxtaposition against estimate of own ability; (6) initial evaluation; (7) second assessment, which combines perceived value with attributed assessment by peers (group); and (8) second evaluation within a global-self and peer-group context.

An Attributional Response Model for Adolescent Interim Assessments

The condition of frameworklessness in the period when the self is in formation makes the attainment of definite conclusions a complex matter. Uncertainty is the defining posture of the adolescent, and this necessitates outside validation. For adolescents, the peer group's standards, established through a group communication and consensus serve to represent objective standards. However, these peer-group values and standards are not stable. They shift and change in a way in which objective physical standards do not. Thus the status of a target characteristic is subject to change at any moment, complicating the task even further. Accordingly, each peer-group member may be conceptualized as being identified by a changing number of Individual Attribute (IA) scores as well as a Total Individual Attribute (TIA) score (see table 9-1). Any individual talent seen as outstanding or as lacking may dictate one's status. More generally, the characteristic is viewed in relation to the general valuation the group accords to the individual; it is viewed as a proportion or ratio (see table 9-2). In some settings the Individual Attribute (IA) scores define the adolescent as the upward/downward/middle figure; in others the Total Individual Attribute (TIA) score is the identifier.

The adolescent not only carries general notions of his own IA scores and of the more general TIA score, but also carries these estimates in relation to his peers. His perceptions are at all times couched within continuous fine tunings of IA and TIA scores. They are applied to his own performance weighted against the performances of selected targets and then weighted in conjunction with the perceived valuation by his peers of the resultant score. In sum, the variables the adolescent assesses in deciding whether to retain an ability or characteristic in the cognitive structure or whether to invoke ESA in another substituting action are the product of his own internalized valuation of IA

Table 9-1
Peer-Group Status Profile

Score (high-medium-low)

Individual Attribute	Hanna	Jon	Aery	Franccy
1. (e.g. Appearance	M	H	H	M
2. (e.g.) Math ability	H	L	H	M
3. (etc.)				
4.				
5.				
6.				
7.				
8.				
9.				
10.				

Score (high-medium-low)

Total Attributes[a]	Hanna	Jon	Aery	Franccy
Average	M +	M	H	M

[a]Synonymous with total individual attribute scores (TIA).

Table 9-2
Ratio Profile—Group Status: Individual Attribute/Total Individual Attributes

Individual	Attribute	Individual Score	TIA Score	Ratio Score
Jon	(e.g.) Appearance	H	M	H/M
Aery	,,	H	H	H/H
Franccy	,,	M	M	M/M
Hanna	,,	M	M	M/M

Note: Illustrates individual attribute in relation to total individual attribute status.

and TIA scores and an assessment of the status accorded the IA and TIA scores of others in the group, couched within relevance to present concerns and to future utility (see tables 9-3, 9-4, and 9-5 for graphic representation). This self-reflective or internalized aspect of the IA and TIA score has an

Table 9-3
Pure Target-Other Assessment

	Individual Rating of Other	Group Rating Of Other	Combined I/G
Present value	80	90	85
Future value	90	95	92.5
Combined value	85	92.5	88.75

Note: Strategies utilized: perceptual (look); auditory (listen); olfactory (smell); verbal (talk); nonverbal (act). Can be utilized for self or others on one or many target persons or target characteristics. Can be used with individual scores or global scores. Maximum value 100.

Table 9-4
Contaminated Target-Other Assessment[a]

	Individual Rating of Other	Group Rating of Other	Combined I/G
Present value			
Future value			
Combined value			

Note: Strategies utilized: perceptual (look); auditory (listen); olfactory (smell); verbal (talk); nonverbal (act). Utilization: Self or others on one or many persons and/or target characteristics. Can be utilized for individual or total scores.

[a]Contaminated by other qualities. Error includes extreme stress factors present in maladapted individuals.

Table 9-5
Relative Combined Yield

Own performance	80
Performance of target	90
Product: own relative status	85

impact on the speed of closure on the eventual first plateau of selected self-elements. Those self-elements assessed as positive and functional will be retained; the nonpositive and dysfunctional will be discarded.

After the rigorous action of the $AERR^n$ function and the operations of the composite IA and TIA scores, at this point in the developmental progression those attributes connected with goal achievement become pertinent. Assessments of other are now altered and distinguished in relative terms along a goal—for example, if Jon has less ability in arithmetic than I do but is working at a cash register successfully, my goal of being a math teacher still stands a chance of attainability. Or, if Sue is not as pretty as I but has a part-time job as a model, my chance of becoming a professional model may be good. Or, I am not as good at tennis as Tom; since he has not made the pro team, my tennis skill may not be great enough for me to consider pro tennis. (Data from the Philadelphia Study disclosed that 15.5 percent of all the comparative statements made were comparisons with a goal, ranking third. Of nine varieties of comparisons, those upward and downward ranked first and second. A conscious future-oriented posture was implied.) Elimination of goals takes place as they are tested by the further action of the $AERR^n$ function. As one, two, or three goals are seen to be reality based, the fantasy level is penetrated. The peer-group arena thus provides a base for reality testing. Prior conceptions of the peer group as a preparatory tryout forum need be amended to incorporate the serious reality format of peer operations. It is interaction within a world of present and future fellow travelers. Simply because the significant others are age-mates, the peer group must not be mistaken for pseudo reality testing or a mock city. It is real!

Functional Friendship Configurations

It is clear that a range of friends is essential if the congregation is to be functional for growth. This range should encompass friends who are more skilled, less skilled, equal, well on their way, not yet begun. This variance elicits an assortment of affective responses. Results of $AERR^n$ functions may leave the adolescent feeling inspired by, as good as, better than, inferior to, or wanting to be like the target friend. The chameleonlike moods characteristic of adolescence may be attributable in great part to an affective response to $AERR^n$. These effects may also be a factor in friendship selection. We have recognized the functional necessity friends serve in providing raw material for ESA and then for $AERR^n$. They also assist in relief of tension accompanying the ebb and flow—the ups and downs—of self-perceptions.

Friends not only diffuse anxiety by their similarity but may also increase it through their differences. Negative consequences may stimulate a determined search for friends with whom association will result in an $AERR^n$ eliciting a sense of superiority and thus serving the need for self-enhancement. Feelings of confidence may be revived and, subsequently, readiness again to search out friends representing desired goals. Within this context, revival of interest in a previously "unwanted" friend, or a sudden drop of an existing friendship, may be understood as a manifestation of an intensely experienced internal need.

This analysis sheds light on the high intensities of adolescent friendships, their sudden endings and frequent changes, which have been seen to reflect the general instability of the period. With an understanding of the function friends serve for one another in actualizing the dynamic functions of ESA and AERR^n, the earlier attribution of instability to friendship selection can be more correctly understood within a context of the unique significance adolescent peers hold for one another.

The primary peer group is the initial forum of the aggregate peer arena. Within this arena dynamic functions stimulate the adolescent to progressive growth. After an initial scan for general assessments, the ESA-provided elements are than experienced as one's own. These plus one's actual self-elements are actualized on the basis of present reality through the path adolescents come to use in this vulnerable period of life when they lack objective standards and must cope with the tasks of preparation for adulthood. Their spontaneous involvement with functions of the preprogrammed Adolescent Dialectic (AD) are an index to a creative life force and to the adolescent adaptive potential, which intuitively brings them to their peers to accomplish the necessary preparatory work.

A Different Stability—
Functional to Change

Observers of groups of adolescent peers customarily note the wide range of conversation and discussion. Closer attention uncovers fast and furious action with little concern for consistency of topic or depth of discussion. Yet the work that is being done is not frivolous. We have seen that two adolescent functions are active—the ESA and the AERR^n. The ESA has supplied temporary elements—the substitution of friends for elements—that supply a temporary equilibrium in the cognitive structure. Assessment-Evaluation-Reassessment Reevaluation (AERR^n) is a close cousin to the Initial Relative Assessment (IRA), but differs in that IRA is a scanning device devoted to the assessment of visible overt characteristics that can be quickly assessed and ranked, yielding an immediate initial rating. I have described the AERR^n as acting to assess and evaluate specific self-characteristics in order to arrive at an estimate of their current status and potential currency in relation to those of fellow travelers. This function is more complex than IRA, necessitating not just one assessment but many assessments and reevaluations before a determination is made. The function AERR^n differs from the processes of comparison that are engaged at other stages of life during periods of self-refinement. The process of comparison yields information about the self in relation to others on specific characteristics (Festinger 1954) which, if desired, can serve as a guide—that is, if Jon finds he is not as good at tennis as Peter, he uses Peter's skill as a model. Social-comparison processes at periods of life other than adolescence are usually limited in number at any one time. They are invoked to assess the self on a specific attribute or attitude as well as for information for refinement of selected elements of an already established self. However, the period of transition between childhood and adulthood requires more than refinement of aspects of self. Adolescence is a period of establishment of the self-structure. Hence, the number and type of assessments are numerous and simultaneously active. The function $AERR^n$ is a uniquely adolescent phenomenon. It engages in continuous, continuing action.

The adolescent exists in a status of borrowed elements. Although initial tension has been reduced by the actions of ESA, this is only a temporary equilibrium. Real elements need to replace pseudoelements in order that true and not facsimile stability prevail. The interrelated functions of ESA and $AERR^n$ focus on each element: each substitute element represented by a friend, borrowed for placement in the cognitive structure, and experienced as one's "own" element must be revaluated and assessed as to its fit (Is this really what I am? What I possess?); as to whether or not it is desired (Will I gain or lose from possessing this element?); and, in general, to future validity (How will it work for me in the future?). Operations of $AERR^n$ will yield necessary information. If deemed foreign and/or dysfunctional it will be ejected from the cognitive structure and ESA must again borrow a replacement pseudo-"friend"-element to take its place as a temporary self-element, which in turn will be subject to the processes of the $AERR^n$ function. If the element feels good or consonant and is regarded as functional, then it is not ejected but remains as an element. $AERR^n$ is again invoked. No longer is it a borrowed, friend's element, but it takes its place in the newly forming cognitive structure as a first-stage element of one's own.

Discussions between peers provide an excellent view of the dynamic activities. The adolescent exercises the function ESA and borrows a position on an attitude. He expresses it. Operation of the $AERR^n$ yields the information that this element is not functional to his goals. The adolescent again engages ESA, easily moves to another position, and substitutes a different position. $AERR^n$ is again activated and offers data as to (1) the response of the group, (2) the response to those others who possess this characteristic, and (3) the response of the group to the presence of the characteristic now manifested in the subject. Adolescent Kinetic forces are active in simultaneous assessments on varying numbers of borrowed elements. Removal or change of a cognitive element is not crucial. This procedure can be engaged as many times as necessary, which is easily accomplished since there is not yet a basic self-structure to be contradicted by the inconsistencies overtly manifested in the alterations. In the stable self, the changing of one element has ramifications for the entire cluster of elements, but this is not the case in adolescence. Cognitive elements are easily interchangeable because each element is borrowed from a relevant friend—a stand-in. When elements are not interrelated, substitution or absence of one will in no way affect the other. A temporary, nonintegrated structure is serving immediate needs for temporary stability. When permanent elements evolve and take their position as interrelated factors in an integrated constellation of elements, the individual can no longer trade as freely.

Adolescent stability is of a different conceptual nature than is adult stability. Whereas adult stability implies consistency over time, adolescent stability implies stabilizing in order that change can take place. What is essential to adolescence is a stability of ground that allows figural change—a temporary stability of a majority of elements so that one element can undergo the changes necessary to achieve permanence. In early and middle adolescence, the peer group serves "adolescent stability" by making available stand-in elements.

Empirical Exploration

Findings from the Philadelphia Study punctuate the propositions of Dynamic Functional Interaction that suggest activity of the dynamic function $AERR^n$ in adolescent-peer-group interactions. We investigated the occurrence of specific comparative actions that were at that time conceptualized as social comparisons, predicted to be present in adolescent-peer-group interactions (Seltzer 1975, 1980). Although social-comparison processes can be operative throughout the life cycle, I now further suggest that in adolescence these processes multiply and join, operating spontaneously not only in present assessment but also primarily in relation to future currency and transforming to an *age-related, dynamic function.* They are regarded as serving specific functions of adolescent self-assessment and self-direction. Since the $AERR^n$ function finds a base in social-comparison theory, findings from the pioneering study that first established the occurrence of social-comparison processes in adolescent-peer-group discussions are offered here.

Eight types of social-comparison processes investigated and a general ninth category ("other") are offered at this point insofar as they constitute the varieties embedded for adolescent idiosyncratic selection. Antecedents draw not only from the Festinger conception of social comparison, but also from post-Festinger research that delineated specific types of comparison into more discreetely defined categories (Latané 1966). From this social-comparison literature, five types emerged as relevant to the theoretical linkage with adolescent theory and were therefore seen as instrumental to the adolescent task of self-definition and self-direction. Conceptual definitions as well as the hypothesized functions were developed.

Upward Comparison

Conceptual Definition. An individual or group of individuals representing a superior condition, attribute, or achievement.

Hypothesized Function. Serves the evaluational and achievement orientation of the adolescent and thus is with a person who has already reached a higher plateau. It is differentiated from the positive instance by its implicit attainability.

Comparison with a Positive Instance

Conceptual Definition. An individual or group of individuals representing the ultimate condition, achievement, or attribute and characterized by a quality of unattainability (the Super Bowl star, the Wimbledon winner, the Hollywood siren).

Hypothesized Function. Offers an uppermost parameter to the quality or achievement strived for, reflecting the valuational nature of a broadened exposure. It offers the opportunity to compare with the penultimate. (This type of comparison provides the shade of fantasy that is not possible with upward comparison.)

Downward Comparison

Conceptual Definition. Another individual or group of individuals representing an inferior condition, attribute, or performance.

Hypothesized Function. Serves the evaluative nature of the adolescent or the defensive needs for ego enhancement.

Comparison with Similar Other

Conceptual Definition. Another individual or group of individuals representing a parallel or like condition, attribute, performance, or point of view.

Hypothesized Function. Serves to strengthen identification of aspects of self and the need for self-validation that accompanies the identification of another who thinks, feels, and looks like one himself. Particularly cogent for the adolescent who is unsure of himself and of the value of his attributes.

Range Establishment

Conceptual Definition. A form of verbal seeking that takes the form of outlining parameters. Search and discovery through citing a variety of instances, each implying a comparison of self with reference.

Hypothesized Function. Establishing the boundaries of an interim framework.

Three comparative acts seen as specific to adolescence were *newly* conceptualized:

Comparison with a Goal

Conceptual Definition. Possessing the quality of going beyond daily parameters or time-limited status.

Hypothesized Function. Serves to accomplish a positioning of the self in relation to a goal, either immediate or long term. Comparison with a goal taps the adolescent awareness of his own transition to adult responsibilities. It catches the adolescent need to go beyond comparison and to relate the results to the peer compared with in relation to similar or different goals and the distance he himself stands with respect to the same or different self-goal.

Satiation

Conceptual Definition. An internal resolution of alternatives manifested by an abatement of the need to compare, reflected in a philosophical stance characterized by a reasoned argument on a given issue, a tendency to attempt to influence, and a willingness to stand by one's own position despite opposition.

Hypothesized Function. This affords an opportunity to experience closure on an aspect of the self or underscores a previous experience of closure. It heralds a transition to influencing and convincing. Satiation taps the incremental transition into a status of greater certainty on specific issues, reflected in the lessening of the need to compare.

Comparison with a Dissimilar Other

Conceptual Definition. An individual or group of individuals representing a condition, attribute, performance, or point of view unlike that of oneself.

Hypothesized Function. Serves to strengthen the identification of aspects of self through identification of characteristics in the other that are not those of the self. Comparison with a dissimilar other is the converse of comparison with a similar other and occurs as a consequence of having already engaged in sufficient comparison to make a distinction between self and other. It is seen within this model as a forerunner of or integral to the process leading to satiation of comparison. This type of comparison is indicative of an increasing ability to affirm what one is through a consciousness of what one is not.

Miscellaneous comparisons that did not fall within these definitions were coded as "other."

In sum, the types of comparison may be conceptualized in a unit. The adolescent, in transition between childhood and adulthood, perceives the similarity of peers and shrinks his world to a manageable one—the peer group. It is within this world that he now searches for self-knowledge in the service of self-prescription. His frame of reference is bounded by what he finds to be the *range* of the opinions and abilities of his peers. Within this range, he establishes and assesses his own opinions and abilities, comparing with the *positive instance* for his criterion. He may engage in *upward* comparison (with someone superior to him on the criterion) and in *downward* comparison (with someone inferior to himself on the criterion). In order to validate an aspect of himself, he may look for a *similar other*. By comparison with a *dissimilar other*, he can distinguish himself against a foreign ground. He may be motivated or disillusioned by his own performance or the accomplishments of others with whom he wishes to identify as he assesses his advance to the *goal*. He may move in the direction of closure, which heralds the *satiation* of comparison. Along the path he may alternatively experience confidence or self-doubt and may react affectively with consonance and/or dissonance (discomfort). He may affect agreement or disagreement. Increased involvement or withdrawal may be manifested.

Each of these concepts was operationalized so that the behavior could be observed for occurrence, and, if present, documented. Within the context of fresh findings about the relevance adolescent peers hold for one another vis-à-vis other reference groups (Seltzer 1975), this interactional study pioneered the examination of what actually happens when peers congregate in groups. (Preliminary to the major study, perceived influence on the adolescent of fourteen major reference groups, including five discrete groups of peers, on ten discrete issues was examined. Results strongly supported the predicted presence of a broad adolescent influence field. The data also strongly add support to the well-known position that the peer group is a relevant reference group, but departed from the literature in the presentation of five discrete groups of peers, rather than a global model of a peer group.) A basic assumption of the interactional study was an adolescent in the developmental posture of transition, instability, and uncertainty, identified with neither child nor adult status. It followed that since the peer is perceived as most similar, it would be with the peer that the adolescent would seek to establish the parameters of an interim, if not a future, framework. Festinger's formulation—that in the absence of a physical-reality, evaluation of abilities and opinions would take place by way of social-comparison processes—was applied.

Subjects were achieving members of the senior class of an all-male academic high school, which drew from a citywide rather than a neighborhood population. They represented a broad spectrum of the general population: three races, five major religions, and four ethnic backgrounds. They were similar in having stable home backgrounds, smooth developmental progression, and goal orientation. The sixty-six boys were grouped into eleven units of six each, simulating a small group of peers.

Students were asked to discuss each of four topics for eight minutes, respectively. Two were achievement-related topics: (1) the possibility of a pass-fail grading system, and (2) the possibility of a student-administered ranking system. There were two value-related topics: (1) student life-style philosophies and (2) interpretations of friendship. The order of topic presentation was rotated for the eleven groups of six boys. Each successive group began with the topic that was first for the preceding group. A minimum of one and a maximum of three short probe questions were allowed for facilitation of discussion in a retiring group. The experimenter's only participation was to present topics and probe questions from an unobtrusive position in the back of the room. Pretrained research assistants observed verbal interaction and nonverbal behavior. The verbal observer recorded behaviors predefined into specific categories. Interrater reliability was established at 94 percent for verbal observers and 90 percent for nonverbal observers in pilot studies and from videotapes.

The sessions were taped so that records of the complete discussion would be available for the coding of social-comparison content. Both the speaker and the person addressed were observed and documented by the verbal observer during the course of the discussion group. Therefore, in analysis of the types of comparison behavior engaged in, the verbal-interaction ("who-to-whom") data were available for analysis, as well as the content of the discussions, for determining the type of comparison engaged in. For example, if a perceived downward member said directly to a member of his group other than the other downward figure, "I would like to attack that problem as you do," the direction of the comparison would be identified as upward. If, however, the two individuals were speaking of a third individual not in the group, the content of the remark itself would be the determinant in analyzing the type of comparison, if any. For example, a remark such as, "Tom was always worse at chess than anyone in our clique," would be a downward comparison, whereas "Tom was as good a man as any of us" would be comparison with a similar other. Interrater reliability on distinguishing types of comparisons was 92 percent; interrater reliablility on distinguishing statements containing comparison from those not containing comparison was 98 percent. In addition to the coding of comparisons within one of eight types of comparison, comparisons from the interaction observation were coded as "direct" if they were expressed by one member to another member in the discussion group proper; as "content" if they were not expressed directly to or about another member of the group; as "peer" if they referred to a member of any peer reference group; and as "other" if they referred to a member of any other reference group.

Since an analysis of variance computed on each of the eight types of comparisons over the eleven groups of six revealed no significant differences among the groups, subsequent analyses were based on the total group of sixty-six students. The results were striking (see table 9-6). The presence of social-comparison processes did occur—in considerable number. Nine hundred six (31.1 percent) of the statements contained statements of comparison. Findings strongly supported prior data of the Adolescent Reference Group Index (ARGI) (Seltzcr 1975) as to the primary position peers occupy with one another. Only 9.7 percent of the predicted comparisons were with nonpeers. References to siblings, older relatives, or commonly known public figures were virtually absent. Even those adolescents for whom the ARGI data disclosed preference for reference groups other than peers, compared more with peers than with nonpeers, contrary to prediction (see table 9-7). These various data underline and lend support to

Table 9-6
Statements of Social Comparison in Discussions of Adolescents

Statements	Number	Mean	Percentage
Total	2,913	45.52	
Statements with comparisons	906	14.16	31.1

Table 9-7
Amount and Percentage of Comparisons according to Reference-Group Context

Context	Total	Percentage
Peer	1,118	90.3
Other	108	09.7

the accepted notion of the impact peers hold for one another. However, their emphasis on the functional nature of communication adds a new dimension to the existing literature.

The data on specific types of comparison engaged in supported the prediction that eight types of comparison plus a general other would occur. They fell within two axes, vertical and horizontal, most frequently occurring along the vertical axis where comparisons were evaluational in character. Almost one-half of the total comparisons engaged focused on whether the target was superior (upward) or inferior (downward) to self. Upward comparison accounted for 25.3 percent, and comparison with a positive instance (two varieties of upward comparison) and 22.9 percent were in the downward direction. These two opposite sets of data imply the presence of parallel and coextensive needs. Upward comparisons reflected aspirational strivings of the participants, whereas downward comparison may have reflected a deliberate search for the self-enhancement necessary to balance the affective insult of inferior self-perceptions. Equally intriguing is that the closely similar number of occurrences of upward and downward comparisons lends credence to our "in tandem" conception of the many simultaneously occurring comparative acts component to the AERR^n function. A dialectic of comparative acts, framed by the tension between the two poles of achievement, adds to the field of forces in the adolescent peer group (see table 9-8).

Table 9-8
Total, Mean, Standard Deviation, Rank, and Percentage of Comparison Behavior for Each of Nine Categories

Category	Total	Mean	Standard Deviation	Rank	Percentage
Range	152	2.38	2.45	4	12.4
Positive instance	74	1.18	1.55	7	6.0
Upward	236	3.69	3.57	2	19.3
Downward	281	4.39	4.04	1	22.9
Similar other	117	1.83	2.03	5	9.5
Disimilar other	37	0.58	0.96	9	3.0
Satiation	63	0.98	1.86	8	5.1
Goal	185	2.89	2.96	3	15.1
Other	81	1.27	1.63	6	6.6
Total	1,226				

Cognitive awareness of the operation of what we now conceptualize as Adolescent Kinetic processes of $AERR^n$ was disclosed in findings from a postdiscussion questionnaire administered immediately following each group discussion. By way of example, the responses fell in this manner:

1. I was aware of whether I knew as much as the group as a whole.   71.9 percent agreement
2. When someone said something particularly pertinent, I was aware of whether or not I could have given that reply, too.   87.5 percent agreement
3. I was aware of my relative standing throughout the discussion.   86.0 percent agreement

The data raise speculation about the extent to which selective cognitive awareness and/or denial of affective response may have been operative. The findings reveal an awareness of an affectively positive feeling when the processes of $AERR^n$ disclose that the adolescent is on a par with or above his peers. For example:

1. It felt good when I seemed to know as much or more than others.   98.5 percent agreement
2. I felt good when I knew as much or more than the person I felt knew the most.   60.9 percent agreement

However, when $AERR^n$ resulted in a dissonant affective response, there was a distinct difference in the level of cognitive awareness.

1. I felt badly when the others did not receive my contribution well.   61.9 percent disagreement
2. I felt badly when I felt I knew less than the others.   82.9 percent disagreement

Other responses suggest subjects did not experience the affective discomfort.

1. At various periods of this discussion, I had negative feelings about myself.   75.0 percent disagreement
2. This was an uncomfortable experience for me at times.   96.9 percent disagreement

The pattern of these responses raises the issue of operation of selective awareness. The data reveal a positive awareness when the adolescent is received well by fellow peers and is on par with or above them. More painful feelings were either deliberately not acknowledged or unconsciously denied. The myth of the affable adolescent peer group may reflect postures publically attested to even as the more difficult aspects remain consensually under cover. The findings to be discussed later on the unexpectedly high numbers of nonverbal behaviors expressed, and on particularly dissonant responses, may represent the behavioral outlet.

Still other responses appear to reflect the operation of the in-tandem functions AERR[n] and ESA toward clarification of whether a pseudo- or self-element should be (1) retained, (2) dropped, or (3) borrowed.

1. This discussion helped to confirm an idea or two I have had about myself.   68 percent agreement
2. I learned something about myself during the discussion.   70 percent agreement
3. Recognizing attributes in others stimulated me to look at myself to see if I had them too.   98 percent agreement

Most strikingly, notwithstanding the painful affective response, students felt positively about the group experience and/or desired a second interaction experience.

1. I was interested in finding out the views of others.   98 percent agreement
2. I would like to join another group.   90 percent agreement

Clearly the presence of numbers of relevant others is necessary to actualize the dynamic functions fully. A field of observations and an almost constant bombardment of stimuli is required to index selectively and reindex identifiable qualities and evaluations for effective utilization. An assemblage of numbers for sufficient raw material from which to determine the validity of direction setting is essential. Hence, a "peer group"—not a group of selected peers—is required at this moment in the developmental process.

The Paradox of Peer-Arena Friendship

The atmosphere of the peer-group arena is thus paradoxical. Adolescents strive to be alike; yet it is their differences that motivate them. An interesting phenomenon occurs. The peers who empathize with each other on the affective level as they experience a similar present stage become increasingly aware on a cognitive level of their functional relevance to one another. As they privately begin to regard their futures, they realize that the peer is not only a fellow traveler at present, but also will continue to be so in diverse settings and situations. Intuitively, adolescents sense that the use of one another is central to the quest of arriving at a discrete picture of "who" they wish to be and "how" they can be. Accompanying the expansion of new cognitive abilities to include future concerns is the sense that a place in an adult world will be occupied, but that it will be a relative place.

Hence, pressures to remain in the group are felt from two directions: (1) the self, in order to continue to avail the self of its functions, and (2) the other group members, who need numbers of peers. Thus a cascading effect of individually felt need sustains the group assembly, which in turn creates the dialectic in which raw materials abound, serving to activate appropriate functions.

We have seen that this field of forces activates the latent Adolescent Dialectic (AD) and its appropriate functions, first the IRA and then the ESA and $AERR^n$. These functions are socially based and are active over a period of time, weaving developmental threads of self-identification, self-integration, identity, and direction setting. Along the way, the tension resulting from the loss of earlier frameworks is reduced as members of the peer group represent positive or negative extremes (positive or negative instances) of specific characteristics, attributes, and abilities as well as the average range, thereby providing an relevant interim structural framework to which they now refer. Assessment and evaluation of fellow members is component to the course of each member's self-evolution as self-rank and the ranks of others becomes facts of group membership. ESA provides temporary self-elements, and action of the $AERR^n$ assists the adolescent in evaluating the presence and/or quality of his capacities and talents relative to the status of pertinent others on the same characteristics. Results of the $AERR^n$ function help the adolescent assess which substitute characteristics are viable for refinement into self-elements. When $AERR^n$ has been completed on one characteristic, the same process proceeds with another characteristic or ability, and the adolescent is ready to add others—invoking ESA and then $AERR^n$. As self-development progresses, adolescent selections narrow to prioritize the replacement of psychologically borrowed elements from peers with complete assembly of his own self-elements. Each active member of the adolescent peer group engages in this process. This simultaneous activity defines the group as one of functional interaction.

Therefore, the nature of the relationship with one's peers is crucial. One's behavior in relation to peers becomes a delicate matter. The adolescent must exert care not to alienate peers and risk losing the privilege of membership in the group. Elimination from a group of generally similar peers enormously reduces opportunities for actualizing ESA and $AERR^n$ and the relevant comparisons and evaluations. The adult group is not similar. Groups of children have lost relevance. Movement to another group of adolescent peers might well suffice, but the time gap, the possibility of nonacceptance, and even the affiliation process itself with a new group might reinstate former anxieties. How much better to remain where it is safe and where the intricate process of measurement and discovery of relevant peers will not suffer delay. Self-security is not yet established. The wounds of recent separations still fester. A consideration of adolescents from this perspective clearly suggests an alternative view of forces stimulating the observable group cohesiveness, whose dimension is often mystical and confounding to the adult and/or nonpeer observer.

As suggested earlier, however, peer-group affiliation and continued membership are not without their costs. Experiences of painful self-appraisal and dissonance may result from dynamic activity of the operative mechanism of $AERR^n$, suggestive of yet a second paradox. Part of the adolescent motivation for affiliation with peers is escape from the uncomfortable comparison level experienced with adults. Affiliation with peers appears more tolerable and does bring initial reduction of tension. But the intensive activity of AD functions may alter unexpected areas of former comfort. Fortunately, stand-ins for the missing elements can balance these new perceptions until acceptable or even superior elements of self are determined, absorbed, and integrated. A fascinating third paradox is also a component of peer-group relationships. On the one hand, the adolescent must retain membership in a group of peers to avail himself of sufficient choices and reconsidered choices of "pseudo" substitute elements. On call, a friend must be immediately available as a stand-in to fill any open element space. Having sufficient peers will permit the adolescent comfortably to place, uproot, and substitute each peer who represents a stand-in in the cognitive structure as he proceeds through trial and error to construct those knowledges that are his own. Hence, even as numbers of peers are essential, a paradoxical condition in which the peer is both essential and dispensable exists simultaneously. This paradoxical descriptor of an adolescent peer group defines the peer in a peer group as *peer, not friend*. The "other" is not yet a friend in a group of friends. At the stage of the primary peer arena, the other is related to within a pragmatic context. They are at one and the same time essential and dispensable, not yet couched within a value-associated belief system.

Thus adolescent friendships must be understood as being of a *different nature* than adult friendships. At this point of development, friendship is uninvested in the other, except for the other's service to one's current stability or growth needs. Such "friendship" is indeed egocentric, but egocentrism characterizes this entire developmental period. Hence, egocentric use of friends to further one's growth is pragmtic and functional, not aggressive or hostile.

This intrapsychic process is overtly manifested as easy exchange of friends with no apparent loyalties. This behavior may appear to be contradictory to the observed preference to be with peers, expressed as a strong allegiance to peers. From a position of maturity and an adult perspective, where friendships reflect exchange and involvement, this confusing behavior is often negatively perceived, even stimulating concerns by parents about their offspring's character formation. The emphasis placed by Dynamic Functional Interaction on a sequential peer-arena model and on the major task orientation of adolescents within a functional-interaction system offers some clarification of existing confusions about overt behaviors.

The apparently extensive length of time the adolescent is involved in peer-group activity can be viewed as necessary to full, spontaneous, and natural engagement in interactions with enough peers to test out the elements on trial incrementally and idiosyncratically. True assessment depends on appropriately utilized, unhurried time with sufficient numbers to integrate valid conclusions. Integrative construction of a network of stable elements is developed through initial trial and error onto more precise calculation within a contextual action by two interrelated spontaneous dynamic functions, Element Substituting Action (ESA) and Assessment-Evaluation-Reassessment Reevaluation ($AERR^n$) which supply, measure, and fit the elements along a variety of indexes. During the period of primary-peer-group membership necessary for completion of these processes, the adolescent becomes incrementally more aware of his own characteristics and those of other peers in relation to fellow peers as he forages to establish a beginning sense of his unique self-definition. Activity with ESA and $AERR^n$ have stimulated some painful consequences of dissonance, but consonance also begins to be yielded in the now deepening sense that important steps in completing the tasks of adolescence are underway. Accordingly, an adolescent imperative to remain a member of the peer group and to proceed with transitional tasks is strongly felt.

A New Dependence

Within our notion that the adolescent needs peers to borrow from and to compare against until such time as his own state of readiness to leave the source of this raw material is reached, a constant threat exists against which he must ever be alert and poised—possible rejection by the group. Developmental work must be accomplished within a group of peers. Interactive processes feed raw material. Elements of the self are borrowed, redefined, and decided on. The adolescent moves back and forth in the dialectic between self and other, assembling a beginning sense of self, testing this self out, assessing and reassessing. Each adjustment is successively more finely tuned. They are then categorized into clusters of self, so that an interrelated network of self-elements becomes integrated. They make up the internal structure used by the adolescent to coordinate appropriate goals. Since he cannot achieve developmental progress without his peers, the adolescent is bound by necessity. He can leave the peer group only when this work is finished.

Within the peer-group interactive arena, the adolescent comes face to face with a mirror held firm by his peers. In that mirror is reflected his current status as well as that of his age-mates who are fellow travelers and who will inhabit the world in which he will continue to live and operate. In this reflection of fellow travelers he sees himself or senses that others see him in an altered potition from that disclosed in his previous isolation. He can see the relative position and progress of each and can assess himself in relation to others. Similarly, he is reflected in the glass that the other peer holds. At this point in the developmental process, the mirror glass cannot yet be put down. The adolescent must still use the other in order to know himself.

Note

1. In his initial presentation of social-comparison theory, Festinger's (1954) hypothesis of a unidirectional drive upward, at least in the case of abilities, implies that social comparison might also serve an ego enhancing function. Issues relating to the affective component of social comparison were developed further for exploration in post-Festinger research and reported in a collection of studies on social comparison published as a supplement to the *Journal of Experimental Social Psychology*, September 1966.

10 The Primary Peer Group: The Milieu

As already noted, adolescent stability differs from adult stability in that adult stability implies consistency over time, whereas adolescent stability is stabilizing so that change can take place. Observers of groups of adolescent peers customarily note the wide range of conversation and discussion. A closer look uncovers that the action is fast and continuous with little attention to consistency of topic or depth of discussion. Yet the work that is being done is not frivolous. The milieu of the peer arena outwardly reflects the surface structure, but the dynamics of the latent structure are less readily manifested. Of necessity, a skillful adolescent navigates a cautious course. This chapter discusses the terrain and the travel.

The serial nature of the assessments, approximations, and refinements encompassed by the spontaneous activity of the Adolescent Dialectic and its various functions have been identified here as necessary to the decision to pursue closure on a particular trait or to discard it. Not only cognitive action but also affective components are connected with both the experiences and the decisions with which the adolescent must cope. Satisfaction with the end-product quality of a trait usually yields a positive affective response— pleasure or consonance. The decision to discard the trait, on the other hand, is more likely to be accompanied by a dissonant tone, perhaps even a serious discontent. Self-devaluation may be experienced when there is a great disparity between what the adolescent sees in himself and in the other.[1]

Whereas the previous chapter concentrated on the cognitive work in the peer group, this chapter will introduce notions on the affective milieu of the peer group. We have established that sufficient numbers ensure an appropriate context in which ESA and AERR^n can be functionally operative, and that the peer group is the forum that provides access to environmental elements that substitute temporarily for elements of the integrated personality. We have traced the beginnings of awareness that the peer group is the arena in which developmental tasks are being mastered. As a consequence, we have suggested, the adolescent for the first time begins to experience some type of stability that, despite its facsimile nature, sustains him. Encouragement and sustenance are necessary since continued engagement in the dynamic functions of peer-group interaction carries a heavy affective component. Forces to withdraw or to assume a facsimile status can become strong, as will be seen in a later chapter. The initial experience of equilibrium, though temporary, adds a necessary consonant support.

An ironic parallel occurs. Just as the adult, in possession of self, resists tampering with the cognitive anchor and sets up powerful resistances to encountering dissonance with a "core-self" value, so the adolescent becomes subject to a corollary resistance to tampering with the temporary cognitive anchor. Despite the nature of the adolescent anchor as facsimile, with friendships filling in for undeveloped cognitive elements, the adolescent experiences a stability he does not want to give up. Outwardly, he appears stable both to himself and to others, although actually he still engages the ESA and $AERR^n$ functions in the peer-group arena. As the adolescent enjoys the benefits of the stability the functions yield, the desire to remain is further reinforced. Therefore, he experiences an imperative to conduct himself in a manner that will ensure continued membership.

The Intricacies of Peer-Membership Management

Caution is necessary for the adolescent. The degree to which peers can be alienated must be closely monitored; confronting peers verbally is done at great risk. Excessive expressions of dissonance with friends has the potential to disturb the equilibrium. Dissonance must be avoided at the outset. Therefore, the phenomenon of "avoidance of dissonance" with peers is a characteristic of peer-group interaction. Implementing $AERR^n$ becomes a more complex threefold task: (1) engaging the Adolescent Kinetic for one's own developmental purposes; (2) effectively coping with the experienced affective responses to Adolescent Kinetic action; and (3) skillfully handling relationships with fellow peer members so as not to risk premature dismissal from the group. Careful inhibition of verbal exchange that might be interpreted as offensive is called for, as is timely insertion of positive verbalisms.

Verbal Management

The findings of the Philadelphia Study (Seltzer 1975, 1980) help us to comprehend the skill with which the adolescent accomplishes this threefold challenge. Findings reported earlier implied that the peer appeared to be the relevant other since social comparison with nonpeers was made only 9.7 percent of the time. But an unexpected finding was that 98.2 percent of these comparisons were not with individuals present (see table 10-1). They appeared instead in the content of discussion about a peer who was not present. Although some of this behavior could be considered natural, the fact that only 1.8 percent of the comparisons were with peers immediately present is stunning. The natural question is, If the peer is pertinent, why not the immediately present peer? Initially the two findings appeared contra-

Table 10-1
**Number and Percentage of Comparisons according to Direction of
the Communication**

Direction	Number	Percentage
Direct (peer present)	22	1.8
Content (peer not present)	1,204	98.2

dictory since the former data reflect that comparative acts were almost exclusively with peers. However, the subjects all but ignored their immediate peers. Confusion lessens when we recall the vulnerable status of the adolescent, which at this point is not only a product of dialectical tensions resulting from straddling two worlds, but is also the result of eagerness to be part of the peer world. If nothing else, borrowing facsimile elements allows the adolescent a new, if temporary, stability. He does not wish to jeopardize the little he may have out of fear of returning to the former frameworkless state. Hence, in avoidance of the direct confrontation that statements directed at a peer who is present might yield, postures of caution were adopted. Consonant, positive peer relationships are essential to continuance as a member of the group.

These data imply an intuitive response to the climate. The adolescent handles himself so as to be able to proceed with the functional potential of the arena. He continues to engage the Adolescent Kinetic but does so creatively, through comparisons with adolescent peers not in the immediate group. Exchanges by subjects of the Philadelphia Study about other peers afforded the dual blessing of freedom to concentrate on relevant concerns, coupled with a minimum risk of offending. Furthermore, from the perspective of continuous operation of peer-group dynamic functions, whereas the AE portion (assessment-evaluation) of the AERR[n] could be activated with respect to target adolescents not present, information gain about the group response to specific attributes or characteristics of this outside adolescent could then be utilized in relation to the RR (reassessment-reevaluation) portion. Thus a double plus was yielded. Feedback could be requested on the objective target without the risk of alienating. Expression of an untested conclusion openly might mean offending the peer addressed or the peer omitted. The data connote a subliminal, privately tended alertness to the delicate manner in which relationships of primary importance must be handled, lest they be injured or lost.

Findings from the Philadelphia Study on amount of comparison according to topic under discussion add additional perspective. Apparently, the topic under discussion itself is subject to very discreet handling. The data reveal that topics that explicitly involved peers elicited fewer verbal statements of comparison than topics that did not. Hence, discussion of a peer ranking system and the topic of friendship elicited fewer total comparisons than did the topics of a pass-fail grading system or of whether to be an all-around man or a student with a straight-A record. These latter topics seemed to permit the adoption of a philosophical stance (see table 10-2). Explicit demarcation of peer topics appears to have automatically stimulated a more cautious approach. By contrast, the adolescent engages his peer directly in consonant interchange. For example, agreement, most often interpreted as confirmatory and experienced pleasantly, is expressed directly. These two discrete actions—inhibition of expression of comparative acts that run the risk of being received negatively and disapprovingly, and direct expression of agreement—may be more correctly seen as alternative forms of the same motive—the motive to maintain consonant relationships with peers.

Data on agreement and disagreement included in the analysis of the verbal behavior in the Philadelphia Study offer fascinating punctuation to this observation. Findings disclosed that of 2,913 communications, more than one-third (842) contained statements with some type of agreement or disagreement (see table 10-3). Of this number, 70 percent (590 of the 842) were statements of agreement. The findings point to the readiness, if not eagerness, of the adolescent to be congruent, to appear positive (see table 10-4). A close look at the data reveals that only 18.5 percent were clear statements of disagreement. The pattern of the disagreement offers additional perspective. More than one-third of the 29.7 percent of the statements of disagreement (11.2 percent) took the form of "yes, but." Hence, it can be seen that difference was tempered with a posture of agreement. This qualified expression of disagreement is functional in serving the adolescent intention to maintain an overt posture of consonance with peers. Furthermore, it beautifully characterizes the adolescent condition—one unique to the adolescent state. Like the adolescent himself, the character of the "yes, but" is tenuous; its dimension is bipolar. In this period of both fragility of self and pressure to establish what the self is, the affective need to be similar to others is represented in the "yes"; the impulse for individualization is present in the dissent—the "but." "Yes, but" bridges the gap.

Table 10-2
Number of Comparisons per Discussion Topic

Topic	Number	Mean	Standard Deviation
Pass-fail	344	5.38	4.50
Straight A	380	5.94	6.04
Peer rank	255	3.98	3.98
Friendship	247	3.86	4.00

Table 10-3
Total Number of Communications: Communications Containing Agreement or Forms of Disagreement, Standard Deviation, Mean, and Percentage

	Total	Percentage of Total	Mean	Standard Deviation
Communications	2,913			
Communications containing agree-disagree, "yes but"	842	28.9	13.16	12.17

Table 10-4
Number, Mean, Standard Deviation, and Percentage of Communications Containing Agreement or Forms of Disagreement

Type	Total	Mean	Standard Deviation	Percentage
Agree	592	9.25	9.25	70.3
"Yes, but"	94	1.47	2.19	11.2
Disagree	156	2.44	2.74	18.5

"Yes, but" also poignantly expresses another of the dialectical complications of change as a part of this adolescent developmental period. It succinctly catches a developmental consequence of the AERR[n] function, namely, that discovery of one's own position brings a corollary awareness of the potential consequences of forthrightly and openly expressing or occupying the newly discovered position—an almost intuitive awareness of one's tentative status in relation to others. In other words, simultaneously accompanying the cognitive assessment is the intuitive affective corollary experienced in a signal warning of the risks of "nonsimilarity" and "nonagreement"—the potential to be interpreted negatively. For the adolescent the immediate risk is expulsion from the group. But there is still too much to be done, too many tasks uncompleted. I suggest that the caution of a "yes, but" is defensively adopted. This stance reveals the rudiments of a developing *contextual sense* of appropriate behavior, evidence of maturation. "Yes, but" reflects behaviorally psychosocial growth as the adolescent recognizes that actions are not regarded positively or negatively in and of themselves but are seen in relation to the social context in which they are expressed. This formulation sets forth that the "yes, but" of peer-group interaction is a concrete demonstration of growth along a continuum of adolescent social development, a milestone in social awareness. Within the adolescent peer group, approval is not the end goal of the "yes, but," as it may well be in other contexts. The response is more properly comprehended as a necessary means of retaining membership in a group of peers.

Nonverbal Management

Affective response to the cognitive functions operative in the peer group do not go entirely unexpressed. Although verbal expression is guarded and then measured in its expression, nonverbal behavior is usually not so guarded. The nonverbal expression of affect is immediate. It appears the safer vehicle for private expression, one not subject to group consensus. Findings from the Philadelphia Study (Seltzer 1975, 1980) reveal 7,810 total instances of nonverbal behavior observed to occur among sixty-six students (a mean of 122.03 per subject) in thirty minutes of discussion (see table 10-5). This implies a considerable need for release of tension. Comfortable consonant behavior—defined as an outwardly manifested expression of joy, pleasure, or satisfaction—accounted for 39.3 percent of the nonverbal behavior, whereas discomfort or dissonance—defined as an outwardly manifested experience of discontent, pain, or anger—accounted for 59 percent of the behavior. In order to differentiate a dissonant affective response from a cognitive disagreement, disagreement—defined as a cognitive experience of difference, incongruity, dissent, or disapproval—was included in the design. The operational definition involved head-shaking in a variety of forms, expressed individually or in mutual eye contact with peers. This occurred 1.7 percent of the time. Data on the orientations selected for expressing either the consonant or the dissonant responses were striking in the extent to which caution with peers was observed (see tables 10-6 and 10-7). Of the dissonant response, 99.8 percent was expressed in private—individually, not on a mutual basis. Data on consonance showed a reverse phenomenon. Of the consonant behaviors (39.3 percent of total nonverbal behaviors) operationally defined as exchange—where two or more subjects communicated or shared a response with one another, as in eye contact—11.8 percent was experienced privately, whereas 75 percent was experienced in mutual nonverbal exchange with another peer. Viewed together, the data unambiguously suggest that when these adolescents experienced discomfort in the group, their nonverbal expression was *private*, not shared. By contrast, consonant experiences in the group are shared openly with peers (see tables 10-8 and 10-9).

Table 10-5
Amount, Mean, and Percentage of Three Types of Nonverbal Behavior

Type	*Total*	*Mean*	*Percentage*
Consonance	3,066	47.90	39.3
Dissonance	4,608	72.00	59 0
Disagreement	138	2.16	1.7
Total	7,810	122.03	100.0

Table 10-6
Amount of Nonverbal Behavior according to Type and Orientations

Type	Orientation		
	Individual	Mutual	One-Way
Consonance	362	2,325	379
Dissonance	4,599	3	6
Disagreement	41	66	29
Total	5,002	2,394	414

Table 10-7
Percentage of Nonverbal Behavior according to Type and Orientations

Type	Orientation			
	Individual	Mutual	One-Way	Total
Consonance	4.6	29.80	4.9	39.3
Dissonance	58.9	0.04	0.1	59.0
Disagreement	0.5	0.80	0.4	1.7
Total	64.0	30.6	5.4	100.0

Table 10-8
Amount, Mean, Standard Deviation, and Percentage of Dissonance in Three Orientations

Type	Orientation		
	Individual	Mutual	One-Way
Total	4,599.00	3.00	6.00
Mean	71.87	0.04	0.09
Standard deviation	29.12	0.21	0.52
Percentage	99.80	0.07	0.13

Table 10-9
Amount, Mean, Standard Deviation, and Percentage of Consonance in Three Orientations

Type	Orientation		
	Individual	Mutual	One-Way
Total	362.00	2,325.00	379.00
Mean	5.64	36.33	5.39
Standard deviation	4.44	22.34	7.85
Percentage	11.80	75.50	12.70

On most descriptive variables the subjects were quite similar and were assumed to experience consonance with similar persons. The volume of the discomfort expressed in the nonverbal conduct of the subjects implies that a considerable amount of the verbal expression may have masked the actual affect experienced and that tension is expressed nonverbally witout the risk of alienating others. Verbal behavior of the subjects in the Philadelphia Study appeared oriented toward promoting consonance with peers, nonverbal behaviors to express the actual affective consequences. These alternative forms of behavior imply that the interaction is in great part measured and purposeful. The relevant other is recognized as a necessary target. Completion of the tasks of self-growth requires other peers. Behavior that is overtly less accountable offers a release for tensions. Implicit in this deliberate functional handling of affective response is an unspoken, intuitive awareness of the delicate manner in which relationships of primary importance need to be handled.

The Individual-Member Stance

The adolescent appears unable to adequately explain his constant readiness to be with peers, a readiness sometimes approaching urgency. However, data from the Philadelphia Study did disclose cognitive awareness of a preference. Responses to questions such as, "It is a relief to be with friends away from the pressures and expectations of the adult generation," and "I prefer to be with others who are in the same stage of life as I," yielded responses of 84.8 percent agreement and 75.7 agreement, respectively. Generally however, the imperative to be with peers remains at the deep-structure level, as does awareness of the functions of the Adolescent Dialectic (AD). The adolescent in the primary-peer-group period senses that he has become involved in a new type of dependence. In the service of his own development, the adolescent has merely changed hosts. Ironically, the adolescent has attempted to escape dependence on and expectation of the adult or parental community. In doing so, however, he has become involved in a *new kind of dependence*. He now depends on the peer group for nourishment.

Along the developmental route, the adolescent has unknowingly changed from an assumption of adult prescriptions of performance to one of peer-group prescriptions. The price is conformity to standards of a new authority, from which any strong deviation carries the risk of expulsion. Absence of an arena and its guideposts leads to nonresolution of adolescent imperatives, reactivation of anxieties of nonprogression, and a return of instability. Cognitive awareness of the need for membership, on the one hand, and of affective discomfort with dependence, on the other, may be sensed but not understood. What is clearly grasped is the need for actions of agreement and conformity.

The specter of loss of access to essential developmental resources makes the adolescent posture in the peer group one of compliance and conformity. A posture of nonconfrontation appears functional to retaining membership and avoiding expulsion. Political management of feelings is functional to the necessity for maintaining membership in the current relevant peer group and continuing accessibility to the dynamic functions of the primary peer group. Dialectics operative in the adolescent peer group are so crucial for adolescent growth and progression that a variety of creative deliberate and semideliberate strategies are invoked by the members to eliminate the recognition of a dissonant response. A *self-protective censor* operating in the service of maintaining a necessary balance, wherein the positive rewards of the functions served by peer-group membership outweigh the affective costs, is evident in behaviors ranging from readiness to express verbal positive responses to the withholding of negative ones, sometimes going as far as actual denial of the negative experience. Openness to awareness of negative affective response might tip the balance, endangering membership.

Since continuing membership in the arena is essential to completion of adolescent tasks already underway, during this period there may be an increase in the use of whatever external outlets for tension release are accessible, in order to maintain the composure necessary to continued affiliation with a peer group until the developmental work has progressed sufficiently to permit a modicum of risk. A portion of the aggression expressed by adolescents against societal institutions may represent a projection outward of anger that cannot be expressed, for fear of expulsion, toward the dominant peer-group standards and norms. The dilemma differs idioscyncratically in relation to internal and external realities en route to an ultimate stable self-conception and relaxation of dependent vulnerability.

The tension that emanates from the push of wanting to avoid the pressures of the peer group, coupled with the developmental pull of needing to stay, makes up the *dialectic* of the adolescent peer group. Forces emanating from the tension of passage backward and forward between the two affective poles of the positive and negative affective consequences of the dynamic functions make up yet another dialectic. The aggregate volume of affective ups and downs, resulting from the pace of the simultaneous actions of the Adolescent Kinetic, contribute to the tension—the dynamism of the arena. Thus membership in the Primary Peer Group acts dynamically to *maintain the adolescent* in the developmental stage by (1) offering an inventory of elements of self and opportunity for trial and refinement, and (2) affording a sense of progress, not of retrogression or stagnation. No other arena offers as relevant a setting.

Alternating Climates: Freedoms and Constraints

Amid its tensions and seriousness of purpose, the peer arena also has a lighter component. Since the adolescent self has not yet been orchestrated, the task of self-discovery, definition, and integration can be depicted as a process of assembly of cognitive instruments. Within a period of general turbulence and the tensions and insecurities that define it, experimentation in the service of establishing a belief system called the *self* can proceed with little concern for the actual content of the topic under debate. The adolescent can move among a variety of positions, can be relaxed or heated at will—he can have some fun taking wide liberties since he does not yet experience the painful distress that comes when a challenge to an integrated self-system is confronted. The duration of the ups and downs experienced, however, is by definition short since the challenge is not to an integrated self. In the primary-peer-group period, it is more likely directed to a facsimile element than to an "own" element. Hence the adolescent seems to manifest an inscrutable ability to bounce back. As adolescent development progresses toward a more mature status, this freedom is reduced, as will be seen later in the discussion.

Some of the notions of Milton Rokeach (1973) on attitudes and values offer an interesting framework within which some adolescent behaviors can become clearer. When we apply Rokeach's view of the position of values as contrasted with the position of attitudes in relation to a total belief system to the unique, transitional, formative status of the developing adolescent, fascinating implications ensue. Recall that the adolescent is aware of the noncurrency of his former childish ways and that he must construct a relevant new self, integrating what he was, is, and wants to be. Old beliefs appear obsolete and irrelevant, but new ones are not yet anchored. New values must be formed, beliefs reexamined, and the attitudes that accompany them reworked, accepted, or rejected. In his work with values and attitudes, Rokeach departs from existing literature and argues against the notion that values are harder to change than attitudes. To the contrary, he contends, if a value threatens or contradicts self-conceptions, it is more likely to undergo a change than is an attitude, which may be discrepant only with a communication or with a behavior. He further suggests that change of values in service of stability of self-conception is more central than removal of a discrepancy that emanates from a position occupied by attitudes. Rokeach's general position emphasizes the centrality of consistency of self as a prime motivator for change.

Rokeach's organizational structure involves a number of levels. Distinct components, including countless beliefs, combine into thousands of attitudes. These attitudes are hierarchically arranged into several dozen instrumental values. From these instrumental values several handfuls of terminal values are organized into a functionally related belief system. Within this system, a subhierarchy is structured. Terminal values are more central than are instrumental values. In turn, instrumental values are more central than attitudes. Another class of beliefs that is even more central to the person is the self, or self-concept, an organization of distinctive cognitions, unconscious and conscious, and their affective connotations. These values must be maintained overall since they are functionally related to self-conceptions.

Rokeach's model sees the individual as involved in identifying instrumental values (based on countless beliefs), and then selecting out and integrating terminal values, which will ultimately be functionally related in a belief system. In this manner attitudes are seen to be the least central. Instrumental values make up the next plateau, out of which selected instrumental integrations become terminal values. The highest integration in this refinement evolves the belief system, which is the self or self-concept. Values and self-conceptions are functionally related. Values provide the person with a comprehensive set of standards to guide actions in the service of maintaining and enhancing the total conception of self.

Functional Inconsistence

The fact of adolescence that is pertinent to its essence is the absence of a real self. The core of the adolescent task is the construction of a self-structure. Hence the adolescent must be viewed as one in a condition of nonself. Adolescent values, beliefs, and attitudes are not yet formed but are in formation. Loud proclamations of attitudes and beliefs are deceptive. If, as Rokeach states, a highly developed belief system is the self, then what the adolescent loudly claims is what he does not yet have. For purposes of intermediate stability and status, he must present a self. Therefore, the facsimile model of a cassette system of friendship is activated. The peer group provides opportunities to place and/or replace friendships as stand-ins that constitute pseudo elements of the cognitive structure. Until the belief needs to be incorporated into the self-image, there is no investment in whether it is accepted or rejected by others. It is an open area—neutral turf. Positions can be changed at will since inconsistency does not yet carry a threat to a core self-system. Adolescents are free to argue a point with conviction. Heated arguments are related to self-experimentation and to AERR[n] processes, not really to content or to substance. Interaction energizes; information exchange, support, and discourse can be active. Conditions are excellent for free exchange since no basic self exists to be challenged or disrupted by any of the expressed points of view.

The component of the self with which Rokeach deals can be seen as a process of refining that occurs subsequent to the establishment of the self.

Since Rokeach also suggests that self springs forth out of a belief system, and since adolescent espousal of attitudes and values occurs in the absence of that core of self, no matter what his stance or apparent posture, these are actually facsimile, utilitarian, and functional in intent. The expenditure of sufficient labor and time in rehearsal will yield more mature postures, which will be no longer facsimile, but real.

The milieu of the peer group society offers the adolescent a sphere in which to try out new points of view and new perspectives without confronting the differential emotional feedback that accompanies interpretation of the expression of dissenting views as antagonistic to a belief or value that is part of a consistent self-system—as is the case when the adolescent talks with generational elders. Development of a belief system requires a special type of atmosphere, wherein the lengthy intellectual discussions characteristic of this age of increasing horizons, new options, and expanding vistas are engaged, positions are offered, argued, and/or accepted freely. The adolescent peer group—a unique assembly of like individuals wherein few have yet evolved stable self-conceptions—provides this arena common to all in which discussion can proceed freely because no stable self-structures need to be defended.

The adolescent has so few permanent self-conceptions that a new perspective or belief is not considered a threat to either the speaker or the listener. The positive relation between strength of self-conception and resistance to value change of which Rokeach speaks is relatively absent. Hence, being in agreement with peers when necessary (or at odds with parents, if desired) is facilitated. Whereas adults must seriously confront the meaning of a new attitude or value as possibly threatening consonance of the self, the adolescent need exhibit no such caution. Not yet in possession of a stable set of cognitive elements or a stable self-perception, the adolescent is free to flit from attitude to attitude or belief to belief, inconsistency notwithstanding. Responding to cues from the social environment, the adolescent moves in the direction that appears most propitious at the moment. If incongruities are expressed, they are not experienced as related to any completed integration of self. These ever changing postures of the adolescent's incomplete self can be considered either his charm or his frustrating potential.

Two Postures in Coexistence: Public and Private

Accordingly, the adolescent's external behavior is misleading. The nonadolescent is often confused by the assumed meaning of the external behaviors involved in adolescent interaction. The overserious discussions are in reality adolescent counterparts of play, of trial and error. Conversely, the activity that appears to be play is in fact the business of the adolescent peer group. Play masks the dynamic operation of deep-structure functions such as ESA and $AERR^n$. Observable behaviors reflect any attitude or belief that conforms to current normative behaviors that reinforce active-member status. The true light involvement in heated discussion is masked by the drama of the exposition. Consequently, it can be seen that in adolescence two sets of attitudes and beliefs coexist—a public set and a private set. The public set comprises those that seem instrumental to success with peers and that serve the purpose of retaining membership in the peer group. These attitudes are expressed. Positions spawned by the rejection of traditional values and the introduction of new "teenage" forms may be loudly expressed, strengthening the notion of adolescent separateness from generational others. Those beliefs closer to the evolving self-system and hence more vulnerable may be carefully guarded if the adolescent is unsure or they are deemed unacceptable to the group. What is adopted privately in the construction of one's own belief system and what is expressed publicly may not coincide since pressure to remain in the group acts to effect and support a peer consensus. Present in latent posture but in highly active form are the ESA and the $AERR^n$, consistently serving the functional, instrumental need. The dialectic shuttle between private and public stance contributes to the field of forces in adolescent-peer-group interaction.

It is helpful to consider the overt manners or behaviors between adolescent members within a context of the quantity of energies expended to cope with peer-membership demands, both open and subtle. Again, overt actions may mask inner states. The prevalence of the detached "live and let live" attitude often observed might best be understood as an effort to maintain a system in equilibrium. The large energy quotient that may well be expended in continuing $AERR^n$ dynamic activity leaves little for real psychological involvement with others. Hence, an active motive may be to free oneself from concern with the behaviors of others not seen as immediately relevant to oneself. The slogan of "do what you want so long as you do not harm others" reflects a posture keyed to the developmental stage, rather than acceptance or even altruism. Here the adolescent actually reflects lack of real involvement or caring. Adolescents are egocentrically still involved in themselves. They do not yet invest in an "other" as occurs in a true friendship. They can easily leave the peer free to carry on as he wishes since any potential behaviors or attitudes expressed will not threaten a set of integrated self-elements, which remain to be achieved. A second major factor behind the adolescent resistance to passing judgment on fellow peers can be found in their daily latent posture. It is precisely because the constant adolescent posture is one of self-evaluation ($AERR^n$) that an opposite stance is stimulated in relation to peers. The position adopted overtly covers up the *almost constant private psychological activity*. The developmental status of the adolescent therefore stimulates a predisposition to adopt a nonjudgmental stance, often misperceived by the adolescent himself as "sophistication." Certainly, this laissez-faire position meets other functional needs for peer-group membership since it is congruent with the need not to alienate. Older-generation protests (of parents, clergy, or teachers) such as, "A true friend cares enough to judge and to share those judgments," are hence premature. They are sounded to individuals at a period of social development at which the protests cannot be heard.

Clearly, interaction at this primary-peer-group period is essentially still coaction. Peers, though physically closely associated, are psychologically disassociated. They are available to be used by one another. They engage one another in conversation and activity. But they are not involved with one another. Each is still egocentrically related to his own task needs. External conformity, functionally motivated, serves to mask this real individualism. Conformity and membership are not ends in themselves. Conformity assures the adolescent the continuity of membership that is necessary if he is to avail himself of the dynamic functions of peer-group interaction. Friends serve important stabilizing and growth functions. It is the function that is essential, not *the* specific friend; others will do as well. Adolescents at this period of life have too much work to do with themselves to be more than tangentially available to others. They are not yet developmentally ready for "true" friendship.

The milieu of the peer-group arena is one of opposites: freedom to experiment and conformity; a fun-loving stance and a functional preoccupation; strong positions and absence of an integrated self-core; pleasantries exchanged and hostilities handled indirectly or taken elsewhere; a public, busy, loud lightness of spirit and a private deliberate, withholding, serious stance. The nature of the primary peer group is paradoxical; its group character is molded by the dialectics of its members' development.

The Redefined Secondary Field

An anchor of interrelated cognitive elements of self-structure is in the process of construction but does not yet exist. This transitional status offers conditions that free the adolescent to exchange elements and to try out knowledges. At first, this small replacement activity endangers no stable whole; but as the adolescent progresses along the continuum to formulating stable elements, each projected change becomes increasingly interrelated and hence more complex. Clearly, this adolescent condition now differs from the condition of frameworklessness with which initial membership in the peer group was approached. Its current complexity reflects the adolescent imperative to engage the functions of the Adolescent Dialectic (AD). With incremental changes, the relative potency of environmental figures as well as their priority status undergoes change. With placement comes displacement. As the adolescent peer comes to occupy the primary position of relevance and import, former primary nurturant figures (parents and perhaps other relatives) move to positions of less prominence. This temporarily or possibly permanently altered relative position is *not* a rejection of parental meaning or function. Rather, it is a manifestation of the changing relevance of the parental generation to the developmental needs of the child now in transition to adulthood.

Developmental work of major proportions now takes place with peers. The home becomes the secondary field, still serving important and distinct functions, but of a different order. The necessary functions served by this now secondary field are *supplementary supportive* functions that act to foster and reinforce the adolescent's strength and energies necessary for active return to the primary arena wherein his social development is now centered. Up to now parenting functions have been clearly nurturant and overtly caretaking functions. Now, more often than not, the parenting of the adolescent needs does not require the same degree of observable presence; hence, unlabeled and (in comparison with former times) unseen, parents may go unrecognized, unacknowledged, and undesignated. With this change in the form of parenting, little continuing reinforcing feedback from offspring or from environmental figures in the context of parenting is offered. This distancing may be experienced as obsolescence and/or rejection.

A Port for Respite

The adolescent incorporates the now secondary field of parents and home with ambivalence. It is valued for its life supports; yet its affective potency has declined. Actually, it does serve as a safe spot to which adolescents bring leftover tensions from daily contests with self and with others. Earlier literature depicts the peer group as a haven away from pressures, but this formulation sees the peer group as an active, even taxing forum. Furthermore, it is the secondary field of the *home* that *provides the haven away*. Now that active developmental work is to be accomplished in the appropriate peer arena, replete with the pressures and tensions of the dynamic activity, only at home are individuals of immediate relevance and potential to elicit swings in affect absent, so that the system may rest. Notwithstanding protests to the contrary by the adolescent, even assigned tasks, if unrelated to social development and goal attainment, provide temporary respite from the demands of life with peers. They represent an opportunity for acceptable "diversionary" effort. Generally, the relevance of "home-assigned responsibilities" has been overestimated, often reflecting an assumption that the adolescent attributes as much relevance to the effort as does the adult whose psychological field is related to the character building, educational, or nurturant benefit of the task. In fact, any urgency for task completion that is exhibited by the adolescent may be a behavioral sign of the deep-structure imperative to get back to relevant concerns in the primary, not the secondary, arena. School-related tasks, work, and family relationships draw less energy than before since they are not perceived as the currently pertinent fields.

Inhibition of expression of negative affect with peers also holds implications for adolescent-parent relationships. In this alternative view of the adolescent-peer-group experience as necessary and not as choice, I conceptualize both consonant and stressful affective consequences of peer-group interactions as stimulating an assembly characterized by numerous tensions. Findings from the Philadelphia Study disclosed nonverbal expression of tension in the peer-group proper. Since at this primary-peer-group period of development, home and family are no longer experienced as constituting the primary arena, the quality of the relationship with these formerly potent environmental figures is seen as not immediately crucial and therefore as able to be risked. Suppressed tensions and angers, offshoots of peer-group activity that layers additional tensions onto the already precarious status of an unstable developmental stage, may be expressed in unexpected confrontations with parents, siblings, teachers, and assorted authority figures—sometimes hostile in character, even from a previously mild individual. Intensity of affect may be a remnant of a peer conflict, a peer-induced psychological injury that has remained unexpressed, a response to a disappointing AERR[n] experience. In the safety of the secondary field, an explosive response may erupt over a minor event or topic of discussion. Actions of others that ostensibly provoke and to which the outburst may be attributed may reflect only an opportunity grasped by the adolescent to expel angers, tensions, insecurities. Inhibited affect stirring within the adolescent, rather than the overt act of the other, is often the germane factor. But parents characteristically engage in self-searching to discover the new flaw in themselves or in the child that occasions such outbursts. In adolescence it is more likely the primary peer group, not the secondary field of the home, that can be the locus of the genesis of the affect. But responses are stored for expression with the safest targets—loved ones who may be angered but who usually do not reject.

A gulf—a no-man's-land that neither side can bridge—may be active. General communication difficulties of varying degree may surface between adult and child. The change in relationship and in the milieu of the secondary field is experienced but is not cognitively understood as a consequence of what is in fact appropriate developmental progression. The parent may again be mystified by the sudden distance that supplants a formerly close attachment. The expressed desire to attend a dance for a "fun time" does not communicate the urgent pressure of the adolescent imperative. Cognitive accessibility to deep-structure needs that motivate the adolescent to seek functional-interaction opportunties with peers is not easily translated, often stimulating frustration and guilt in the adolescent. Parental confusion is compounded by the inability to comprehend and hence to communicate on any common level of understanding. Thus another paradox surfaces: the safe secondary arena, viewed by the adolescent as the true haven, also frustrates. Although communications may begin affectionately, they may end quite differently.

The adolescent's stage is the peer arena. Though publicly present at home, more often than not he is privately absent. He seems to come to life on the phone or when a friend appears. Flexibility, flux, and instability are touchstones in the adolescent's primary arena. However, in the supplementary support field he needs stability, certainty, and structure. An appropriate role for parents often lies in firmness, not in the popular and more easily mounted flexibility. Notwithstanding verbal protestations, the adolescent needs a firm forum to which to return. Nor do adolescents need innovation. Changing values and postures may be requested but are not necessarily desired. A strong, stable, supportive secondary home field buttresses developmental struggles, thereby helping the adolescent maintain stability in an unstable period.

Progressive "Give and Take"

Notions of the hierarchical prominence of the peer group and the supplementary status of home and family offered here set a perspective for beginning to alter a conception of the structural relationship between parents and adolescents. Affective bonds undergo a change, which must be accompanied by a corresponding change in the functions of environmental contexts. Confusion for the parent may ensue. For example, somewhat after the advent of adolescence when the family's altered functions as life-support and emotional-support systems begin, the now secondary field is called on for a third function. It is couched within the context of a "next step up" toward adulthood. The adolescent condition at the primary-arena stage of social development is one of lack of anchor, wherein interrelated elements are not present in the cognitive structure to yield any constancy of self. This status has been described as one of mixed blessings in that the adolescent can easily exchange elements of his cognitive structure without upsetting the whole. He can swap attitudes, reject and accept beliefs and values as he pleases. In the peer-group arena members experience similar rights since there is no challenge to a basic core self, as would be the case with a group of adults. Discussion can be intellectual, experimental, humorous. Interaction is bipolar in nature—on the one hand, carrying a deep-structure $AERR^n$ dimension, but superficially a game—pleasant, light, challenging, enjoyable. With the adult, the adolescent confronts a well-thought-out belief system integrated over time; hence, the adult is a far more serious conversationalist. Furthermore, the adult may find the adolescent's skepticism or his challenge to basic values jarring, disruptive, and serious, and therefore may not respond easily to trial-and-error debate. An attitude close to the adult core may be threatened, possibly stimulating the adult to reevaluate attitudes or to remove or change a belief or even an element. Since for the adult, adding or changing elements, even in the service of achieving consonance, runs the risk of upsetting the balance of an integrated whole, he does not engage lightly. How understandable then that the adolescent would prefer discourse with peers. But with the passage of developmental time, $AERR^n$ yields conclusions that earmark specific elements as potentially eligible for incorporation into a self-structure. The atmosphere in the peer group at this developmental point becomes incrementally more serious. The quality of discussion in the secondary field now changes, also. At this more advanced point of progress toward the completion of adolescent tasks, the more serious quality of adolescent discussion in the home field may reflect an attempt by the adolescent to test a second level, perhaps the beginnings of an $AERR^n$ search for value and relevance beyond peers. Although peers represent a relevant group of fellow travelers who will also be future fellow travelers, parents represent the broader arena in which the adolescent soon will also compete.[2] Thus an important third function of the secondary field as a "tryout stepping stone" is now invoked. A more involved, less challenging, and more inquiring verbal interactional posture, now manifestly obvious in the adolescent in the home field, suggests that satiation of need for actions of the primary-peer-arena dynamic functions may have begun. Increased shuttling back and forth between the primary peer arena and secondary fields evolves as functions that are worked on in peer-group interactions begin to move toward satisfaction.

Notes

1. In his work on social comparison processes, Festinger (1954) established that hostility may be present as accompanying the cessation of comparison. He suggested that derogation may be present to the extent that continued comparison implies unpleasant consequences. Recent research (Mettee and Smith 1977; Brickman and Bulman 1977) has begun to pursue questions of the affective consequences of comparisons.

2. Findings from ARGI disclosed that among a choice of fourteen reference groups on ten separate issues, parents did in fact occupy a strong position of influence, particularly in future rather than present-related areas (table 10-10).

Table 10-10
Mean Percentage of Influence Accorded Reference Groups per Issue

Category	Amnesty	Haircut	Year Off	Cheating Friend	Shop Jacket	Drug Use	Living Together	Qualities to Look For	What College	Day Off
Brothers and sisters, older	9.6	8.7	13.4	8.4	9.3	10.0	10.3	10.0	10.8	4.2
Brothers and sisters, younger	1.2	5.2	0.6	0.7	3.1	0.7	0.9	1.2	0.5	1.7
Friends 2-5 years younger	0.9	1.5	0.7	0.8	0.9	1.3	1.0	1.5	0.8	1.5
Friends 2-5 years older	9.6	5.9	10.4	6.2	8.9	7.3	5.9	7.0	6.5	5.2
Friends over 5 years older	4.2	1.4	6.4	1.9	2.6	7.8	9.9	7.2	5.3	0.5
Media	25.5	1.1	4.3	1.2	7.8	21.0	5.6	3.6	6.8	4.5
Clergy	3.9	0.4	1.2	1.6	0.0	4.2	7.4	4.6	0.6	0.0
Neighborhood age-mates	5.0	9.8	4.2	7.2	16.1	10.1	6.5	8.2	1.8	23.1
Parents	17.8	27.1	29.7	14.2	22.5	11.8	18.4	27.5	25.8	9.1
Relatives, older	2.6	1.4	2.4	0.3	1.7	1.2	2.0	4.1	3.6	0.2
School age-mates	9.7	12.7	6.2	34.5	20.0	14.1	9.2	10.4	8.8	18.3
School personnel	5.0	0.3	14.8	8.7	0.1	3.1	1.9	3.6	25.2	0.8
Special friend	2.0	17.3	2.4	7.2	6.5	3.2	18.6	9.0	2.7	24.7
Other (please specify)	2.9	7.3	2.0	7.0	0.5	4.1	2.6	1.5	0.8	6.1

Note: N = 66.

11 The Primary Peer Group: Forces for Leaving

In the period of primary-peer-group membership, the dynamic functions of major impact are ESA and $AERR^n$, the former providing the raw materials and the latter refining and weaving the unique pattern. The action of ESA also allows the individual to maintain the adolescent state by affording him a pseudo-self-structure. Hence at each moment in time the adolescent is an individual with distinct opinions and values. Quick change is possible because the facades are temporary. Concurrently, he can borrow, try out, substitute, or keep. Engaging these two functions of the Adolescent Dialectic (AD) in trial and error and reconsiderations within the peer-group interactional system affords the adolescent a means to test and confirm characteristics as relevant, functional, and congruent.

The adolescent comes out of frameworklessness by borrowing elements of self-structures via ESA and by constantly altering these borrowed elements of a temporary structure in a posture of consistent openness to change. During these primary stages the adolescent lives in the present in a more literal way than adult minds perceive. Each moment past is history, each next moment future. The atomization of time is a function of borrowed knowledge and of an awareness of being in a state of changing and seeking. A unique quality of the peer group is the existence of its *present orientation concurrently with its future imperative.* Thus even in the present moment an element undergoes distinct functions to ascertain the present and future values the adolescent may want to keep.

Impostor elements are gradually replaced by evolved elements perceived as one's own. Outward behavioral expositions and loud defenses of borrowed positions subside as the selection of potentially stable self-elements proceeds. Anchoring of each element after careful coordination with each of the others leads to an end result of balance and harmony between individually satisfying cognitive elements and defines the completion of that primary task in which the adolescent is involved in his passage through adolescence. This chapter and the next will set forth criteria for identifying the incremental points of passage along the way.

Advent of the Future Imperative

A significant milestone in the smooth progression through the stage of adolescence is the initial replacement of pseudoelements by permanent elements. The acquisition of some general attributes and some notion of feasible future directions provides both status and the beginnings of self-assurances. At this time, in service of the adolescent task of self-direction, a second-stage activity of $AERR^n$ becomes active. More and more, $AERR^n$ is now characterized by emphasis not only on "Do I have this characteristic or how much of it do I have," but also on "What goal will this attribute help me achieve?" or perhaps by a more directed focus on a specific goal.

In the initial peer group, the Adolescent Kinetic processes of the $AERR^n$ function focus on the presence or absence of the attribute and the relative merit of the characteristic under examination. As initial integrations of characteristics cluster, a longer-range dimension of testing becomes prominent, one that incrementally becomes integrated into all evaluation and selection functions. "How will this characteristic serve me in the future?" is a future weighting applied to element examination—an F valance—imposed on the $AERR^n$ function. Ever pragmatic, this $AERR^n$-F function is the future-goal criterion directly applied to test the future usefulness of any and every element. The greater the amount of integration taking place, the closer the adolescent is to establishing real self-elements, the more quickly future-goal focus is added to the $AERR^n$ function. As this functions grows in strength, it progresses from $AERR^n$-f to $AERR^n$-F. Gradually, and as later stages of peer-group membership advance, the F emphasis of $AERR^n$, the $AERR^n$-F, becomes the primary valuation criterion. $AERR^n$-F will merge with the related goal to $AERR^n$-FG (future goals) or $AERR^n$-G (goal). The latter significate is applied when the goal becomes specific and future related but is not immediately potent. (In arriving at the future goal, there may be a series of intermediate goals—$AERR^n$-IG. The latter will be subsumed under FG).

A future goal grows out of alternative choices and perceived posibilities. While these choices are extant, elements can be judged for future general utility instrumental to these various alterntives or to the choice itself. During this activity, the $AERR^n$ function might be symbolized as $AERR^n$-fg (lower-case letters indicate beginning stages of F and G). Eventually, a specific goal is selected and $AERR^n$ narrows to $AERR^n$-g. Emphasis is on direct utility to the end in sight. According to status or state of development, the focus of $AERR^n$ on individual elements narrows or widens. Each element under consideration must be applied to the clusters of elements to test utility, flexibility, interface, and so forth. "Does this fit with others?" "Together, are they functional to any selected goal?" "How about other goals?" "Under those or these circumstances, does this element fit?" In the interests of $AERR^n$-fg or $AERR^n$-g applications, the Adolescent Kinetic process supplies specific others who appear to possess similar element clusters and/or others who express some experience with the desired goal for evaluation. Functional assessments are arrived at by $AERR^n$-fg or

$AERR^n$-g through a consideration of blend and utility of several integrated attributes to the specified goal attainment.

As seen in earlier chapters, widely scattered, gross action of the Adolescent Kinetic has been necessary to gather a spectrum of information with which to assess easily and then reject or retain the first-stage inventory. The second-stage review now under discussion then permits a narrowing of the scope of inquiry. Certain attributes no longer need the broad-scope $AERR^n$ or a more focused $AERR^n$-fg function. The global, rapid volume of the more active primary period no longer meets these new needs since no new source of information on the attribute is seen as available in the primary peer group. At a point at which the Adolescent Kinetic activity has actualized resolution of an ESA element as having sufficient or insufficient potential for acceptance into the self-structure, the initial $AERR^n$ function begins to approach satiation. (Active in helping to achieve this satiation of elements and the beginnings of self-structure are both $AERR^n$-fg in the latter part of primary-peer-group membership and the beginning $AERR^n$-F of that same developmental period).

Satiation: Pathway to a First-Stage Self-Structure

When new information sources on a specific attribute are no longer available within the primary peer group, not only is a stance of lack of inquiry manifested by the inquiring adolescent but also definitive statements on the matter are issued. This behavior signals the beginning of a state of satiation on that attribute. Since the peer group is an assembly of adolescents who reach different points of development at different times, each also reaches satiation on one attribute or another at his own pace and in his own style. Hence, at any given time each individual adolescent may be invoking some form of $AERR^n$ on x attribute and simultaneously may be serving as the positive instance to another on an attribute for which his own state of satiation is overtly manifested.

It is important to distinguish the condition of satiation from the idea of closure. The latter infers finalization and full acceptance, contract, or cementing. Satiation, however, is not permanent; rather, it is satiation of the hunger, or sufficient answer to the instant question, or adequate examination of the object. Closure, on the other hand, eliminates once and for all any other alternative and determines a finite ending (of element selection of direction or choice). In later, secondary-group periods we see closure; but here, at the end of the primary-peer-group period, satiation on elements represents a starting point for the eventual closure process.

Contrast between the adult condition of satisfaction of comparison and the adolescent condition of satiation may be pertinent. In his work on influence and social comparison, Gordon (1966) delineated behavior that reflects a state of satisfaction of self-questioning yielded by sufficient social comparison. He suggests that once an individual is satisfied with the validity of his opinion (and is thereby freed from the need to continue to engage in social comparison), a desire to demonstrate the ability or opinion is activated and expressed by attempts to influence other people. Implicit in Gordon's work, as well as in Festinger (1954), is the notion that the processes of inquiry and satisfaction occur at all stages of life.

The present position is that in the period of adolescence, the developmental condition necessitates a substantively different kind of comparison than is needed at any other period of life. In fact, the Adolescent Kinetic energizes great volumes of simultaneous inquiries for concurrent functions of the AD. This tumultuous condition contributes to the instability of adolescence, on the one hand, and characterizes its uniqueness on the other. Crucial in differentiating adolescent satiation from Gordon's adult satisfaction is the fact that the adolescent has no integrated self-structure with which a new posture must fit. Gordon does state that the adult experiences a need to demonstrate the new ability or opinion. What Gordon does not discuss, however, is that perhaps the adult must influence in order to eliminate any dissonance aroused by introduction of the new element. By contrast, the adolescent need feel only that he has sufficiently utilized Adolescent Kinetic to establish the positive valence of the attribute. It does not have to connect with other elements; the adolescent may not yet have many "own elements." Hence adolescent satiation needs to establish nothing more than the currency of the attribute as "possible." Results from the Philadelphia study (Seltzer 1975, 1980) disclosed that satiation occured in 5.1 percent of the statements of comparison (rank 8 of 9). Satiation was conceptually defined as "an internal resolution of alternatives manifested by an abatement of the need to compare, reflected in a philosophical stance characterized by a reasoned argument on a given issue, a tendency to attempt to influence, and a willingness to stand by one's position despite opposition." This finding implies the lack of readiness of this group of subjects to discontinue comparison behavior or, conversely, the strength of the desire to continue comparing. The fact that comparison with a dissimilar other, conceptually defined as "an individual or group of individuals representing a condition, attribute, performance, or point of view unlike that of oneself," its conceptual partner, ranked last and just below satiation at 3.0 percent underscores the lack of interest in the individual who seems different. Findings on satiation imply that the adolescents were in the primary-peer-group stage and not ready to stop looking and measuring. Results of comparison with dissimilar others might imply either primary- or secondary-peer-group level. In the primary group the members are interested in specific, not general, elements.

Adolescent satiation is neither related to nor affected by congruence with an already existing self-element. The only elements present are pseudoelements postured for replacement by permanent, stable self-elements yet to come, or perhaps some initial stable-element applicants.

Whereas adults experience satisfaction in having reached a conclusion, the adolescent is not yet concerned with congruence of the attributes that achieve satiation of the initial $AERR^n$ function. Only validity of the attribute is tested. Four conditions must be met: (1) that it really exists; (2) that it is functional in the present; (3) that it is functional in the future or to a specific future goal; and (4) that it possess its own combinatory, integrative potential to blend with other attributes. In the period of peer-group interaction, a general potential for combinatory action is determined. Although condition (4) implies that satiation of $AERR^n$ has occurred in each projected temporary element, yielding a completed set of cognitive self-elements, the actual work necessary to achieve combinatory integrative potential of specifically selected elements is actually accomplished in the next period of peer-group interaction (the secondary peer group), where selected implementation of the function $AERR^n$ in relation to specific goals is imposed. Reference to these acts of consolidation and integration are included here since they may appear prematurely despite the fact that the dimension of future goals within adolescent identity tasks and its integration in the $AERR^n$ function are more active in the secondary peer group. It is important to recognize that this process straddles both primary- and secondary-peer-group dynamic activity. Therefore, although we isolate $AERR^n$-G as more heavily active in the secondary peer group (transformed into SER-G) it might also be recognized as active in the primary group, conceptualized a $AERR^n$-g and/or $AERR^n$-G. An attribute medley that has fugue potential is established in relation to specific goals as the classification process is repeated over and over from the most open and general to an ever more refined and complex orchestration.

Satiation Levels

During the initial period of primary-group membership the large volume of new data available to be assembled calls for the Adolescent Kinetic to be poised constantly and activated instantly, whether in random scanning or in purposeful invocation. The ESA and $AERR^n$ functions, which worked most often in tandem during this earlier period, used the full potential of Adolescent Kinetic to evaluate discrete elements for appropriateness and fit.

As the adolescent moves toward satiation of the need for primary-group functions, the assessment process narrows its focus and the Adolescent Kinetic broadens its scope to bring several attributes into one focus for evaluation by $AERR^n$ of potential blend and combinatory utility. This second-stage function of $AERR^n$ does not interfere with the other, still ongoing, first-stage discrete functions. Both first- and second-plateau processes are active. To first-plateau activity is allocated discrete individual attributes, whereas the second plateau deals with combinatory attributes, and a third plateau is devoted to assessing functional quality or the attributes' relation to potential goals:

First level	Do I have a talent at math?
Second level	Do I have a talent at math *and* chemistry? Math *or* music?
Third level	Will my level of talent at math and chemistry be an advantage to being a physical scientist? Jon is going to be a doctor. I am as good at math and science as he, but not as good as George who will be a physicist.

First level	Satiation.
Second level	Combinatory satiation (includes first level).
Third level	Goal-integrated satiation (includes first and second level).

Clearly, second- and third-level satiation does not occur in isolation, but rather in relation to the first plateau, and to the first and second and the second and third plateaus, respectively. At the point in the process of development at which satiations begin, not only is each individual attribute in its own orbit of relative readiness for satiation, but at each plateau differing degrees of readiness are operative within the same model.

Satiation at each level involves an $AERR^n$ function sufficient to arrive at closure for that level of acceptance or rejection. Satiation takes place when enough time has elapsed for the various dimensions of $AERR^n$ to gather enough evidence for eventual closure. When satiation of attributes begins, more often than not, it occurs on many attributes simultaneously rather than sequentially. Therefore, what is unique to adolescence is the numbers of first-stage resolutions and that they occur so close together in time, even simultaneously. It is this coming to satiation that culminates the most active functions of the Adolescent Dialectic (AD) and the indefatigable Adolescent Kinetic in gathering endless data for those functions. It is also the culmination of large-peer-group experience.

Transitions

The appearance of satiation heralds the passage through major functions and their processes in which the adolescent has moved from bondage to objects in the social environment to the beginnings of a status of pseudoelements and on to identification of true self-elements. It is this appearance of *satiation that marks the coming to an end of the primary-peer-group activity stage.* It is not abrupt or clear or discrete in any way—this primary stage ending is merely schematically drawn.

The adolescent must now hew, polish, and refine the elements for permanent installation. A stable self-structure is in the process of formation. In the beginning of the process, adolescents use others to stand in for a network of elements not yet possessed (ESA). The adolescent engages $AERR^n$ in assessment and evaluation of elements. At any one time actual adolescent elements are evolved and others are borrowed. Elements are dropped or retained as assessment of both self- and pseudoelements occurs. Satiation via $AERR^n$ is accomplished, and the element is either identified as one's "own" or is rejected. As an "own" element is identified and retained, a pseudoelement can be replaced, and the self-structure will continue to retain its stability. The self stabilizes and defines itself as an aggregate of anchored elements, not ungrounded or labile pseudoelements.

Therefore, the initial self-structure is built of elements and clusters of elements integrated for present utilization and capable of future flexibility. A relationship exists between elements as well as a capability to blend them and to substitute one for another. Closure on self-structure occurs incrementally at different levels of satiation and integration. However, the dialectical imperatives have moved in contrapuntal waves. As a consequence of their actions, satiation on some attributes has occurred, whereas new needs for continuing Adolescent Kinetic activity may have surfaced. Some characteristics now are perceived as strong, others as weaker. When the need for the action of $AERR^n$ is stated, the relative status of each element (ability, personality characteristics, and so forth) is sufficiently resolved to be seen both individually and in cluster. Self-conception is the ultimate product—an amalgam of individual assessments and perceptions of reflected group assessments.

Advent of Self-Elements

Self-perceptions now replace the pseudoelements supplied by friends, acquaintances, and relatives whose characteristics have "stood in" as replacements for the absent self-elements. (This developmental progress may have some surprising manifestations, such as the abandonment of what had appeared to be a treasured friendship.) As the adolescent moves closer to the completion of permanent identification of self-elements for incorporation into his unique self-structure, he is increasingly less dependent on the friendships he previously held essential for the two crucial functions of (1) relative assessment and measurement and (2) provision of pseudo-elements to stand in temporarily for his missing "own" elements.

As more pseudoelements are replaced and the adolescent's constellation comes to include more and more of his own elements, the adolescent experiences the mixed blessings of both opportunity and new responsibility. No longer a dealer in stand-in pseudoelements or borrowed attributes, he must now refine, select, and choose among self-elements those that will become the foundation blocks of his self-structure. ESA and $AERR^n$ functions honed in the Adolescent Dialectic are now narrowed to Specific-Element Selection (SES) and Selected-Element Refinement (SER). The action changes from assessments of "Do I possess the borrowed attributes?" to the weightier "Is it of the quality I want?" "What use will it be to me as mine?" and "Do I have enough of it to utilize functionally within the time I have for the purposes I want?" This more selective selection and more refined refinement are altered functions of Element Substituting Action (ESA) and Assessment Evaluation-Reassessment Reevaluation ($AERR^n$)— more concentrated and more limited in scope. Specific Element Selection (SES) and Selected Element Refinement (SER) grow in frequency of use and importance as the adolescent progresses toward a full self-structure and self-elements are built into the structure. Substitution of an own element for a pseudoelement—one at a time—retains the system in equilibrium as the assembly of a true self-structure proceeds. Once real self-elements, no matter how rudimentary in form, have become an established part of the self-structure, the adolescent has moved beyond the functional need for a stand-in for the self.

Satiation and establishment of elements are the products of a hard-fought internal resolution of alternatives. Behaviorally, we may observe a sudden burst of confidence and of the desire to influence. With the achievement of satiation on a sufficient number of attributes, the adolescent may begin to feel more certain of who and what he is. Imperceptibly at first, the outward manifestations of the decreasing need for the ESA function become apparent. Simultaneously, with the Adolescent Kinetic action reduced, outward behaviors may also reflect a growing internal equilibrium. The adolescent may appear less tense, able more easily to choose between alternatives and to stay with a task or activity longer. Outward manifestation of some inner resolutions sporadically begin to be obvious.

Rumblings for Leaving the Primary Peer Group

This more stable base of initial equilibrium is shortlived. Soon a new tension arises, stimulating a new set of forces—forces to leave the primary group. Tension again increases. The self-elements that have been selected are recognized as needing further exploration and perhaps refinement. Fortunately, the tension level does not reach the former pitch of the frameworkless state in which the intense need for affiliation with peers was first experienced. Unlike that earlier undirected, abstract anxiety, now a more conscious tension manifests itself, incorporating a direction for its own reduction. Many quests satiated diminish stimulation of the Adolescent Kinetic and reduce the need for high-volume interactions. Thereby a different relationship to membership in the peer group begins. The experience of satiation brings on a diminished necessity for global data on cotravelers. This may yield a somewhat disquieting period for the adolescent since the reduced need for a library of raw data begins to suggest that it is time to leave this comfort. Ironically, as urgency is reduced through the beginning of satiation, the similar others come to appear *too* similar.

Needs that only membership in the primary peer group could satisfy now feel near completed. The adolescent has established an interim framework. The primary peer group and its supply of pseudo-self-elements has served well to stabilize the self and to continue the utilization of these pseudoelements in a beginning effort to assemble one's own elements. Now the adolescent has some general notion of who he is and of his tentative direction. Since the functional properties of the peer group are now losing their potency, a sense of the nonutility of continued primary-peer-group affiliation begins to stir. Since such large numbers are no longer needed, the costs of membership may be greater than the gains. Still not ready for the adult arena, the adolescent experiences an initial sense of nonfit with the large peer group. As the urgencies of the early primary period abate with gradual satiations, the derived strength of the cohesive group (in which membership was a must) ceases to provide the bulwark it heretofore has offered. Fewer friends, fewer gang clusters, fewer data, fewer substitutions are now needed.

Forces in the service of developmental readiness to leave the primary peer group become activated when developmental needs met by the membership have been sated. Forces for leaving the primary peer group gather when the conjoint actions of the dynamic functions of $AERR^n$ and ESA have been sufficient to yield a set of potentially stable elements, which in fact is the end result of their combined actions. Accompanying this developmental milestone is an intuitive sense that (1) additional information on global abilities or opinions to be yielded by continued interactions in the present adolescent large group are not necessary, and (2) raw material for more exact assessment of specific selected elements will not be gained in the large group. *Movement to a new group is experienced as necessary.* The progression of development that activates forces to leave the primary peer group does not eliminate the need for continuing peer contact. However, the desired interaction now has directed goals. Now that identification of potential self-elements has taken place, it is refinement of self-elements for permanence that is necessary. The focus has been narrowed. The desired peer group is therefore a smaller, more differentiated group, one identified as closest to the dimensions to be refined.

In order to avail himself of the appropriate arena in which to carry forth transactions with peers perceived as more similar to himself on those dimensions that he has selected as consonant with the beginning rumblings of his self-identity, the individual adolescent uses one or a series of secondary groups to gradually complete the task of self-definition. The large numbers of the adolescent peer group are no longer necessary. The adolescent is generally cognitively attuned to the new group in which he now needs to seek membership. This choice varies according to the degree of closure already accomplished. When the adolescent achieves the ability to factor and select variables out of "own elements" or clusters of discretely identified elements within the greater peer group, the movement to a secondary group can proceed directly. Others not quite so certain of closure may require an interim group or groups, or even tangential memberships in a variety of special groups in order to refine an array of possible talents or directions. Some may need to return for short periods to the primary group. Each adolescent has his own individual style, pace, and unique time span on the path to achieving closure on the developmental tasks. Hence some may remain members of the larger peer group longer. Others may come and go several times. Still others may leave once and not return.

It may be in order here to differentiate the adolescent who has achieved sufficient closure from one who needs to leave the group temporarily (from time to time) to gather strength in order to return. Some adolescents have not yet fully completed the developmental work of the primary peer arena but have defined some self-elements. In order to reduce some of the tension that may intrude on their capacity to continue as members of the primary peer group, they may need to refine and achieve final closure on these elements. Arriving at some aspects of closure permits them to continue to participate and risk exposure to the continuing forceful dialectical intensity of the functional interaction in the primary peer group. They need to separate themselves from the intensity and the global experience in order to refine one or two elements firmly. Then they set these aspects aside, no longer having to deal with them actively. They feel satisfied because they have less to juggle. Behaviorally, this inability to handle the intensity of stimuli may be manifested in a temporary departure from the large group of peers—perhaps to a special interest group—followed by a return. Certainly, occasional movement out is used by many adolescents for brief periods only. When the element has been refined and feels like a part of the self (or perhaps has been rejected), the youth more comfortably returns to his peers.

This new orientation to self-elements that need firming up and refinement toward closure lead to a new comprehension of self-evaluation. Whereas earlier concerns were weighted toward group opinions and other peers' evaluations of himself or of borrowed self-elements, the adolescent now turns to questioning and examining his own closely. An equation of "self to other" changes to one of "self to self." This change is far reaching in that it opens the adolescent to consider outside reference groups heretofore avoided or relegated to lesser importance. Any number of variations can occur in the transition from primary to secondary peer groups. In general, there is no preferred model. The route selected is based in part on the history of reinforcements and the conditioned responses that form the habit structure. The essential features include involvement first in a large peer group, followed by selective movement to a smaller, less global, more homogeneously identified group. The precise process, however, varies idosyncratically.

12 The Secondary Peer Group: Functions and Processes

Although overlapping in time and rarely a discrete event, readiness for entry into a smaller, more clearly defined group of peers and the transactions that commence represent what is outwardly perceived as the beginning of maturity. In fact, the refining processes and transactions that will follow over a considerable period of time continue to mingle and merge with still unfinished functions to refine a "maturing" process of weeding out and cementing in.

Movement to the Secondary Peer Group

Schematically, a movement between primary and secondary peer groups reflects the accrued self-elements translated into the beginnings of self-structure, the achievements of ESA and AERR^n, and the organization and utilization of AD functions. Some adolescents shift in one motion; others shuttle back and forth, in the same or different groups.

Alternate Routes

1	2	3
Primary peer group	Primary peer group	Primary peer group
Secondary peer group	Secondary peer group	Secondary peer group
	Primary peer group	Primary peer group
	Secondary peer group	Secondary peer group
		Primary peer group
		Secondary peer group

Once the adolescent has completed the first plateau of assembly of instruments of cognitive structure and has moved to the secondary peer group, the now more mature adolescent wishes to refine specific elements for permanent inclusion or rejection. Elements have been chosen that may relate to a vocational or personality goal. Now more refined contours must be discovered and the feasibility of achievement determined. Hence the criteria on which the secondary arena is based are that it contains similarly perceived, not diverse others. Diversity of relevant others was necessary for the value of global attributes needed as raw material, but specific specimens of selected similar types make up the contours of the secondary arena. The interaction with smaller number of peers who meet specified descriptors calls forth slower, more deliberate precision. Both ESA and $AERR^n$ take on altered forms to serve newly constituted AD functions. The character of Adolescent Kinetic changes. Its intensity, its whirlpool nature, and the pressure of immediate action now are all dysfunctional. Its scope is reduced to a changed arena, but its action is still necessary. Adolescent Kinetic must now be used for slower refinement over time. It will be recalled that sufficient utilization of Adolescent Kinetic in the large adolescent peer group yielded Jon the information that he had ability in music that was stronger than he had previously recognized. Furthermore, it was greater than his ability in math or science. Now, in the secondary smaller arena, the question changes from a reflexive, qualitative, "Am I good, as good as, or better at math, at science, at music" to an outer-directed positional question: "I have chosen music. Within this area, I must know my relative position to others who have also identified music as an element of self." Forces are active for Jon to pick out peers who are musicians—and perhaps then musicians who are not peers at all. Adolescent Kinetic slows in motion, transformed from Ado K to Ado k.

Forces for Action in the Secondary Peer Group

The small secondary group is perceived as specialized, a more relevant arena in which to refine or reject elements in the service of cementing elements in the orchestration of cognitive self-structure. Indeed, several or many smaller groups may be needed to seek refinement and closure, all of which constitute the secondary arena. In this secondary arena the derivative functions Specific Element Selection (SES) and Selected Element Refinement (SER) serve inventory and refinement functions, just as ESA and $AERR^n$ did in the primary arena. But the operative mechanisms are slower and more specific, more intense, perhaps to all appearances more serious.

Second-Stage Functions

Refinements of self continue in relation to elements already in the cognitive structure. SES and SER represent the same inventory and refinement functions that served in the primary-peer-group period to acquire and assess temporary elements and stopgap structures. They might be viewed as "second-stage" ESA and $AERR^n$. Whereas the expansive scope and breadth of ESA and $AERR^n$ were impressive and the enormous power of the

Adolescent Kinetic (Ado K) to energize their activity seems infinite, the focused, confined activity of SES and SER seems, by comparison, of a reduced order of magnitude. However, SES and SER are no less intense and no less serious than the parent functions. However, their more finite productive ends are more measurable, more specific, and more likely to remain with the adolescent longer, perhaps permanently. Thus a subtle quality attaches to SER and to SES that gives the appearance of more seriousness and more gravity applied than to the more ubiquitous ESA and $AERR^n$—which are still functioning actively.

Earlier, broader-scope functions were activated almost at any time as the high-powered Adolescent Kinetic (Ado K) brought volumes of elements for selection. ESA was in a constant motion of supplying substitute elements, but SES is slower and more deliberate in its one-at-a-time pace since it is now drawing from a much reduced inventory. Similarly, $AERR^n$ worked at cosmic speeds at many levels simultaneously, (and conjointly with ESA), whereas its secondary-arena derivative, SER, must work sequentially and thoroughly toward more serious closure and permanence (element cementing). The Specific Element Selection (SES) must supply specific elements for adolescent self-structure refinement. The Selected Element Refinement (SER) must test utility and tolerance and must synchronize in cluster with other elements. Elements now contend for ownership and permanence, quite different from the earlier "rental" arrangement.

Again, as with congregation of the primary peer group, the state of readiness of the functional assembly itself gives rise to the Adolescent Dialectic (AD), activating SES and SER into spontaneous action in much the same way as it had activated ESA and $AERR^n$. This time the measurement is with a similarly perceived individual whose SES has selected the same element or particular cluster of elements. It may be a music and theater cluster; it may be a scientific cluster; it may be a political cluster. Individuals and small groups have been selected for perceived similarity on these elements for purposes of refinement of these very same elements. In the secondary arena the adolescent deliberately chooses the target person because of perceived element possession. Whereas the original function, IRA, quickly scanned the primary peer arena and selected another for a global rating, the global other (or total other) is no longer the object of the deliberate process. ESA and $AERR^n$ functions together yielded satiation on potential permanent characteristics or elements. In the secondary group, however, the target of the refinement process yet to follow is selected because he possesses the identified element. This time it is neither the person who is the object of SER, nor even the person and the characteristic; it is primarily the selected attribute(s) or characteristic(s) that are focused upon.

The dynamic functions SES and SER serve an in-depth experience of closure. That operative satiation in the primary peer group, which wrought an initial element self-structure (through the AD functions ESA and AERR^n), contributes an essentially "qualifying informational" closure. Satiation in the primary peer group implies that enough confidence has been achieved in one's own perception of both consonance with and quality of attribute so that any additional information available from the larger group is no longer necessary. Decision for acceptance or rejection of an element can be based on information gathered on the element alone. Closure accomplished in the secondary peer arena is the actual end process after the AERR^n has contributed its information, which occurs only after the point at which the SER—the careful honing process that clarifies uncertain aspects of the projected self-attribute in order to satisfy internal questions—has also been satiated. Only then can the decision for permanent adoption into the self-structure be made.

In this sequential second motion, operationalized within the secondary arena, an important dimension of the SER function is displayed. Whereas the AERR^n-g (lower-case g to indicate that its action is goal related-goal seeking) was inherent to the primary-arena AD function of AERR^n, actual consideration of the functional relevance of the element to the goal is emphasized and becomes more prominent in the secondary-peer-group period. Consideration of permanent adoption of the already selected element in which the adolescent feels personally confident takes place in relation to the SER-G function (capital G representing a goal finalized in more substantive form within a more precise inquiring posture of an adolescent dealing with fewer selected integrated elements of the secondary-peer-group period).

SER's sequential process follows the AD functions (ESA and AERR^n) that initially identified goals by asking questions about which characteristics are essential to goal achievement and, of these, which the individual has. Functions activated by the Adolescent kinetic (Ado k) in the secondary peer group provide raw data on other peers seen to possess the desired characteristics isolated by their own SES. Those seen as having the necessary groupings are targets for the SER function of self-assessment in relation to eventual fit and feasibility. The concept of *goal* permeates Ado k information gathering in the secondary arena. Self-elements are tested as to their quality of instrumental goal validity and accorded a place in a range. This unique adolescent "focused" dynamic SER function injects a *reality-based* component into the potential self-element evaluation that ESA had provided and SES had selectively isolated as a potential permanent element. Fantasy in relation to a goal is penetrated by the action of SER and a focused Adolescent kinetic (Ado k) that energizes the process. For example:

1. You proceed to think of ballet as a profession.
2. You begin to believe you have dancing talent (AERR^n).

3. You begin to notice the attributes of ballerinas in the real world (AERR^n-f).
4. You are attracted to other dancers and join their group (SES).
5. You study those who are good dancers, especially those who have achieved or demarcated dancing as their goal (SER).
6. The abstract goal of becoming a ballet dancer becomes real as you need to confront relative dancing skill and assess your suitability for the goal (SER-G).

In the Philadelphia Study (Seltzer 1975, 1980), goal-oriented statements for the middle to late adolescents were conceived as incorporating more than an estimate of "How far am I from the goal," which implies that a goal is settled. A measurement process of the self in relation to one or a number of goals was seen as more characteristic. Therefore, statements of adolescent comparison with a goal were conceptualized to reflect a continuous process of back-and-forth evaluations of self in relation to the feasibility, fit, and attainability of a specific goal or goals. The results disclosed the prominence of the comparison with a goal. It was the third most frequently appearing type of comparison, ranking at 15.5 percent, just under upward and downward comparison. Findings lent support to the strong presence of a goal-oriented cognitive stance in the comparison behavior of the seventeen-year-olds.

Integration and Flexibility. A subdimension of SER specific to the integrative potential of the cognitive self-structure under construction is also active at this point, SER-IF—representing integration value and flexibility. In considering the permanence of an element, the element must not only be consonant with the other elements but must also possess a quality of flexibility so that it is accessible for differential utilization, in service of goals and a future that are as yet relatively uncertain. Beyond this, the element must obtain congruity with other elements and exhibit tolerance or malleability to adjust into a cluster with refined elements already in place, as well as with goal demands yet to come. Thus internal consistency of elements is not sufficient. Flexibility for an unknown future must be field tested and fit—goal oriented and integrated. Hence, closure on a self-element must be recognized as a complex process involving present value, goal relevance, integrative adaptability, and flexibility for maximum utilization. No wonder the Adolescent kinetic process must be slow and focused. Ado k is no less active by virtue of its slower limited focus, but the lower-case k of the secondary group reflects the slower pace. This Adolescent kinetic impact continues its process, energizing SES and SER in serious, demanding, functional work with deliberate and focused diligence. As new groups of selected peers become necessary, the now educated scanning and selection functions carry a different urgency to the self-imperative. The general AD does not slacken; neither SER nor SES can be a casual, weak function. The decision to select an element for cementing as part of the permanent cognitive self-structure is consciously one requiring careful deliberation—hence the necessary extended duration of the secondary peer arena.

The Milieu

The affective milieu in the secondary peer group is also different. The desperate state of frameworklessness is no longer present. There is less of an immediate sense of crisis. Less initial tension allows for more precise deliberation. The Adolescent kinetic (lower case k) is slower and more directed. The Adolescent Kinetic (capital K) processes of the larger primary peer group were engaged to gather data for eliminating frameworklessness and to establish self-parameters by gaining information and insights into the frameworks and guideposts of fellow travelers. By now members have achieved the beginnings of a framework. Tasks in the secondary arena deal with the details of that frame. Adolescents do not experience the same degree of bondage to this group. They do not fear expulsion from the group. Since their stay may be short, they work intensively in refining the hues and colors of their frame. In service of the refinement of the selected specifics from within this framework, the Adolescent kinetic energizes the SES and SER functions of the AD. It may be that these hues and colors can be worked to sufficient clarity within one group, or they may require membership over time in a number of defined element groups or defined cluster groups in order to complete the process. Adolescents can more easily move from secondary group to secondary group since the anxieties of leaving or entering are not embedded within those affective consequences of a state of frameworklessness. The secondary arena is experienced as a more independent and affectively more secure environment.

Stances of Idiosyncratic Response

The adolescent's overt behavior at this point in time may be confusing. Although on the whole the adolescent posture is one of a more global composure, periods of intense, though not necessarily prolonged, preoccupation may surface, in which behaviors or opinions are expressed that seem to defy logic. The adolescent may demonstrate a specified interest or talent, yet appear indecisive in his allegiance to it. Although the skill may be manifestly unquestioned, on the deep-structure level the adolescent may be struggling with one of the many dimensions of the AD, perhaps even the final SER-IF dimension. He may not be sufficiently satisfied in it for closure. For some adolescents the period of membership in one or many different secondary peer groups may be the longest in duration. Their struggle may be not with the identification of self-elements, but rather in decisions relating to the flexibility and goal-related functions. For others a condition of premature satiation may need to be remedied. If anxiety has brought them to premature satiation in the primary peer experience, they are now challenged to undo some of that premature satiation and move forth to appropriate elements in the secondary-peer-group period. This may appear an extended secondary-peer-group period, although in actuality it includes shuttling back to the primary group. For some this is further complicated by energies expended in face-saving needs that may deflect direct remediation.

The self-imperative that the adolescent, fresh from his prior group imperative, assumes now has added complexity. Clearly the adolescent faces difficult choices, rigorous work, and dedicated effort in achieving closure on a self-structure. Decisions to reject can be as troublesome as those to accept. Alternative possibilities beg future questions; indecision and equivocation are often easier than resolution. Yet the self-structure presses for progress and for confirmation. Substitute offerings of ESA and a constant plethora of $AERR^n$-digested data now seem inappropriate and counterproductive to the self-imperative. Adolescent mood and overt behavior may reflect this new posture. Among the more serious of the new orientations the adolescent brings to the secondary arena is an intensity of goal emphasis. Taxing decisions must be made, wherein elements are evaluated and integrated with direct regard to function. The type of person the adolescent is to become must be addressed. The intellectualizing and posturing of the primary arena has yielded temporary, initial attitudes and values. The new, smaller groups necessary to refine the self-elements bring closer exposures and more serious, perhaps deeper insights. As selected similar others in the chosen secondary peer group are surveyed, there is also an increasing openness to outside reference groups offering real-world verification. The functional utility not only of goals but also of values is measured in the secondary arena within the models set forth. Variations in closure and self-structure are available within the schematic of SES to SER.

As the condition of end closure is reached, identification of the selected attributes of self-construction in relation to one another, to relevant others, and to their future utility as well as their relative status has been resolved to a great extent. Increasingly, further refinement of structural and functional features of each element in the potential self-structure appears less necessary. Clear decision making about elements to be integrated into a permanent self-structure generally has been accomplished through the dynamic functions of AD actualized in interaction with a second, smaller, more select group of others who are perceived as exhibiting desired attributes and as yielding a context in which to critically examine initial closure on "Who am I?" and "Where can I go?"

After these experiences of closure, the adolescent who has identified and assembled his cognitive instruments experiences satiation of the need for continued intense involvement in the group. The need for numbers has diminished, if not disappeared. Occasional self-questions stimulating the need for comparative acts may still be necessary and will probably continue throughout life. But movement to groups is no longer necessary. Rather, it will be the processes of social comparison that will be invoked; no longer the peer-group dynamic functions of $AERR^n$ or SER nor their dynamic adolescent kinetic processes (see tables 12-1 and 12-2).

Table 12-1
Progression of Cognitive Status in Adolescent Social Development and the Behavioral Component

Time	Cognitive Status	Cognitive Activity	Behavior
Entering	Frameworkless	IRA	Lost
Early	Borrows elements	ESA	Carefree
Middle	Borrowed elements in beginning flux	ESA $AERR^n$	Preoccupied, intense, tense
Middle	Borrowed: own elements forming	$AERR^n$	Relative calm; pain
Middle/end	Borrowed/dropped: own replacements/trial	SES SER	Directed concern
End	Integration of elements	Social comparison	Calm

Table 12-2
Progressive Course of Tension Levels of Adolescent Social Development

Time	Tension Level	Peer-Group Period
Entering	High	Primary
Early	Reduced/Tolerable High	Primary
Middle	High	Primary
Middle	High Reduced	Primary
Middle/End	High Reduced/Tolerable	Secondary
End	Relative equilibrium	Secondary

The peer-group experience takes the adolescent from a frameworkless sense of no self to an identification, organization, and integration of self-elements and the achievement of a self-structure. Precisely such a frameworkless state will not again exist. The numbers of peers necessary to effect the essential inventory of combinations of attributes in order to select, assess, test out, and reflect will never again be necessary. Adolescent kinetic processes in service of the sequentially released functions of the Adolescent Dialectic will no longer be active. With passage through the developmental stage, the AD is sated, as are the functions and processes spent. At this point the process takes a new course as another phenomenon begins to act. Forces for leaving the secondary group now gather, just as forces for leaving the primary adolescent peer group appeared as adolescence progressed. Together, these constitute forces for leaving the peer arena.

13 Forces for Leaving the Peer Arena

As the adolescent process of social development progresses through satiations in the primary-peer-group interactions, and then through closures from the secondary-group interactions, outward manifestations of these achievements may be observed in a decrease in the number of peer associations and in a reduction in movement from one friendship to another. Possessed of a newly owned sense of self and posture relative to fellow travelers, the adolescent's criteria for friendship selection change fundamentally. The desire for a wide variety of friends, often so mystifying to the observer but so necessary to the adolescent at first, loses its potency. The adolescent no longer needs friends in order to borrow their elements, to assess them, or to be as similar to them as possible. Neither does he need to polish or integrate his own elements in relation to admired sets of similar clusters of elements. The adolescent is freed from indiscriminately seeking volume, from satisfying the forces to affiliate and to join—pressures that characterized his adolescent entry status. A new freedom is expressed even in the more deliberate search for affiliation with those perceived as similar. Pressure to conform, refine, or polish is no longer a defining characteristic. He is free to seek out others merely to interact.

The unstable pseudoself has been replaced gradually by a stable set of elements, which allows for the risk of closer relationships. The threat that intimacy may reveal the absence or instability of the self, or even may threaten emerging but not yet fully consolidated self-elements, is no longer at issue. Now the adolescent can confront difference, which no longer necessarily threatens. Integration of an achieved structure of self-elements yields a newly experienced sense of self to be offered. He himself, having something of his own to offer, is ready to test real relating.

Indexes of Readiness for Relationship

Generally, the course of movement is from large numbers of peers to smaller, more select numbers; to more intimate relating; to a few friends. Allowing for idiosyncratic variations, this individual change occurs simultaneous to the processes of one's age-mates. Each, in the course of his own idiosyncratic use of the interactional dynamics of the peer arena, has stabilized his individual constellation and his own functional relationships.

179

This new stability is reflected in fewer and more predictable friendships. Some old friendships may survive the vicissitudes of substitute elements and movements to new groups for refinement. Others may dissipate as their specific function proves to have been temporary and tangential.

Now the desire for more unitary relationships is activated. Others are no longer desired in service of the establishment of the self, but in order to explore the self in relation to a second person. The adolescent is now prepared to become involved. Formerly, he took from the encounter what was needed for purposes of his own self-growth. Now he has moved beyond the former stance of mutual barter. The motion turns and changes. In the ebb and tide of their own development, adolescents are now ready also to give. They now desire to give and take, to exchange. *Exchange* implies involvement, not defensive distance. Hence, an in-depth style of "relating," a vertical orientation, replaces the superficial, horizontally oriented, and voluminous transactional styles of former years. Intimacies begin.

Peers: No Longer the Peer Group

I have presented in considerable detail my formulations on the beginning period of adolescence, when the impact of frameworklessness and strangeness even to oneself is experienced. I have further suggested that membership in a group of age-mates is essential to maintaining stability in a condition of deliberate, psychological separateness from one's former guides and guideposts—parents and elders. The need to separate is stimulated by growth experienced in several developmental domains. The pain of aloneness and frameworklessness raises conflicts and presents sobering difficulties that sway the adolescent's resolve. The peer group offers a place and a community of like others experiencing similar pushes and pulls. Supports alone do not suffice, however. Active developmental tasks are also at hand. Identity must be achieved, and it must be an identity that is functional to life in a complex Western society. Although adolescents join peer groups to answer the first set of needs, upon membership they become involved in the collective dynamics of the members of the peer group. Circumstances and conditions act together to create an arena for working out the second set of needs. Thus the adolescent peer group serves two basic functions in adolescence. First, it provides the adolescent with a relevant setting that offers a temporary framework. Anxiety is reduced as temporary guideposts are incorporated. Thus the adolescent is supported in tolerating some stress and escapes the need for a defensive response—regression to childhood or premature adulthood. Second, peer-group membership serves functionally in solving the essential tasks of adolescence—self-definition and self-direction.

When primary tasks are accomplished, forces gather to stimulate the individual to leave the primary peer group. The first departure is from the large group to affiliation with a small secondary peer group, marking entry into the secondary arena. The second departure, from this smaller arena, occurs when a self-structure is constructed and is integrated with self-direction. The third advance is on to individual peer associations and from there to intimate relating. Friends are now seen as persons with whom to interrelate, not as concrete targets of the physical environment. Interpersonal exchange begins. This affiliation with peers is different from affiliation with a peer group. Unlike those of the earlier period of development, when affiliation with many individuals in a group of peers served distinct developmental functions, affiliations with individual peers now reflect an advanced stage near the end of adolescence when the adolescent is developmentally ready for true relating. Sometimes, however, a unitary relationship does develop at an early point in the developmental process. It may be a defensive reaction, an attempt to reduce the stress of peer-group interaction with many peers—hence, the monopolization of another youth. This adolescent, on the one hand, experiences the comfort of the defense; on the other, he may experience conflict and discomfort as a product of this precocious involvement prior to psychological readiness. Premature involvements are discussed at greater length in the next chapter.

Cessation of need for a large group and the appearance of forces to leave the peer group provides the complementary concept to "freedom from bondage to the concrete" that Piaget and Inhelder (1958) have suggested accompanies the acquisition of structures of formal thought in late adolescence. Acquisition of the formal structures of logical thinking frees the youth from the limits of abstraction only on the concrete, to the ability to abstract on abstractions. Dynamic Functional Interaction sets forth a complementary notion in adolescent social development. With the completion of an assembly of self-elements, the adolescent is freed from the need to continue with large numbers of visible, concretely available peer-group members. Membership in a peer group provides interaction with those concrete aspects of the physical environment necessary for looking and listening and essential to the exercise of preprogrammed Adolescent Dialectic functions. Through participation in the sequential peer groups, the adolescent gradually identifies a constellation of self-elements and constructs a defined, refined, and eventually identified self. Successful resolution of adolescent tasks is marked by the construction of a self-structure and the setting of a direction. The need for the concrete presence of a group of others, essential for exercise of the initial dynamic functions, has now ceased. Further refinements to the self can continue largely on an abstract level. This posture approximates that of the continuing adult condition of ongoing self-refinement on abstract rather than interactional levels, although forays into the concrete may occasionally be necessary (see table 13-1).

Table 13-1
Function, Awareness Level, Activation, and Type of Interaction in Primary and Secondary Group

Progression	Time Orientation	Cognitive-Element Operative Function	Function	Activation	Awareness Level	Peer Group	Type of Interaction
1	Present	Absence	IRA	Automatic	Manifest	PPG	Collision Intra-action
2	Present Future	ESA	$AERR^n$	Automatic Deliberate	Latent	PPG	Intra-action (more) Coaction (less)
3	Present Future	SES	SER	Deliberate Automatic	Latent	PPG	Intra-action (less) Coaction (more)
4	Future	SES	SER	Deliberate	Latent	SPG	Interchange
5	Present Future	SS	Social comparison	Deliberate	Manifest	Friends Mate	Exchange

Notes:

ESA	=	Element-substituting action
SES	=	Specific-element selection
PPG	=	Primary peer group
SPG	=	Secondary peer group
SS	=	Self-structure
$AERR^n$	=	Assessment-evaluation-reevaluation-reassessment
IRA	=	Initial relative assessment
SER	=	Selected element refinement

The Peer Arena Renewed

A condition of developmental readiness leads the adolescent to join a group of peers. Dynamic functions of the Adolescent Dialectic are progressively activated, and their processes are exercised within the peer arena in sequential service of adolescent development tasks. As dynamic functional interaction first yields satiation and then moves to successful closures, the magnetic pull of the group begins to weaken. As the peer-group experience increasingly meets its functional imperative, the forces to remain in the group weaken and those to leave the group gain in strength. Less conforming behavior can be risked. Expulsion from the group has lost its former potency since self-stability is no longer dependent on maintenance of group membership and accessibility to its functional interaction. Neither is the group as essential in assuring a sense of self-stability. Its functional field-of-force system has successfully energized growth potential to be identified and to be sequentially organized so as to identify and assemble the sought-after integrated and directed self-construct.

But new members with developmental readiness revive the system. When they join, their initial needs stimulate readiness of the potent dynamic functions that activate the group field of forces. The functional interaction system of the adolescent peer group is reinvoked and reenergized.

14 Irregularities in Development and Functioning

The peer-arena model of adolescent social development that is offered in the theory of Dynamic Functional Interaction states that the interaction processes between adolescent peers in groups, over the course of early to late adolescence, is central to their construction of an integrated self-structure—who I am and where I may be able to go. Irregularities in smooth passage through the adolescent stage occur when adolescents do not experience a full period of participation in the adolescent peer arena and its sequential developmental functions. Implicit is the notion that irregularities of development can be initially stimulated as defenses against the cognitive conflict and affective pain occasioned by the peer transactions. To the existing orientations on defenses active during the adolescent period and their behavioral manifestations, this book offers a social-environmental perspective with the peer arena as a central structure.

By no means is an abbreviated arena experience that may have stimulated the irregularity considered to be the only causal factor. Nor can the explanations assembled here delineate that categoricals be applied individually without full knowledge of the individual. Each adolescent brings a continuum of psychological strengths as well as a continuum of environmental factors; each adolescent is unique. However, problems connected with peer-group membership are considered to have a primary impact on each unique constellation of personality and to contribute to irregularities in social development. In order to understand effects, this chapter uses categorical models to delineate types of situations and classes of conflict.

The focus is first on those adolescents for whom the duration or quality of the involvement in arena membership is insufficient for them to complete the tasks specific to this period of development. Some of the irregularities to be discussed are immediately recognizable as maladaptive by virtue of unacceptable overt behaviors. The more subtle irregularities are not, however. Overt postures may mask dysfunctions for some time, perhaps forever. However, these individuals also may be subject to situational stresses later in life that may unmask them as underdeveloped individuals as their behavior regresses to the adolescence they have never outgrown.

Some hitherto puzzling behaviors become clear in the light of unfinished adolescent passage; they can be seen as compensatory reactions to extreme dissonance or deprivation. Again, however, caution is essential before any conclusions are drawn, given the complexity of the human personality. This chapter attempts to present some of these irregularities in the context of an insufficient peer-arena developmental experience. They have been developed out of new theoretical postures and are introduced here in skeletal form.

The Characteristic Adolescent Countenance

The achievement of an integrated set of cognitive elements to anchor a self-structure is the goal of the adolescent developmental period. The adolescent begins in an aura of frameworklessness, removed from the guideposts of the borrowed self-structure of his parents, eager but unequipped to forge his own path. He seeks out others just like himself for comfort, unaware that his peers represent the instruments he will use to compose and orchestrate his emerging self. This will be accomplished within a field of forces organized in an arena to which he is innately drawn, as are his contemporaries. Involvement in the primary and secondary arenas, despite dissonance and turmoil, should engender a smooth, progressive accomplishment of the adolescent tasks of self-identification, self-integration, and self-direction.

The spontaneous product of adolescent peer congregation is the activation of the Individual Adolescent Dialectics (IAD), which then intersect and energize sequential evolution of appropriate dynamic functions to guide individual quests. There are considerable costs along with the ultimate gain. Inquiry into self and other and inquiry of self in relation to other are hard work. Conformity and good fellowship are required. The affective consequences of assaults to one's self-conceptions must be cautiously balanced against perceptions of accomplishment and emerging new vistas. Most adolescents traverse the path of peer-group involvement. Some, however, never enter the arena; others try to withdraw; still others leave through early closure.

The internal adolescent state of transition is commonly manifested externally in behavior that is consistently inconsistent—chameleonlike. Although it is congruent with the developmental period, this behavior may appear unstable and even alarming to the observer. This range of behaviors is the overt behavioral response to the operation of functional development processes of the Adolescent Dialectic (AD), whereby self-elements are removed, replaced, expelled, or retained. Any number of varying self-postures follow one after another.

Absence of self makes the adolescent feel unsteady. Hungry for self-stabilization, he wishes to fill in the missing elements. Attractive characteristics, attitudes, and opinions of fellow peers are available to be borrowed as psychological stand-ins for still undeveloped self-elements.

Once chosen, the stand-in elements feel firm. But the borrowed elements may not constitute complete, whole elements. Insofar as the donors—adolescent peers themselves—may not yet be fully developed, the element available for borrowing may or may not have stability. Once it is borrowed, strange and irregular behavior may surface. A previously steady individual may suddenly appear unstable. Even when borrowing for stability leads to internal consonance, the overt behavior can be alarming. Such manifestations may be in evidence under three conditions. First, the adolescent may assume behavior that seems totally out of context with the person he has previously projected himself to be. Second, the imposter element may be extraordinarily weak, rendering appearances even more unstable than before. Third, since the element is an imposter element, it can be quickly replaced. Rapid turnover of self-elements is behaviorally displayed in confusing, even contradictory behavior. External expression reflects the internal variations. The vicissitudes of adolescent behavior reflect a responsiveness to both environmental and internal cues. Within the peer-arena model, it is also an external manifestation of the incorporation or exchange of a foreign or pure self-element.

Accordingly, a tumultuous, *chameleonlike adolescence* is seen, within the peer-arena model, as developmentally appropriate. Those in the arena arc rapidly turning out new self-elements. For most, the complex adjustments throughout adolescent development are not smooth or untroubled. For some the road is tortuous; for most it is turbulent; for all there is some stress. Inner turmoil and changing perceptions assail them. Bursts of energy followed by exhaustion and rapid mood changes attest to the unsteadiness of the individual en route to self-structure. The tasks of self-identification, self-integration, and self-direction hammered out in the primary and secondary arenas require quick and unpredictable shifts in posture and mood. The adolescent inside the arena is himself part of the arena forces that intersect and permit each to use the other as instruments of his own respective development. Intense latent concentration is required for inquiries into self, self in relation to other, and self in the group arena. Careful, modified behavior is mandated and mediates conformity and good fellowship. Many project outward behavior opposite to their inner responses. Masked confusion and pain are among the consequences of peer-group membership. Affective consequences of new pieces of cognitive weight and information must be handled with caution and care. Assaults to self conceptions must be balanced with news of accomplishment and hope.

These are demanding and trying events that occur constantly over an extended period of development to produce gains and progress, but also considerable costs and pressures. Yet some handle the progressive states more easily than others and in fact accomplish a relatively smooth passage to self-structure and onto closure. For most, however, the journey is hesitant if not zigzag and is full of confusions and tensions. These adolescents—the majority—are resolving and integrating a self-structure that will bring them to full maturity.

For the most part, the literature is in agreement that some peer involvement is necessary. Membership in peer groups has been conceptualized along a continuum ranging from minimal involvement to membership in an adolescent subculture (Burlinghame 1967; Offer 1969). As early as 1948 Newcomb, in his classic study of attitudes in a college population; Sherif and Sherif (1954) in participant-observer studies of Oklahoma boys; and Konopka, in a 1966 study of influences on girls released from delinquent institutions all suggested that adolescents with greater youth-culture affiliative needs manifested a type of deficit in the circumstances of their social development, thus needing compensatory encompassing relationships. Investigations into the continuum of normal adolescent-boy peer groups and youth cultures set peer affiliation at one end of a bell-shaped continuum and the adolescent subculture at the other (Offer 1969; Burlinghame 1967). Although the uncommitted adolescent (Keniston 1965) and the adolescent in the subculture (Goodman 1956) have been examined, little attention has been paid in the literature to the adolescent who does not meet these more extreme descriptors and is neither totally uninvolved nor heavily committed—the adolescents ranging between minimal involvement and those who are not at all involved in peer-group activity or appear to do well without it.

Since the peer-arena model suggests that full participation in the peer group is a developmental need in order to effect the full social growth of the adolescent period, we must look beyond observable social adjustment to a consideration of irregularities that occur when full participation is not operative. I will therefore emphasize the necessity for a close watch on the extent and nature of peer-group interactions, not as a measure of a deficit in the circumstances of social adjustment, but rather as a developmental necessity. Its presence connotes positive developmental potential; its absence raises concerns about what will come after, not only about what has preceded. Within the peer-arena model of a progressive course of interaction in developmental integration, the absence of sequential peer-group experience spells irregularity in development.

Types of Irregularities

Despite many trying and demanding events, most adolescents experience relatively smooth passage. However, irregularities in passage do occur and are categorized here in four major dimensions: (1) *The Pseudoadult,* (2) *The Settled Adolescent,* (3) *The Low-Threshold Adolescent,* and (4) *The*

Adolescent without a Group. Within the third dimension of irregularity, the Low-Threshold Adolescent, are two subdimensions: (1) *Early Closure*, and (2) *Suspended Closure/Dropout.* Further within the Suspended-Closure/Dropout subdimension are four categories of dropout: *Temporary* (ranging from withdrawal to dropout), *Secret, Masked,* and *Solo.* None of the adolescents in these four dimensions of irregularity successfully complete peer-group tasks, and their entry to mature status is affected. The Pseudoadult and the Adolescent without a Group never really engage the adolescent peer group. The others represent the low end of the scale of minimal involvement in the peer group. Overt manifestations of their developmental postures differ. Some postures are considered adaptive and successful, others are easily recognized as maladaptive, and one dimension is seen as irregular and sympathetic. None are truly successfully adaptive modes.

The Pseudoadult

The Pseudoadult is the adolescent who seems more mature than his chronological years. He appears stable rather than unstable. Paradoxically, however, he is not experiencing appropriate developmental progression through the adolescent growth stage. This type of adolescent may never have experienced the same sense of frameworklessness as did his fellow peers. His history of reinforcements has taught him to imitate adult choices, and continued reinforcements may appear achievable with adults if he continues the adult stance. These rewards overshadow those available with peers. The Pseudoadult appears settled and does not fit the stereotype of the laughing, talkative, freethinking, changeable adolescent. In contrast to the turbulent motion of other adolescents, his maturity is often noted precisely because of its striking deviation from the adolescent norm. Usually such adolescents do not affiliate with peers.

David Ausubel (1954, 1977) suggests that not all adolescents are afforded an experience of the devaluation that stimulates a resatellization, although he contends that adolescents need to resatellize (join with a group of peers) in order to desatellize (achieve independence). Nonsatellizers cannot risk the possible assaults to self-esteem that are involved in leaving the adult environment. Ausubel suggests that this adolescent has been either overvalued or rejected. The overvalued child has had no opportunity to confront tasks and conflicts by himself. The rejected child, overdominated, needs to adhere to stringent standards of behavior. Both types perceive mature behavior as a necessary precondition for primary status. But their status remains an attributed one. Ausubel refers to a basic core of personality developed by the resatellizer but not by the adolescent who does not resatellize. Thus Ausubel, too, seems to correlate peer-group membership with developmental history. His view is that if the developmental history is strong enough, the original location (family) can be left, and the next stop (peer group) can be risked and endured. However, if developmental strength is weak or absent, the original location cannot be left. The implication is that if the adolescent is strong enough to enter the peer group, he will be strong enough to stay. Ausubel emphasizes the predetermining factors. His formulation does not examine the specific processes active in the peer group proper and the impact of the peer-group experience on the future course of development.

Proper management of the field of force dynamics operative in peer-group interaction requires a sophistication of balance and coordination not usually attributed to a developing child. Incorporating painful affective data in a face-saving manner and suppressing personal expressive needs in favor of acceptable group behavior may be difficult for any adolescent. It is even more of a challenge for adolescents such as Ausubel's "overvalued" ones. Adjustments have always been made for these individuals, just as decisions have been made for the rejected child who cannot risk potential negative outcomes of experimentation for fear of misbehavior and rejection. Although this behavior is based in a habit structure of conformity, peer-group membership asks much more than merely conformity. The freedoms of frameworklessness coexist with conformity requirements, juxtaposed with a formidable task of managing the actions and reactions of AD functions. Coping requires high motivation as well as multiple energies expended in self-adjustment and fine tuning.

Internally based directives are self-motivated, self-modulated, self-energized, self-regulated. The conformity required in the peer group calls forth energies toward the achievement of new skills. It differs from the earlier submission, which served family norms. Overdominated households usually provide a focal cue, but in the peer arena many cues are active, requiring instant coordination and response, even selective skill in determining which external cues to follow. This flexible posture operates on external cues mediated by internal integrations. Although the rejected or the overvalued child has habitually responded to external cues with internally directed actions, such children have not acquired the ability to perform the mathematical manipulations both cognitively and affectively necessary to conform to many individual peer expectations plus group expectations simultaneously. The flexibility essential to this level of sophisticated coping may be underdeveloped in this more conservative adolescent.

Furthermore, for those adolescents who always appear mature, the load of requirements of peer-group memberships may be more than the prospective gains, since active forces for affiliation with peers may be low. Satisfying positive reinforcements from current reference figures/groups/parents, and/or an affective sense of ego enhancement based in identification (on a level of unreality) with a positive-instance model of a desired set of characteristics may yield sufficient positive environmental feedback to dispel the discomfort most adolescents feel in comparison with adults. Hence, these adolescents choose to continue a habitual pattern with an actual or fantasized reference figure or group. They retain those characteristics in the repertoire that have been received positively. The sense of frameworklessness may be minimally present if at all. Therefore, forces do not mitigate toward searching out another arena.

Since there is little or no peer-group involvement, friends are not used as pseudoelements to stand in for missing pseudoelements. Parents or other adult reference figures are selected instead. Hence, the overt manifestation of "pseudoelements" of these reference figures appears quite different from behavior based on the utilization of the borrowed characteristics and skills of friends. These pseudoelements do not include the unstable, disconnected self-element extremes and inconsistencies characteristic of the substitute adolescent peer elements. Substitute adult elements are usually more consistent and smooth. A facsimile of internalized maturity is manifested with external behavior that reflects the smooth pseudoelements. Since the adolescent who does not join a congregation of peers and who does not utilize friendship inventory as a source of pseudoelements cannot manifest the behavioral counterparts of these nonmature elements, the overt manifestation of the borrowed mature elements contrasts strikingly with the behavioral vicissitudes displayed by adolescents who borrow peer elements. The change from frameworklessness, through erratic and erratically changing behaviors, to stability is dramatically apparent in the adolescent who has participated in the peer group. As the element is cognitively shaped (or perhaps rejected and then replaced with another pseudoelement) in the course of the adolescent selection of his "own self-elements" on the road to maturity, the vicissitudes of immaturity and instability may be even more obvious. But as the adolescent replaces pseudoelements with selected self-elements, each element individually is anchored more stably, whereas the pseudoelement replaced was not anchored. When a number of pseudoelements have been replaced by real elements, behavior begins to be markedly less changeable and more regular. The transition to maturity becomes obvious. The before-and-after contrast is dramatic. This process of replacement of pseudoelements with elements of self is far less observable in the adolescent for whom the foreign element has been adult and not peer.

With the adolescent whose upheaval is open, the vicissitudes of the transitions are visible along the way; resolutions reflect a movement toward stable, more mature behavior. We can assume that a process of self-development has taken place. For the Pseudoadult, for whom adult elements have always stood in as the temporary self-constellation, behavior remains relatively unchanged at the mature level. As the peer-related adolescent nears the end of the period of the secondary arena and approaches closure, the degree of difference perceived between the immature, peer-related adolescent behavior and that of the non-peer-related adolescent begins to alter. The behavior of the peer-related adolescent is now also perceived as mature. However, whereas one type of adolescent has experienced the internal, incremental buildup of his base of internal stability, the other has coopted stability from external sources.

The continuum of borrowed pseudoelements ranges from a totality of adult elements at one extreme to a totality of peer elements at the other. The outwardly observable stable or unstable component of the behavior will correspond to the number borrowed from each category. The range, accordingly, extends from (1) the pseudoadult who borrows the entire set of adult elements and does not rework the elements but retains them as they are, to (2) the adolescent who borrows and reworks some or all of them, to (3) the adolescent who selects almost exclusively from peers and reworks these elements with the $AERR^n$ in the adolescent peer group. Borrowed adult elements are often taken into the peer group and made relevant in relation to a peer who models the peer version of the element—at which point the $AERR^n$ becomes active. In this designation of the Pseudoadult, I am referring to the adolescent who identifies and takes as his own the adult elements, without involving himself with peers.

The Pseudoadult has not affiliated with peers, has not been automatically involved in the functional interaction of peer congregations, and has not reached out to utilize fellow peers in the process of his own self-definition. The structure of the elements taken on is not experienced as his own. He continues to live with a borrowed set of elements, acquired through an identification process. It follows that the immature behavior manifested by those adolescents who construct their own set of elements usually will not be observable. Erratic behaviors reflective of the process will not be present. The individual's mature behavior has always reflected an end result, not a process. Hence, it is difficult to ascertain whether real maturing has taken place or whether the behavior is facsimile and will remain so. There are no overt significates of change that advise whether there has been an exchange of Pseudoadult elements for real self-elements. With the minimally peer-involved adolescent who manifests a quality of early maturity, it is uncertain whether the process of social development that takes place when peer pseudoelements are involved has in fact taken place when the borrowed elements come from adults. Adolescents manifesting "early maturity" may be developmentally in the opposition condition. The "mature" posture may be a manifestation of protracted childhood—where the individual still proceeds on parental imperatives and is still satisfied by positive reinforcements that serve to overpower (or at least help to defend against) the rising dissonant and unsettling ramifications of individual change. Questions and parental concerns may be abortively eliminated, if only temporarily.

Thus the maturity of the adolescent who manifests no upheaval may not be evidence of maturity at all, but rather may actually reflect a developmental delay in psychosocial progression through the adolescent period. Strongly active physical, cognitive, and affective forces of change stimulate defensive suppression of anxiety. A fragile self is reassured by positive reinforcements from major actors in the social environment. This reduction in tension encourages identification with adult models as further protection against increasing inconsistencies and upheavals.

The Settled Adolescent

On the continuum of involvement in the peer-group AD functions, a second category, the Settled Adolescent, stands between the outwardly obvious adolescent and the Pseudoadult. This person neither copies a cognitive self-structure (as does the Pseudoadult) nor constructs and integrates his own. Although he does borrow pseudoelements in much the same manner as the adolescent in the peer group, he is not a member of the peer group. The temporary pseudoelements are borrowed from adults rather than from peers. But the process differs from that of the Pseudoadult. Whereas the Pseudoadult imitates the adult to the point of taking over the adult self-structure as his own, the Settled Adolescent borrows elements of adult references to assemble his own self-structure. He does not copy the adult or identify in wholesale fashion as does the Pseudoadult. The anxiety of the Settled Adolescent is not as great as the Pseudoadult's; therefore, he does not need to utilize defensive identification. However, although the degree of anxiety is not strong enough to call forth total identification, it is strong enough to discourage full and open movement toward peers. Hence, although they engage in the same process of substitution of elements, they adopt a cautious practical stance. Indeed, the Settled Adolescent might just as aptly be named the Cautious Adolescent. Caution is the pivotal fulcrum on which his involvement with others rests.

Because the elements are adult elements, the crucial difference is that the dynamic functions of ESA and $AERR^n$ do not operate; neither do the subsequent SES and SER functions. Weighing and judging are not a part of the settled adolescent's experience. Neither is the sheer volume of exposure and risk. Instead, elements are tried out in relation to adults in an older generational context, *not* with age-mates and fellow travelers. The Settled Adolescent escapes the intensity and functional relevance of involvement with age-mates. Forays into the peer-group arena are brief and experimental. From them he flees to adult models. Consequently, he is denied the experience of satiation, the satisfaction of true closure.

The outward behavior of the Settled Adolescent is changeable, but the specific behaviors themselves appear stable since the risk of borrowing built-in instability is reduced greatly when the pseudoelement is borrowed from an adult. Therefore, although this middle group does not manifest the anchored posture of the Pseudoadult, its members present a much more regular, even posture than do peer-oriented adolescents. They are similar to Pseudoadults in that their developmental deprivation is not outwardly apparent. The relative evenness of the Settled Adolescent masks his developmental dysfunction. Social approval, even commendation, reinforces the mask.

The Pseudoadult and the Settled Adolescent do not appear on the continuum of peer-group involvement in AD functions. They represent an *avoidance of adolescence.* The Settled Adolescent engages in some limited tryout, in facsimile $AERR^n$, SER fashion. But since the elements are borrowed from adult models, they are not the raw material of the peer-group ESA and thus are not subject to the rigorous Adolescent Kinetic processes in service of $AERR^n$ functions. Therefore individuals do not construct an "own set" of integrated cognitive elements. They do not experience the richness of the contrast between true self-stability and the instability of the adolescent years. The action involves identification with elements in an adult cognitive self-structure at an early point in adolescence. It is maladaptively stimulated and contributes to eventual developmental delay. The natural processes of involvement in the dynamic functional interaction system of peer-group membership are resisted. Discharge of the dynamic functions of the Adolescent Dialectic is suppressed. Self-assessment and evaluation in relation to fellow peers, selection and tryout of self-elements, and isolation of desired self-elements and self-integration are all inactive. Inhibition of AD functions is a defensive response specific to adolescence. Full development is delayed.

These individuals may continue throughout life in an undeveloped stage. This may be manifested in a tenuous hold on one's own adult role and adult direction, evidenced by chronic anxiety about "being adult" and "feeling adult." Regressive behavior later in life may be manifested. Interesting paradoxes can occur, whereby immature behavior is exhibited in later chonological life by persons who displayed seemingly mature behavior in early life. Inappropriately early maturity is followed some years later by the sudden eruption of suppressed adolescent forces. Behaviors inappropriate to an older adulthood or middle age may erupt, quite in contrast to the individual's characteristic steady personality. Situational factors that constitute a reality blow to a fantasized self can stimulate these eruptions that have heretofore been held in check (for example, a career crisis, romantic rejection, physical problems). Depending on when the individual avoided adolescence, he may either return to a partial adolescent posture or may actually enter it for the first time and attempt to work out cognitive and libidinous adolescent tasks.

Since the forces of suppression have been weakened either by the impact of the traumatic happening or by its stimulus value to reenergizing internal adolescent forces previously held in check, true adolescent behavior may ensue. The behavior may vary decidedly from former postures. Another personality may suddenly be in evidence. The anecdotal reference to a "second childhood" should more correctly refer to a "second adolescence." This behavior may continue for an extended period of time. If it is replaced by behavior that appears more age appropriate and characteristically adult, it may be either that sufficient closure of certain absent elements has been achieved—or, on the other hand, that a new anxiety has been elicited that has in turn stimulated a return of suppression. If in fact closure has been effected, it is not the same closure as that achieved within the operative dynamics of the adolescent peer group. But some additional development has indeed occurred. Some anxiety has been released, some energies have been put to the task, and some degree of satiation and closure has taken place.

Time is an essential ingredient for proper processing of the sequential functions of adolescent social development. A rapid passage through adolescence is maladaptive, leading to irregularities. Outward manifestations of an unexpectedly early mature stance, either philosophical or behavioral, should be cautiously regarded. Adult behavior is inappropriate in adolescence, just as adolescent behavior is inappropriate in a child. Uneven levels of comprehension of what is developmentally sound and desirable and what the vicissitudes of the period represent contribute to a readiness to accept the "mask" of maturity as developmentally desirable and sound. Quite the contrary. When behavioral maturity appears quite early, and particularly when it operates in tandem with no involvement or minimal involvement in the peer group, it should be seen as a red flag of irregularity in smooth progression.

The Low-Threshold Adolescent

This category of irregularity—the Low-Threshold Adolescent—involves a response of two types of maladaptive closure, which can be seen as two sides of one coin. The following discussion encompasses various behavioral manifestations that differ overtly but are dynamically of very similar origin. The first subcategory, Early Closure, is generally seen as socially acceptable, whereas the second subcategory—No Closure, or Suspended Closure—is considered distinctly maladaptive. Several forms of the latter subcategory will be delineated.

Early Closure

Some adolescents possess a low threshold for dissonance and, after making an initial attempt at membership are unable to manage the intensive peer-group experience. This type of adolescent spends an insufficient length of time in adolescent-peer-group interaction. Although the adolescent may be ready and the beginning functions may have been ignited, the peer group is abortively left before the various sequential AD functions can be released. Although rapid operation of ESA affords immediate facsimile stability and reduction of anxiety, the laborious Adolescent Kinetic processes of $AERR^n$ do not yield early satiation, nor do the slower SER functions yield quick results. Appropriate closure is achieved only with a minimum of two peer-group sequences, each requiring an investment of significant time.

Adolescents whose history of reinforcements is antithetical to tolerating suspended resolutions (those who cannot, figuratively speaking, juggle many balls in the air) will experience more discomfort than those who are less compulsive. Long periods of nonresolution may increase anxiety. Difficulty is experienced early, perhaps even with the initial IRA scanning function, in managing affective responses or handling perceptually received information. It may be that readiness for the AD is accompanied by an inherent early-warning system that stimulates a level of caution upon entry. This type of adolescent may quickly sense that the processes of interaction with the peer group could result in debilitating increases in tension connected with perceptions disparate with former estimates of self. A possible outcome might be a precipitous drop in self-evaluation. Intellectual rationale or even defensive rationale may fall short, with consequent anxiety mounting to an intolerable level.

An intact developmental history, of course, affords supports necessary to buttress new stress. Internal strengths are lower among adolescents whose history is anchored, to a major degree, in adult reinforcements rather than in some experiment and risk. These adolescents are more prone to suffer self-doubt and periods of self-devaluation. As members of an adolescent peer group, individuals who have been overvalued may have to deal with unbiased, more objective information for the first time. Furthermore, their assessments may identify peers who surpass them in skills and abilities that are targets of their own.

Actions in Service of Consonant Equilibrium

Notwithstanding the strong forces for affiliation, the Low-Threshold Adolescent will experience considerable pain early in the peer-group period. The adolescent may act to shut down—not to open up. Attempts will be made to keep stimuli in check to lessen dissonant reactions. Action is initially cocoonlike and self-protective. Outwardly observable behavior may include anger, aggression, frequent altercation, verbal projection of anger or upset onto a moral or philosophical matter, and perhaps an abrupt rejection of a former ideal. Communications may ensue over "red herrings," uncharacteristic behavior foreign to formerly stated goals or ambitions. In this manner the adolescent expresses negative affect that might otherwise be turned inward. Engulfing anger stemming from the effects of dissonant self-perceptions cannot be handled safely within the peer group itself. Expression in the home field, which formerly sufficed, may now no longer do so. For a few, aggressive response to other institutions of society may be an outlet. But the majority of those who find the pain of realizations discrepant to prior perceptions threatening an even greater upset move to early closure.

Hence, for both types of response—withdrawal and aggression— when efforts at management are unsuccessful, the adolescent may choose a more drastic action in the service of self-stabilization. He can choose to withdraw from the peer group. The removal can be deliberate; he can look for a different group or remain isolated from any group at all. However, the withdrawal may be accomplished without any awareness that it has in fact been withdrawal. It is accomplished through early closure. In this case the adolescent quickly arrives at conclusions to his deliberations. Options are limited; decisions are made quickly; little is left in suspense. Dealing with readjustments of self-perceptions and effects of peer-group interaction drains strengths and energies, particularly when new perceptions contradict those previously held. Rather than continue to undergo assessments, and subsequent reevaluation, early closure on adolescent tasks is chosen in service of stabilizing the flux of self-perceptions. If elements of self-structure are abortively delineated and if early decision on self-direction is grasped, the stress of validation of self-perceptions along a variety of dimensions can be avoided. Overwhelming upset is no longer risked.

Conceptually, Early Closure on the task of selecting and organizing elements of the cognitive self may be viewed as another form of defense against the excess affective stress that accompanies the vicissitudes of the dynamic functions of interactions in a group of adolescents. External determinants also may contribute to the rise in anxiety levels, thus intensifying the need for relief from any available area of stress. Economic, academic, or family-based stress leaves reduced psychological energies for assault from other sources. Relief is sought, which, if found by early closure, inhibits important developmental processes.

Early closure is manifested in diverse areas of development in service of current stability. An early decision about self-characteristics is outwardly reinforced by an overt, rigid, almost impenetrable resistance to a reconsideration of their functional merit. Not uncommon is the same stance on early closure on identification of skills and abilities, with accompanying set definitions of one's present and future self-direction. A range of overt behaviors and attitudes toward others designed to protect the psychologically premature resolution may be evident.

The adolescent may avoid the peer group, totally protecting himself from the action of its automatic functions, or may remain physically present without involvement in latent functions. When membership is nominal only, it serves to support the cognitive awareness of a need for social connection with a group as well as to fill the face-saving need for friends. In fact, an ego-enhancing component now exists. Such adolescents, who appear assured and "together," are present to serve as "objects" for others but not as subjects for themselves. They make clear to both self and others that their goals are set. Ironically, they may become comparison objects of the "positive instance" and excellent candidates to represent pseudoelements in the cognitive structure of other group members.

The character of the interactions of Low Threshold Early Closure adolescents reflects their posture. Interactions are objectively oriented, with a concomitant lack of the intensity common to others. Relationships that can be engaged in on a fairly superficial level are preferred. Communications are characterized by attempts to influence, characteristic of satiation—in this case, a pseudosatiation. Statements expressing "I'll tell you *what* I am going to do" are more prominent than those explaining "*why* I am going to do this." The "what" reflects the decision for closure; the absence of the "why" reflects its prematurity. Other members who have also effected early closure (early or actual) on self-definition and future-oriented goals are content not to ask why but to engage the what.

Early Closure is not limited to personality characteristics or vocational goals. Early Closure can be active in mate selection and may even be a factor in selection of mate gender. While the current child-development literature identifies an early critical period for sex typing (Biller 1974), another strong branch of theory has long identified the adolescent period as one of finalization of gender and of choice of mate (Freud 1905). AD peer-group interactional functions do encompass self-questioning, comparing, and definition in the area of sexual identification. Various degrees of internal stress as well as the stress stimulated within the context of evaluations by peers have the potential to encourage a route to short circuit painful assessments by self and others through early closure on sexual preference. The anxiety that may have already accompanied conflict stirred by a self-evaluative process of same-sex, incestuous, or forbidden-object preferences may have intensified through observation of socially appropriate sex preferences of fellow peers or, perhaps, through sensitive antennae that received the beginning of a nuance of disapproval in peer verbal responses and nonverbal behaviors. Early closure on selection of a mate carries the potential to be interpreted as a defensive effort to reduce stress of $AERR^n$ feedback. It may be that the dissonance accompanying the vicissitudes of attraction or the process of courting itself is too stressful; hence the decision is made to marry early. Conflict with moral teachings, disapproval by parents—conscious or unconscious, verbally or nonverbally transmitted—are exemplary of situational determinants that increase dissonance and a defensive response of early closure. It may also be a socially acceptable resolution to socially taboo areas, such as homosexuality or incestuous desires. The degree of anxiety experienced may have activated defenses of early closure on a mate—going steady, living together, early marriage. Later in life, if dissatisfactions begin to press too hard and defenses weaken, the true preference may surface.

Developmental Fictions in Socially Approved Decisions

Early Closure runs a high risk of being misinterpreted as adaptive since it is generally seen as a socially acceptable action—for example, choice of a mate, career, set of interests. As long as the closure is in a socially acceptable direction, early decisions are generally not frowned on. They are not commonly recognized as aberrant or as representing a malfunction in smooth developmental and psychological progression. Often, the outward manifestations of early closure are greeted as evidence of precocious maturity and reinforced as developmentally advanced (this external support of early closure may be seen as a reflection of a general societal predisposition to precocity). Dependent on the personality variations of the major environmental figures, early closure will be encouraged or not. Late Closure may appear to be an opposite phenomenon, but it is not. (The type of closure overtly opposite but dynamically similar to early closure is "Suspended Closure," to be discussed shortly). The adolescent who remains in the peer group and participates in the sequential functions and their processes will eventually move to closure. Some may take a longer period of time than others and the closure may appear to come late. Their process may be slower, or they may have psychologically begun later, regardless of chronological age. The adolescent who takes longer to make up his mind may use more small groups and may go back to the primary peer group for a time, but will move through the process to successful closure.

By contrast, the Suspended-Closure Adolescent utilizes a variety of postures to move away from the stimuli of the adolescent-peer-group functions and their oppressive consequences. Suspended closure, more colloquially seen as "dropping out," is a way outwardly different from Early Closure to respond to the same phenomenon of overwhelming stress, contributed to in whole or in part by activity of AD functions.

Suspended Closure: the Dropout

Paradoxically, the Dropout, a close cousin to the Early Closure Adolescent, is generally seen as embodying a socially unacceptable resolution. Although the underlying dynamic is similar, Early Closure is interpreted as success and Dropout as failure. More explicitly, the Dropout is considered a quitter. It is considered implicit that he cannot or will not cope. The social posture of each of these "close cousins" may be determined in great part by the history of social reinforcements and conditioned-behavior preference selections. The adolescent who has a history of positive experience with adults is cognitively attuned to what behaviors will continue to bring approval and thus reduce anxiety as a consequence of positive reinforcement by relevant adult figures. If the path to constructing his own set of self-reinforcers (which would be an end product of examination of self-elements, selection and reselection, testing, and integration) becomes cognitively and affectively burdensome or perhaps even overwhelming, the adolescent may abortively move to early closure. But the Early-Closure adolescent will select a direction based on an awareness of how the former positive-reinforcement history was achieved.

Actions in Search of Relief of Dissonance

With the Dropout, the motive is the same—avoidance of dissonance—but the pattern and the path are different. There may not be so clearly demarcated a history of positive reinforcements. Congruent relationships and contracts effected with adults may be less stratified and clear, masked, or even absent. Resolution in a socially acceptable direction is unavailable. The comfort of a group of peers has been short lived. Stress emanating from ESA and $AERR^n$, operating in tandem, placing the adolescent as both subject and object, have resulted in a continuing assessment of self in relation to other that has raised anxiety to an untenable level. The Dropout merely quits. Flight is the response.

This model of the Dropout, seen within a context of painful affect connected with a self-evaluation process with relevant peers operative in informal peer associations, can be extended to a variety of settings in which adolescents are present in groups, including academic settings. The educational dropout has been traditionally regarded as either unwilling or unable to do the academic work. The potentially great amount of stress that may be experienced as an affective consequence of AERR[n] functions and processes has not been included in the spectrum of factors considered causal. Despair and disillusionment with the self in not coping with the ongoing personal challenge is added to by the force of Adolescent Kinetic processes that stress the future relevance of the present performance.

Stress can be multiplied exponentially as the adolescent not only confirms perceived inadequacies in the present, but also sees the talents of fellow travelers in life with whom he will continue to compete. For some, dropping out of school and entering mixed society is less painful. There is no guarantee, however, that the adolescent will not experience a reactivation of tension in a different environment with different environmental elements. In the service of seeking shelter, he may confront new feelings of inferiority and self-doubt, perhaps of an even less tolerable dimension.

Flight takes alternative forms: flight away or flight to. Quitting school or the peer group can be considered flight away from an area in which painful effects become intolerable. Activities that lead to feeling good should be conceptualized as "flight to." They include experiences that cover, overshadow, or even depress experience, sometimes to the point of near annihilation (for example, alcohol, drugs). Sexual acting out and antisocial or delinquent activities can offer opportunities to release frustration and angers. A desire for isolation or isolated experiences may serve a protective distancing need.

It is essential to *look beyond* the common assumption of lack of ability or desire to meet an objective standard of expectation. "Flight from" or "flight to" may not be at all related to what is assumed by an assessment of obvious circumstances, as for example, the last task failed. It is far more productive in considering the adolescent period to maintain an awareness of the motion of the interactional peer-group functions. What is happening during the peer-arena period is the ongoing relevant area of inquiry and should be a continuing focus. The priority environmental figure of this specific developmental age is the peer. Peer estimate of adolescent performance and the resultant status with peers is clearly of maximum importance. In early and middle adolescence, the future, couched in a world of abstractions, is not experienced as real. Adolescents relate to the concrete and the visible. Academic tasks are known to be preparatory to life but are not of immediate, concrete relevance. Peers and the group response are, however, concrete and visible. The response of the relevant other, at this stage, is what is certain. What achievement of the task means in relation to the quest for self-definition and self-directive or goal setting is understood primarily in relation to the immediate peer response. Their world is a peer world; there is not yet another real world. The peer world is the center—the core, the plasma, the matrix. The immediate peer response represents, concretely, the levels of one's potential impact in the future world one will share with peers. Peer values do not necessarily mirror those of adults, and adult expectations or standards do not carry the same impact. In the peer-arena period, adult response is relevant for reward purposes, but what the achievement means is reflected in the eyes of the peer. Peers are perceived as the relevant others. They will be the fellow travelers against and with whom the adolescent will continue to interact and transact. Their response is what measures and credits or discredits achievement.

Hence the phenomenon of the Dropout should be examined in relation to the social context and to the press of the developmental period. The former yields data about "where and who else," and the latter can offer a perspective on the appropriateness of seemingly inappropriate behavior. The pain to which the Dropout reacts may be stimulated by an awareness of peer response. More crucially, however, it is to his own despair, tied to increasing concern over his future posture. The dropout phenomenon must be understood in its subtle form as a coping mechanism in a route away from the stress of peers—not in its overt display.

Types of Dropout

Four varieties of dropout, which represent irregularities in development with a common dynamic base of suspended closure, will now be delineated. They are conceptualized as alternate forms of the defensive response discussed earlier as early closure: (1) Temporary Withdrawal/Extended Withdrawal/Temporary Dropout; (2) Secret; (3) Masked, including (a) Cause committed and (b) Person committed; (4) Solo, including (a) Obvious Loner and (b) Parallel Loner. Although temporary withdrawal is adaptive, not maladaptive—and is technically not really dropping out—it is included here since it can be mistaken for real dropout and is, in fact, vulnerable to becoming an extended, maladaptive form.

Temporary Withdrawal/Extended Withdrawal/
Temporary Dropout

Temporary withdrawal represents an interim coping movement. This phenomenon is not the same as dropout; rather, it is a quasi form of dropout and should be regarded as an adaptive movement. For example, at any point in the developmental process, an adolescent may sense a lag, colloquially expressed as a feeling of "not being together." (The popular expression, "I can't get my head together," speaks most pertinently to the adolescent task.) Hence the adolescent may temporarily retreat to assemble and reassemble elements in pursuit of a cognitive anchor.

The relaxed milieu of temporary withdrawal from the affective impact of task pursuit can be seductive. Though recognized as a universal need in adolescence, some temporary withdrawals begun in the service of reassembling strengths become extended withdrawal that can lead to temporary dropout—a first step toward more permanent dropout. Once away, return to the necessary arena is affected by the point of development at which the adolescent withdrew. The extent of task work accomplished and the past effectiveness of affective coping responses substantially influence the degree of the motivation to complete peer-group tasks. The higher the percentage of satisfactory $AERR^n/SER$ experiences, the greater the expectancy for more areas of satiation and closure—hence the strong motive to return to the peer group. The more painful the consequences of $AERR^n/SER$ have been, the greater the tendency to extend the withdrawal period. In fact, the closer the temporary withdrawal is to crucial moments in the peer-arena sequence, the greater the potential for extended withdrawal on to some form of dropout. Since the adolescent experiences an increasing rate of satiation and/or closure the further along he is in the peer-arena sequence, the risk period for withdrawal is in the primary-peer-group period for most adolescents.

To the extent that a temporary withdrawal aids integrative functions, the adolescent experiences decreasing tensions. Stability increases, as does readiness to reenter the appropriate group and complete peer-arena tasks. Shorter periods of withdrawal will ensue. The postures on the continuum from occasional withdrawal to temporary dropout on to permanent dropout are subject to modification and uneven change and should be closely monitored. Constructive use of withdrawal may be viewed as a component part of a developmental process wherein resolutions take place on a piecemeal basis as, one by one, elements are examined, assembled, integrated, reexamined, and orchestrated. Close attention to timing, frequencies, and length of withdrawals may signal irregularities, particularly in the primary-arena period. Notwithstanding the benign respites and positive potential of temporary withdrawal for some adolescents, those who do extend temporary withdrawal to permanent Dropout are clearly deviant from a healthy developmental line. The danger of retreat to maladaptive functioning is real. Antisocial behavior and self-destructive habits or philosophical rejection of life are examples of behavior patterns and attitudes that directly manifest this developmental failure.

Secret Dropout

Not all Dropout is visible. Another type of Dropout exists that is not outwardly observeable—the Secret Dropout. This individual is physically present in the peer group, but psychologically he is absent. Retention of
membership in the peer group does not reflect the internal condition. This
adolescent has decided against physical departure. Psychological departure
with physical presence may reflect the compromise struck. He has closed
out psychological involvement; the functions of AD are rendered in-
operative.

Physical proximity to a group may be desired for many reasons. Obser-
vably, he continues to be seen as interacting with peers in an age-
appropriate fashion. Face-saving needs with respect to self and others are
thus satisfied. Any number of actors could be operative as well. Libidinous
interest or fantasies may be active. The size of the primary arena may shield
intrusive relationships of others—the family, for example. Unless the
adolescent is challenged by other group members, psychological absence
coupled with physical presence may offer a comfortable means to escape
pressures from environmental figures. It also serves the adolescent's own
fantasy of being "with it" and developmentally in tune while still escaping
the cognitive and affective consequences of AD processes.

Overt manifestations may vary from a philosophical, removed de-
meanor to behaviors seen as "just not with it." The Secret Dropout clearly
uses the adolescent peer group in a deliberate manner. Lack of involvement
is subtle and difficult to identify. The Secret Dropout more often than not
remains secret, except for what may eventually appear as an overlong stay
in the primary arena. Physically leaving the peer group carries the threat of
a rise in anxiety level. The adolescent may choose to move to a different
form of dropout behavior or may find another age-appropriate group in
which to be a secret member.

Masked Dropout

A fourth category is Masked Dropout. Two varieties of Masked Dropout
are active: the Cause-Committed Dropout and the Person-Committed
Dropout.

Cause-Committed. The first type of Masked Dropout is one in which the
adolescent chooses to mask his withdrawal from the painful experiences in
the appropriate peer arena through a disproportionate displacement of
energies to an objective cause. Hence, he does not overtly manifest the
psychological separation he attempts. He does not present the traditional

picture of a Dropout. The Dropout is subtly masked by his intense involvement, perhaps even total absorption, in constructive efforts on behalf of a cause or a particular societal group. The power of attraction to cause or to cults of various types can be objectively rationalized by the adolescent as a stance on values. Not yet possessed of his own values—since, developmentally, values can only be attached to a core of self that does not yet exist, the adolescent adopts a stand-in element with which to defend this position. Excessive time expenditures usually are common, thus affording another objective rationale to the self, as well as to others, to foreclose peer-group activity. Investment of energies of a dimension that appears inappropriately excessive to groups or causes other than an adolescent peer group during the adolescent-peer-arena period is suspect. Overcommitment may disguise a subtle form of withdrawal from AD dynamic developmental functions and may mask dropout. In this way developmentally essential functional processes of the peer group are aborted.

Person-Committed. A second form of masked dropout is manifested in overcommitment of another variety—an extended, almost exclusive absorption in another individual. Early in the period of adolescent development, the adolescent may experience a crush on a same-sex peer (Blos 1970) or on an older figure (Josselyn 1952), again usually of the same sex wherein the individual represents an ego ideal of sorts. Some form of temporary imitation or fantasized identification is active. However, the involvement of this variety of masked dropout is characterized by an extreme dedication. Along with the intensity and exclusivity exhibited, a self-effacing quality is often present. A psychological fusion is sought as a bulwark against the pain of isolation and self-doubt. It is as if the adolescent were absorbed by the selected object—or sought to absorb it. The overdedication that allows the adolescent to merge psychologically also serves ego-enhancing needs as the adolescent experiences his own relevance and importance to the selected other. The overdedication reveals the irregularity. Achievement of the maturity to commit psychologically to a second person, often behaviorally manifested in a dedicated stance, is component to the later successful resolution of adolescent tasks. However, when this dedication is engaged prematurely in order to bypass the painful path to constructing one's own maturity, it takes an exaggerated form, as in the Person-Committed Dropout. The commitment to a person is not in the service of true exchange. It operates subtly in the service of flight from engagement of the age-appropriate and developmentally essential AD functions and escape from coping with the affective consequences. True adaptive dedication to another individual is a product of appropriate exercise of the sequential processes of the AD. Premature dedication, behaviorally manifested as overinvestment, represents a form of abortive withdrawal from the tasks of developmental passage.

Solo Dropout

The fourth category of dropout is the Solo Dropout—the adolescent who seeks dramatic means to decrease or even eliminate pain and/or anxiety. Eventual dropout may have begun with temporary periods of withdrawal or with psychological dropout as the adolescent incrementally experienced the painful consequences of peer-group task processes. There may have been an early departure at the first point of the IRA (scanning) function. Two subcategories of Solo Dropout are observable: The obvious loner and the parallel loner.

Obvious Loner. The Obvious Loner has chosen to leave the adolescent peer group. But this drop out prefers isolation to risking additional stimuli with which he may not be able to cope. He has withdrawn from the impact of the peer-group stimuli to a minimum level of exposure to social stimuli. This socially withdrawn or isolated adolescent may seek satisfaction in solitary adaptive practices such as drug abuse or alcoholism, and may move from responsibility to responsibility unsuccessfully. An outwardly observable aloneness is often projected. This type of adolescent may become a true isolate. However, a dramatically opposite path may be selected. As is the case with the Person-Committed Masked Dropout who arrives prematurely at dedication to a second individual, the Obvious Loner may select a hobby or vocational interest to which he is overly devoted. Premature settling on the pursuit is neither the healthy closure that comes as a product of successful passage through the sequences of peer-group activity, nor the early closure of the settled adolescent, whose premature closures extend over a variety of elements. The absorption of the obvious loner in a pursuit (in itself socially acceptable or unacceptable) carries the overintense character that identifies it as extreme. Once again, this overdedication is another means of promoting defensive isolation. This defensive use of energies is designed to keep the obvious loner away from the adolescent peer arena and from the opportunity to construct his own growing maturity. It is evidence of irregularity in smooth adolescent progression.

Parallel Loner. The second category of solo dropout, the parallel loner, is linked dynamically to the secret dropout. Although the parallel loner has left the primary peer group, he wishes to retain a connection with peers. He cannot tolerate participation in a group; he desires instead to be alone, within a group. Therefore, the primary task is to find a group in which the affective consequences of AD will not again overwhelm him. The first obstacle to overcome is in gaining acceptance into a group perceived as more comfortable and safer. Hence the adolescent is attracted first to the new group by virtue of an externally obvious path to becoming a member. A group in which external determinants of status—such as age, socio economic status, or race—will accord him uncontested status may suffice initially. However, lack of similarity with the majority of members has the potential to reinstate dissonance. True membership in a group, a posture he may have never achieved in the peer group, the lack of which contributed to his departure, may be available rather easily if the adolescent is willing to participate in the common-denominator activity. The activities of such a group may be those that meet the critera of "comfort." The use of alcohol or drugs may be the entrance fee if the focus of the group is related to consumption and to the resultant behaviors. Furthermore, since the effects of drugs and stimulants are regarded as casual, the behaviors that result are not seen as really representative of the person himself. Psychological comparative energies focus around the enactment of the objective act. Membership itself is seen as a gesture toward conformity. Initial clumsiness or failure is not regarded as reflective of an internal lack of ability. Assistance is offered at entry. The ego, mercifully, is not involved. It is not an interactional format wherein comparative acts are focused on adolescent task areas. AD functions have not been energized. Self-definition in relation to peers is not at play. Rather, the focus is on the effects on the individual of the objective acts committed. The salient point is what one does, not who one is. Cults offer such assurances in the extreme.

The action in such groups is frankly parallel. True intcraction is blatantly absent. Truer involvement is only with self. The model of involvement is next to one another. Activities are engaged alongside another or others in parallel-play form. Parallel goals are to feel good and to reduce sensitivity to the immediate. Interaction between members takes place in relation to objective factors—information giving, exchange of materials. Drugs and alcohol serve functionally to numb developmental realities, and membership in a group in which others participate in similar acts supports a fantasy of age-appropriate involvement, although abortion of developmental progression into maturity is the true reality. The functional need for peers and peer-interactional processes remains strong but also remains unsatisfied and unsought.

The Adolescent without a Group

The final category of irregularities involves a group of youth that is more often than not overlooked—those adolescents who are without a group. According to the basic premise of the theory of Dynamic Functional Interaction, these adolescents are deprived of a fundamental and essential developmental experience. At any one moment, the adolescent without a group can be identified within a number of different postures, most of which describe the moment in time rather than defining the condition:

1. The adolescent may never have been a member of a group.
2. The adolescent may have experienced rejection from a group and is searching for a substitute group.
3. The adolescent may have prematurely withdrawn from the peer-group arena through a form of closure or dropout.
4. The adolescent may be between groups, having completed the primary peer group period and still searching out an appropriate secondary group.

Variations of position also exist along the developmental continuum. The adolescent between groups has achieved sufficient satiations of primary peer functions to be ready to move to the appropriate secondary peer group. Only a short period may transpire until a satisfactory new group is found. A lengthy search for an appropriate group may involve trial periods in various groups, but in this case the lag represents selectivity or narrowing specific end goals. In contrast, the adolescent who has prematurely withdrawn is at a far more primitive state developmentally.

The Observedly Exceptional

The first category of adolescents just listed meets the criteria for defining the condition. These are the adolescents who are deprived of a peer group. Paradoxically, their lack of visibility as a group reflects with precision the source of the intrusion to their development. This broad and diverse category includes a wide range of adolescents whose circumstances have denied them access to a sufficient number of adolescent peers. Causal factors range from the population limitations of the home community to membership in one of the various nontraditional minority groups for whom sufficient numbers of "like enough" others are unavailable—for example, mentally retarded and physically or disfigured disabled persons. This unrecognized populace represents a deprived group that is not only externally limited but is further excluded from the nourishment of assembling with a large group of chronological age-mates. Deprivation of the opportunity to engage their peer-group assembly and the AD functions adds still further to their burden of handicap. Falling within the same general model, but with a potential for a more temporary condition is the Newly Arrived Adolescent. This category includes those newly immigrated to the United States and those who have moved within the United States,—even to a new school.

The instability of the vulnerable adolescent condition is increased by nonaccessibility to a group in which at least the comfort of "like others" is experienced. More central to developmental delay, however, is that a peer arena in which to exercise developmental functions is unavailable. No matter what the precipitating causes, the adolescent without a group bears a condition of insufficient access to a group of peers. This represents a phenomenon different from a condition of social loneliness. Like all other adolescent categories, these adolescents have access to peers in school classrooms or perhaps in religious activities. But these are primarily objective-tasks settings in which opportunities for natural interaction are highly limited. In formal settings, time constraints inhibit natural interactive processes, since the allotted time is spent in objectively determined tasks. AD processes may be partially activated but short lived, and by themselves alone, insufficient. The opportunity for an informal, frequent, ongoing exposure to adolescent peer groups in which interaction is unstructured and unregulated over a period of time is unavailable. The necessary social context in which adolescent growth-specific tasks can be actualized is denied. The arena in which adolescent readiness for operation of AD functions can be coactively ignited is unavailable. This adolescent must struggle with self-questioning without the social context of relevant age-mates and their evaluative responses. Decisions about maintenance or rejection of characteristics for the repertoire of behavior are made in a vacuum of peer relevance. The adolescent cannot experience satiation and then proceed to complete refinement of self-elements. Experiencing and handling affective consequences of assessments with a fresh awareness of the range of abilities of fellow travelers is denied. Accordingly, the challenge of fashioning a functional framework in a confusing new world with limitless possibilities is also denied.

A finding contrary to prediction in the Philadelphia Study (Seltzer 1975) offers support to the concept that the adolescent without a group lacks satisfaction of a fundamental need to compare with relevant others. It was predicted that the adolescents who had selected peers as their primary reference group would engage in more comparison behavior in the discussion group with peers than would students who had selected nonpeers as the primary reference group. Strikingly the hypothesis was not supported. Data disclosed that the students who had not identified peers as primary reference group did, when peers were available, engage in more comparison with peers than did those who had identified peers as the primary reference group. The conclusion was drawn that it may be the absence of availability of peers as the primary reference group that leads to more comparing with peers when the peers are in fact available.

Findings from a postdiscussion interview in the same study (for the group as a whole) disclosed active interest in the group experience.

1. I was interested to find out the different
   points of view of the other members.   98.4 percent agreement
2. I was not very interested in the opinions
   of others on the topics we discussed.   93.7 percent disagreement

The Observedly Unusual

Adolescents who are not isolated geographically, but who are not members
of peer groups because of some objectively observable idiosyncratic difference may become increasingly determined to ally themselves with a
group in some way, becoming less particular the longer their isolation continues as to just how this need is met. Former discriminatory criteria may
alter as vulnerbility to joining any group increases. Hence, even suscep-
tibility to joining a self-related "feel-good-ethic" group, in which drug
abuse, alcoholism, or sexual acting out may be prominent, increases insofar as membership is accessible by a demonstration of willingness to participate in the group's activities. Frustration of readiness needs for affiliation will abate, and the adolescent prepares to functionally engage the
group.

However, this type of membership does not engage exercise of the
sought-after developmental functions since the motive structure of the
Observedly Unusual Adolescent without a group differs from those of
others who may have joined in flight from AD functions. Quite to the contrary of what may be sought, the physical effects of group activities inhibit
the stimulants to action of AD. Thus the relief of initial affiliation is short
lived. Since these groups serve flight from—not engagement in—the dilemmas of social and emotional growth, for the Adolescent without a group
the path to social growth is further retarded, if not permanently af-
flicted.

Since adolescents in geographically more remote areas lack accessibility
to large numbers of other adolescents (including accessibility to maladaptive groups), a risk is present that the geographically remote adolescent
may seek to flee from a sense of aloneness through private escape, alone or
with a few others. Escape to alcohol or drugs that cloud experience may
represent a temporary reduction in stress. These must be acknowledged as
available means to deal with various frustrations related to deprivation of
the physical forum in which AD functions can be actualized.

The Adolescent without a Group, whether the status is based in defensive withdrawal from previous member status or in nonaccessibility to peer
group, is a member of a senstive population. Consequent nonaccessibility
to the forum in which to actualize AD sequences is a portent of irregularities—developmental lags or maladaptive behaviors. In the absence
of exposure to numbers of peers offering varieties of self-elements to try
out, there is danger of global identification with adults and cassettelike
substitution of adult elements in the cognitive structure. Chances for a
reinforcement of pseudomaturity or an alternate form of maladaptive early
closure are high. These maladaptive choices may be a consequence of
frustration.

A Vulnerable Populace

Anything less than full participation in the functional interaction system of the sequential peer groups in which the dialectics of this crucial period of development are active denies the adolescent the opportunity to construct and fuel his "own" self-structure in relation to his perceived fellow life travelers. The first dialectic engages self and other, self and group; the second maintains the tension between past and future—where one was and where one is going. Where one stands in the immediate present moment is seen within a context of a relevant group of peers interactive with an outer circle of other generations. Irregularities in development occur consequent to this deprivation. Full developmental readiness to enter the adult world is not achieved.

Protective defense activities as a response to stressful conditions are available and can be utilized at any period of the life span. Adolescents, in a temporary condition of possession of little "core of self," are particularly vulnerable to the lure of avenues to reduced stress. Peer interaction is not easy. Most adolescents can tolerate these conditions, but some have greater difficulty than others. The forms of irregularities discussed (see table 14-1) offer escape from the upheaval and dissonance that accompanies adolescence and is intensified for protracted periods by interactions in the peer group. However, any extended period of reduction of participation—and certainly total nonparticipation—interrupts the completion of developmental task functions. The integration of one's own self-structure is seriously endangered. Even when a self-constellation is partially orchestrated, continuing self-refinement will suffer. Full involvement with sequential functions of the Adolescent Dialectic is essential to successful closure on a developmental period that is in and of itself crucially time related.

Table 14-1
Categories of Irregularities

Category	Major Affective Posture	Defensive Action	Group Presence		Outward Stance	Social-Posture Acceptability Quotient
			Psychological	Physical		
Pseudoadult	Equilibrium	Identification with adult	−	−	Mature	+ +
Settled adolescent	Equilibrium	Early decisions	−	−	Stable	. + +
Low-threshold adolescent *Early closure*	Equilibrium	Premature closure	+ −	+ −	Stable	+
Suspended Drop Out						
Temporary	Controlled	Withdrawal	+ −	+ −	Erratic	−
Secret	Dissonance	Withdrawal	−	+	Preoccupied	−
Masked	Dissonance	Flight to	+ −	+ −	Extremist	−
Solo	Dissonance	Flight	+ −	+ −	Removed	−
Adolescent without group	Frustration	Withdrawal/ flight	−	−	Lonely-searching	+ or −
Smooth progress adolescent	Consonance-Dissonance	AD functions	+	+	Unpredictable	+

Part IV
Potentials and Applications
of the Theory

15 Implications for Parenting Adolescents: A Revisionist Design

The adolescent literature generally suggests that separation of the adolescent from the parent is essential in the preparation for adulthood tasks. Dynamic Functional Interaction offers the peer-arena model, which sets a perspective of incremental involvements and separations extending the numbers of transitions the adolescent must engage and conquer with important environmental figures. Earlier theoretical models have leapfrogged the existence of a second crucial fusion and subsequent separation. The adolescent's entry into and departure from the peer group have gone unacknowledged. Since the peer group has been generally conceptualized as no more than a freely available sphere, an unstated assumption has been that it is entered, engaged in, and left easily. Neither entry processes nor functions at play within the peer group have been seriously examined. As earlier chapters have detailed, forces for affiliation are active and forces for leaving are activated. In between, powerful forces are operative in the arena. Leaving the peer group is a process in and of itself. Separation from peers is a function of the ending phase of the period of development. However, prior to completing peer-group functions, the joining of a peer group in and of itself involves separation from parents.

Parenting: Transitions and New Dimensions

The literature has generally not juxtaposed separation from parents and early peer-group membership. Rather, adolescent rebellion has been generally regarded as a function of separation from parents, a cause and effect, conceptually part of the adolescent-parent relationship. Separation from parents has been considered tantamount to the assumption of adult, not adolescent, tasks. The peer-arena model suggests, however, that separation begins at a point at which the adolescent is physically able to be separate for longer periods of time than in childhood and is psychologically able to move toward more egalitarian relationships. Separation dynamics usually begin before the period of primary-peer-group membership, not after. In fact, it is the separation from parents and parental guideposts that leaves the adolescent frameworkless and adds stimulus to forces for affiliation with adolescent peers. The present view represents a departure from the literature that sets the behaviors within a peer-parent model of rebellion, of storm and stress. Neither are the behaviors attributed exclusively to the vicissitudes of the individual personality and his society only. Nor are these the only sources or resources. Dynamic Functional Interaction sets forth that, in part, observable adolescent behaviors are also stimulated by the reciprocal impact of adolescents on one another and that their behaviors should definitely be regarded within the context of overt responses to the dynamic functions of peer-group interactions by youths in readiness.

For the most part, parents accept as an integral task in preparing an adolescent for mature life the responsibility to acquaint the adolescent with various life-styles and to inform him of the necessary preparations for these varieties of life choices. However, only part of the task can be thus accomplished. A complementary area must be self-taught. It is paramount to the adolescent that parents respect the adolescent imperative to manage himself in relation to the emerging context of the adult world in which he will travel in relation to his fellow travelers, with whom he will be cooperating and competing—his peers. A picture of self in relation to peers is information as important as the objective means and information offered by parents and elders. In the process of accumulating his data, the adolescent's day-to-day assessments of self in relation to fellow peers may result in a series of intermediate themes. Integration of data over time may converge into a stable self-picture, possibly at variance from more potent intermediary themes. Even an overriding theme may be reassessed. During this passage, adolescents need support and perspective offered by parents in order to overcome temporary stalemates and to avoid flight to maladaptive defenses.

Interactional Currents of Altering Postures

During the transition from child to adult, relationships with parents necessarily change. Parent-adolescent relationships during this period are known to be turbulent. With the advent of physical maturity and added cognitive abilities and emotional scope, caretaking functions of parents decrease since the strike for independence carries newly relevant guides and guideposts. Behavior that has been interpreted globally as rebellion against control may be better understood as a component to trial and error, necessarily accomplished at a distance from parents in order to identify what is clearly the adolescent's own value system. The peer arena becomes functional as the forum for the nurturance functions toward social growth previously offered at home. Disorientation experienced simultaneous to internal dissonance leads the adolescent to seek others experiencing similar circumstances. Similar end goals of social growth now dictate that the appropriate forum differs from that of former years. The adolescent senses that growth and development will take place in an arena of peers. Enormous energies must be expended to incorporate developmental raw material for processing, to cope with demands for conformity, and to handle the emotional wounds that interaction yields. With these new, taxing demands on the distribution of his energies, the adolescent manifests less interest in parents and home. A depletion of energies is represented, not a rejection of family. Still egocentric, but now future oriented, youth choose—in the service of development—to invest their energies in areas that appear to hold the potential for the most efficient gain.[1] Since parents and family recede in meaning and involvement with family appears generally nonfunctional, energies are delegated to the arena that is functional: the peer group. Global parental impact changes, becoming more specific and limited in scope. Parents are no longer the exclusive arena.

A number of factors can further confuse. First, paradoxically, the manifest picture of the peer arena—good times, laughter, easy discourse—masks the functional nature of the group. Hence most parents regard peer-group activity as meriting only a limited time involvement, and perhaps even consider the time spent as a deterrent to the serious business of growth. Many parents view adolescent-peer-group commitment as competitive with the substantial routes to growth they carefully orchestrate, direct, and even model. Intense involvement is seen as frivolous and dysfunctional rather than as an essential stepping-stone to growth.

Second, the transitional cognitive condition of the adolescent in the process of constructing a self-structure can further confound. In the primary-peer-group period, ESA is utilized for the assembly of a pseudoelement structure. Although the adolescent expresses himself with overt sincerity, the attitude or opinion is frankly a tryout. Exchange in the peer group involves a reciprocal, nonverbal understanding with another who intuitively understands that the concept is under "tryout." Total freedom to advocate six or seven viewpoints, many of which may be contradictory, is accorded. Each peer freely adopts positions with as much vehemence as he offered opposing views only minutes before. Intuitively aware of the exchange functions of the congregation, the respective peers do not attach permanence to values expressed, despite the depth of sincerity manifested. However, the same nonverbally acceptable set of ground rules is not operative at home. Parents usually accept offerings of apparent deep conviction at face value. At home, two different life stages of development are interacting. On the one hand, parents engage in discussion with the seriousness component of a self consisting of evolved self-elements. When values close to the parent self-system are attacked, the parent may feel violated and grow angry. By the same token, the adolescent may experience increasing hostility as he is held responsible for a view he has expressed but does not experience as his (since he is still in the developmental posture of exchange and tryout). He may feel trapped but bound to save face. Consequently, frequency of discourse may decline. Distancing often sets in, initiated either by adolescent or by the parent, who must withdraw for longer or shorter time periods. Some parents internalize the consequences as rejection, operating on what was originally a theoretical concept but has now become a popularized notion of adolescent rebellion. Peer-derived functions and angers overtly misdirected toward family members are red herrings that further compound the confusion, frustration, and hurt and that parents may internalize as a further rejection.

It is crucial to recognize that children and their parents are engaged in a process of altering their postures toward one another. Developmentally, they concurrently experience transitional viewpoints and conditions. The adolescent transitional status from child to adult is in continuous active motion. It is observable physically and is a well-advertised phenomenon. Since parental transitional status involves only changes in function, on the other hand, it is far less obvious. Ironically, parents who formerly occupied the role of guide to the child now find the guideposts that framed their former parenting dysfunctional. They too are left without tools. But a curious omission is found in the literature. Although considerable attention is accorded the lack of distinct role functions for the adolescent in sophisticated Western society in the time span between physical maturity and actual assumption of adult societal roles, little attention is accorded to the parent of the adolescent who is in a similar condition. Skills hewn over a period of years of nurturing and guidance now face no outlet. Years of activity have yielded a strong, intact habit structure that is now obsolete. Within a context of adolescent issues, the adolescent literature generally has not examined in any depth the implications for the parent generation of the adolescent freedom to move away toward the newly relevant group.

Bigenerational Task Model

We have seen that the parent-adolescent separation-rebellion model casts parents as outgrown libidinous objects. Although the model of developmental continuity takes exception, no specific model for parenting is offered beyond an assumed continuity of ongoing parenting practices, unless they have been found dysfunctional. Parenting a transitional "chad" (child-adult) is of a different complexion than is nurturing a child or relating to an adult child. The task of parenting must change in scope, direction, and form. Two major dimensions are encompassed: (1) emotional support and (2) informational reference.

An alternative new framework for parenting is offered within this formulation. It lies within a bigenerational developmental task base. The Bigenerational Task Model collapses parenting into sequences—the active sequence and the *latent specific* sequence. The active sequence is one of active nurturance, including responsibility for health, safety, close direction, and supervision. The latent specific sequence, making its appearance in early adolescence, is one of incrementally increasing reserve rather than active nurturing, of specific consultation, and of active lifeline responsibilities (financial, educational, support and so forth). The Adolescent-Parent Relevance Quotient works hand in hand with and complements the Bigenerational task base. Parental functions are not rejected; they are merely altered (see table 15-1). Some elements are eliminated or reduced, whereas others are increased; for example, responsibility for physical safety has ended. The need for parents as an important information source on relevant areas remains and may even increase as the complexity of issues confronted grows (see note 1). The task of functioning as secondary support is added, whereas that of primary responsibility is ended. The Adolescent-Parent-Relevance Quotient encompasses secondary support, information, and reference group functions. Within this model, adolescent transfer of functional energies into peer-arena membership heralds *successful* closure for the parent on the active sequence of parenting. A helpless offspring has been husbanded into biological maturity and guided through initial socialization. Membership of a child in a peer group is considered a *milestone of passage.*

A utilitarian framework on which parental behavior can be built is available through conceptual utilization of the Adolescent-Parent Relevance Quotient and the Bigenerational Task Model. Patterns of parental nurturance and the transition from primary direct functionary to secondary indirect functionary complement the developmental passage of the child into adolescence.

A Conceptual Lag

Socialization practices in Western society lag behind developmental transitions. Parents in Western society generally yield to necessary separation

Table 15-1
Adolescent-Parent Relevance Quotient

Task	Appropriate	Inappropriate
Advising		×
Guiding	+	
Directing		×
Informing	+	
Doing		×
Supporting	+	

and change of status when a child marries. This transition is not internalized as rejection but is anticipated as a necessary transition. Falling within the traditional parenting framework, they stand ready to be an informational source, to offer guidance and advice. Although adjustment is anticipated, the new status both they and child now occupy is regarded as natural and appropriate. The external significance of mating or marriage signals the necessary set of psychological adjustments for change in role status and role functions to become operative.

The formulation offered here suggests that the existing sociocultural conceptual lag be foreshortened. Mating or marriage is no longer the signal for ending the nurturance period in parenting. The onset of adolescence is such an event. Adolescence also signals the initiation of parenting behaviors of the latent specific period. Now the adolescent takes command of his developmental ship and navigates his course to the transition group. Passage is to the adolescent peer group, wherein necessary developmental nurturance is constructed through interactional experience with peers. Dynamic Functional Interaction suggests that a conceptual complement be added to currently anticipated transitions and resulting behavioral changes of allegiance. Transition to new interpersonal preferences should be anticipated to begin at some point in early adolescence. If expected, this can be planned for and encouraged as developmentally sound and necessary. The transfer of energies from parent and family to the peer-arena field, if anticipated as a naturally occurring transition, can be experienced as a desirable developmental progression. Reduction of parental concern is appropriate to new role functions of reduced general scope that parents can assume in relation to a sequentially appropriate arena. Encouragement and support of the transition as essential to smooth developmental process can reinforce a sense of successful parenting rather than concern that peer membership will rival positive child-parent relationships. The parental task is one of retraining, not "doing"—being available if called on.

The first separation and passage of entry into primary schools, where new environmental figures are added to the child's figural spectrum, is to be followed by a second emotional passage in early adolescence. Recognition of this natural movement will encourage readiness for refashioning the parental posture when this reshuffling of positions in the figural spectrum does occur. Passage from parents to peers will be anticipated. Later, peers too will be separated from.

In sum, the fluid notion of an Adolescent-Parent Relevance Quotient within a Bigenerational Task Model requires a reversal of parenting habits as the child becomes an adolescent. New skills need to be exercised. First, appropriately timed deemphasis of traditional nurturing requires a conceptual temporal reconditioning. The primary period of actual nurturance moves to proud completion at the *beginning*, not the end, of the pubertal awakening. Second, types of parenting functions change: (1) the transition to a more cognitive relationship, which supplants a primarily emotional-affective nurturant relationship; (2) offering of support rather than reluctance about the preference of the adolescent for peer-group affiliation through assuming postures of acceptance and facilitation, if not encouragement. Especially during the beginning period of transition, when the Adolescent Kinetic processess are most active and the adolescent is newly exposed to handling remodeled perceptions of self, parental backing can reinforce the strength of adolescent resistance to dysfunctional escapes.

The Home: New Dimensions as Haven

Since up to now the functional nature of the peer group has not been recognized in its full impact, neither is it understood to be the forum where hard developmental work is operative. Current views of parent and peer functions reflecting this lag need reorientation. They are seen *in reverse*. Contrary to popular positions in the literature, it is *not* the peer group that offers escape from the developmentally relevant pressure. Prior to adolescence, social development has in the main been achieved through integrations made in the home with the home agent. Now, however, the *primary agent* of social development is *out of the home*; the primary home function becomes to *support* maximum functioning in the growth arena. The home offers a release valve to the constraints on behavior that must be assumed for retention of peer-group membership. Home may be the safe haven in which the adolescent can cry out the angers and tensions that must be restrained with his peers. (Although parents and siblings come to understand that some adolescent outbursts originate in conflicts arising from peer-group interaction, the insults experienced from such hostility may not necessarily be erased or excused.)

During this period the home serves as a haven in which the adolescent can "regroup" stimuli acquired in the peer arena. An apparent decrease of interest in familial activities, or a lack of desire to accompany the family, is often the manifestation of a priority need to regroup. This type of withdrawal usually is a functional use of the home field, but it is often misinterpreted. Since the posture is not necessarily cognitively understood by the adolescent, the inability to translate the need verbally leads to frequent assumptions of rejection or of its cousin—rebellion. In childhood the home was where the parent was—literally and concretely. The cognitive advance of adolesence contributes to the ease with which the adolescent can function away from the physical reality of the home or the home figures. As dependence on the concrete image lessens, the adolescent conceptualizes the home far more broadly and can extend his mental conception of home to include physical and topographical aspects. Physical presence near the parent is no longer necessary for the experience of "home." Now the physical experience with the topographical characteristics of home may offer nurturance that at a younger age was available only through physical proximity to the parent. Parents and siblings now merge more into a ground of home, whereas during earlier developmental periods their figural components defined the space. Hence, when the adolescent needs the home field for support, he does not necessarily require the physical presence of others. It may be enough just to be "at home."

The expanded adolescent conception of home is developmentally appropriate, representing an adaptive phenomenon of development that facilitates transfer of energies to a peer involvement without an experienced sense of loss of the home or of its abdication. Whereas for the child parents *were* the home, for the adolescent they are only a part—albeit an important part—of home. Psychologically, the adolescent can incorporate an abstraction of home and hence can readjust the topography of home. Conceptually, the adolescent is empowered to integrate home and peer group and is equipped to deal with the network of combinatory factors. Since this developmental transition is not marked societally by a ceremonious physical leaving of the home, the change remains invisible to parent and child. The necessary adjustments can be elusive. The emotional costs of interactions couched in honest confusion and misconceptions may be high.

A Multigenerational Perspective

Concrete education about the motion of and subtleties connected with adolescent passage seems essential to actualization of effective functioning as a parent to adolescents. Whereas up to now an important task in parent education has been interpretation to the parent of connections between outwardly observable changes in adolescent behavior and internal growth changes in the physical, cognitive, and affective domains of the development, new models are now necessary. The figural-ground realignments of adolescence need explicit interpretations so that parents, once informed, can begin the difficult affective readjustments. To date the conceptual thrust has been based in traditional transitional milestones of emotional passage, spawning parent education models based in a parent-adolescent separation-rebellion model. The Adolescent-Parent Relevance Quotient, based in the Bigenerational Task Model presented earlier, has as its conceptual base notions that separation from parents has taken place prior to peer-group membership and that the salient point of reference in adolescent development is the transfer of energies from the home field to the peer-arena field. A fluid, incremental reversal in the potency postures of parent and peer arena is depicted. Hence, the teaching model is not adjustment; rather, the model is *readjustment*. The two-dimensional model of child and parent, appropriate to childhood years, is dysfunctional in adolescence. An expanded model for expanded needs is multidimensional—to include parent; adolescent; adolescent peer group; and, incrementally, as development proceeds, pertinent reference persons or groups. Concepts of adolescent separation, rebellion, parent rejection, and escape are less useful, if not altogether off the mark. They need to be replaced by more appropriate conceptions, such as: adolescent relevance quotient, secondary nurturance posture, relationship realignment, and bigenerational tasks. Parents and adolescents are not involved in separation and rebellion but, rather, in redesign of roles and redistribution of energies. Each struggles with coordination of bigenerational developmental tasks as well as with the mastery of their own. The model of conflict based in separation and rebellion begs replacement by a model that incorporates a multidimensional figural and task base.

Note

1. Findings from the Adolescent Reference Group Index (ARGI) (Seltzer 1975) showed a very discriminating adolescent who selected the most pertinent reference group to consult for each specific issue: for example, teachers for which college to attend, parents for their opinion as to whether they should take a year off before attending college, school friends for whether to report a peer who was cheating, the media for effects of marijuana (see table 10-10).

16 Educational Innovations: A Peer Ecology

Classroom as Peer Group

The school classroom, an assembly of peers in formal settings, has generally not been regarded as a peer group. Yet the classroom in which the child sits comprises people of the most relevant age group in his life—his peers. When the school and the classroom are conceptualized as a group of peers whose interactions contribute to the milieu of the aggregate peer arena, it clearly follows that the developmental functions of the Adolescent Dialectic (AD) are active in classroom settings, too. Conceptualization of the educational setting as a component part of the arena extends the notion of the affective consequences of AD field forces to the classroom. Hence the adolescent must handle affective responses to AD functions at the same time as he copes with educational content. Implications of effects of feedback from peers extends far beyond the objective subject matter at hand to juggling perceptions of reflected level of mastery of material and its academic stress and implications. Also, the adolescent must balance aggregate perceptions of the effect of the academic position on former peer appraisal of self and then make the necessary self-reassessments onto realigning goals. This mass of intrapsychic activity is masked by an exterior of coping habits.

Given the intensity level of peer interaction, it is clear that a far broader scope of concentrated work is under construction in the classroom than is observable. Comprehension and introjection of the content are the designated major tasks; the working out of AD functions is the corollary undesignated major task. A preoccupied student may actually be dealing with $AERR^n$ tasks. Hence, education issues take on multiple dimensions when appropriateness is assessed within a conceptual framework of AD functions. For example, with regard to the $AERR^n$, on the one hand homogeneous groupings do provide similar peers so that the results of $AERR^n$ processes do in theory yield more benign results. On the other hand, assignment to a non-preferred group may carry a stigma of potent impact toward devaluation by peers. The more beneficial aspects of a more benign $AERR^n$ evaluation may be thus diluted. Furthermore, the observable group assignment makes the devaluation public and therefore factual. The assault endured may discourage motivation, increase anxiety, and/or raise the potential for attraction to the varieties of early closure or dropout. Public devaluation experienced by the adolescent on any criterion may stimulate concerns of

225

generalized devaluation in the eyes of his peers. The debate over the value of homogeneous or heterogeneous classroom groupings takes on a greater complexity when couched within a contextual framework of the classroom as a part of the peer-arena aggregate. Dynamics of the peer arena are active not only within the class, but also in the hallways and on the school bus. Some adolescents may arrive at school already stressed by the morning's AD impact.

Ubiquitous Presence of AD Functions

Crucial to the educational progression of each student is the degree of sensitivity the administration and the teachers have to the ubiquitous presence of AD functions—the nature of their actions and the energy drain this constitutes for the student. Students, particularly those in the primary-peer-group period, usually respond first to the demands of the peer arena and only second to the content assigned. Some students can handle the stimulation well; some retreat from it; some react with overstimulation. Depending on the individual student posture, effects may stimulate or may seriously retard, intensified academic dedication. An educational model wherein educational progression is integrally intertwined with developmental progression includes sequentially scheduled developmental batteries alongside traditional educational achievement batteries. During the period of adolescence, data collected on the peer-group experience can contribute an index to developmental position and appropriate or inappropriate points of passage—for example, the point at which the student has preference for secondary, smaller groups rather than the larger primary peer group. A developmental grade might be conceptually joined with a distinct curricular program, setting incremental goals for relevance to both academic and social growth. Periodic reassessments would monitor not only each domain but also their interactional component. For example, (1) the impact of "peers" on goal setting may come to be publicly acknowledged as an influential dimension; (2) a refocused approach to adolescent peer counseling, as another example, might first entail a functional analysis of the situation within a peer-arena-model framework in order to assess whether peer counseling could be predicted to aid or exacerbate the problem, incorporating timing as a conceptual aid; (3) emotional response to dissonance with peers or the disorientation produced by conflicting perceptions require coping energies that may be drawn from academic pursuits.

A Peer-Arena Progression Profile has been developed for use in educational as well as therapeutic settings. Rather than utilizing a school-grade or chronological-age model, the Peer Arena Progression Profile (PAPP) index can index the position of the student on a developmental continuum.

It provides data by which the educator can produce an available energy profile for each student. Depending on the progressive developmental position of the adolescent student, whether he is in the primary-peer-group period or the secondary-group period or perhaps even further along, the levels of available energy for schoolwork will vary. The educator is thus alerted to whether the student is still in a period in which major energies are being channeled to initial AD functions, or whether he has progressed to secondary-peer-group AD functions, in which more integrations of the self have been constructed, thus holding the potential for a reduction of expended peer-arena tasks, and possible readiness to channel energies to intermediately established goals. The PAPP offers a rich data sheet for educational counseling, if necessary (see tables 17-1 and 17-2).

Academic Under- and Overproduction

Although energies may be dissipated in order to cope with dissonant results of AD functions and processes, most students move forward smoothly both academically and developmentally. However, two quite opposite scholastic patterns each demonstrate the impact of the effects of AD: (1) academic underproduction and (2) academic overachievement. The former type of adolescent may achieve positive reinforcements more rapidly from energies expended outside the academic area, whereas the latter does so within the school setting. Underproduction is an obvious red flag to possible peer-related problems as well. Extremes of behavior at either end of the continuum, whether manifested in a socially acceptable direction or not, should be examined for evidence of possible stress. Overproduction often masks a problem, since generally praise is accorded rather than inquiry. Abrupt precocious or retrogressive academic productions may be overt stress responses or defenses to AD consequences. Dropout proportions may be reached.

Group norms operate as potent silent navigators in a classroom. As is well known, classroom behavior may be affected by continuing concern over rejecting and risking rejection—for example, loyalty to a friend may inhibit an individual from responding correctly. As discussed earlier, in adolescence nonconforming behavior carries a great risk. Much more is at stake than the loss of a friend or one's place in a group. Loss of the opportunity to actualize a developmental necessity is at risk. Therefore, extreme care extends to peer groups, even in the academic setting. It is familiar that conformity to school-prescribed goals and codes, when they are perceived to be at odds with membership norms, is cause for conflict and surprising subsequent behaviors. Although the group has been described by Redl (1974) as a continuously active, persistent, "under the couch" phenomenon in adolescence, fear of potential loss of AD functions (which only the adolescent peer group can serve) has not yet been recognized as contributing to conforming behaviors. Adolescent rooting to peers and the centrality of AD functions may provide insights for puzzled teachers and administrators into mystifying or unexpected extremes of student behaviors and may serve to explain instances of under or over production. Opportunities are rich for educators to work within a pertinent PAPP model from which a functional analysis of adolescent educational productions may be made. The model, furthermore, can occupy a central position in pre- and postprofessional training, as well as in pragmatic planning.

It appears instructive, therefore, for educational planners to take concrete account of the enormity of stimuli affecting the adolescent, to an especially marked degree in early adolescence. The time necessary to integrate newly impacting self-assessments which follow disorientation experienced as a function of operation of AD logically begs practical application in educational settings. Seventh and eighth grades, often those points in the educational process at which behavioral turmoil and problems of control are manifested, exemplify the external response to the AD functions within an educational setting.

Structural Reorientations

The peer-arena model adapted to educational settings suggests that a student option to elect a time for separation from peers should be available, if not required. At crucial, known points in the developmental process where AD functions abound, the adolescent is internally hyperactive and needs relief from stimulation. Settings to which adolescents may go at will for temporary periods should be incorporated. The "quiet room" often used in the treatment of hyperactive children offers a model for extension to the nonobservably hyperactive—that is most adolescents. Small study or relaxing rooms for individuals or small numbers of peers might suffice in providing a quiet experience or as an alternative to large cafeterias. More and smaller libraries where the student can read or just muse, or even silent musing rooms, could be objectively labeled so as to *underline the appropriateness* of the need.

Encouraging a focus beyond objective academic problems to a view of the idiosyncratic impact of groups, associates, and other school customs on AD functions (and their relation to academic performance) may bring insights into those component elements that affect functioning. Ironically, popular problem-focused "rap groups" in educational settings often reenergize already stressful and overstimulating concerns. Redirecting of these groups into "musing groups" encouraging orientation away from concentration on school or current interpersonal problems with peers or home could offer a legitimized opportunity for physical proximity to peers in situations of limited AD-function options. By contrast, other students may need individual help in coping. Academic production can then be viewed within a contextual model, reducing skewed emphasis on natural endowment.

A Broadened Conception of Beginnings:
A Crucial Period

Beginning a new educational experience, such as junior high, high school, or college, generally has been recognized as a significant transition that requires an adjustment period. Physical orientation or reorientation may be necessary; however, necessary adaptations go beyond external adjustments and the energies they expend. Integrations and reorganization of crucial internal processes are also necessary but have generally gone unspecified. Entry into new situations by definition extracts internal, organic reorganizations of the self. Hence, since adolescence is already a period in which there is minimal framework and the adolescent self is still in formation (though composed in part of vulnerable pseudoelements), a crucial period is stimulated by an external necessity to enter into a new situation—for example, a new school. Old guides and guideposts are few or nonexistent, so that most adjustments are made from an internally transitional platform, itself unstable. Reactivation of AD assessment and evaluation functions occurs in a new situation whenever the self is yet unsettled; hence, newly relevant adolescent peers stimulate new self-perceptions and new alterations in a self already under inspection. This condition is not restricted only to early adolescence. Not yet possessed of a stable self, generally every adolescent is still highly vulnerable to perceptions of and by others in any new setting. AD functions are reenergized at a fast pace to offer data with which to traverse the new territory. Those adolescents who have fully completed beginning stages of adolescence will find the new transition less difficult; those who have not may suffer considerable distress. The less anchored in clusters of settled elements, the more fragile the state of integration of self, the more vulnerable the adolescent is to stimulated reactivation of original AD processes brought on by a change of situations.

Seen within the context of notions set forth in Dynamic Functional Interactions, the drain of energies by AD functions brought on by the stress of new transitions, raises dilemmas attendant to the propriety of the pattern of living away from home at school or college during the adolescent period. The adolescent entering a school or college away from home, assumed to be mature, generally adopts a posture of apparent independence. Since his world is almost totally a peer world, he is consistently exposed to the continuums of assessment and reassessment in relation to fellow students. For the adolescent occasional escape from these conditions in order to regroup is necessary but may not be possible at a residential school. If the adolescent commutes from school to home, the return to the home field each evening allows retreat from these AD functions to the extent desired. Furthermore, familiar others react to his known core attributes. Unless the adolescent himself is in a period of reworking these core attributes, the responses of his family generally reinforce specified attributes as still present, thus promoting equilibrium. External touchstones available to the commuter student elude the adolescent who both studies and resides away from home.

Flexible Programming to Include Idiosyncratic Adjustments

No matter what the academic level, educators of early, middle, and late adolescents must recognize that construction of a cognitive self-structure is the primary, ever present, latent psychological goal. Furthermore, instability often is manifested during periods in which the temporary self-structure is threatened or needs reorganization. Recognition by educators that the initial adjustment needs of students in new situations may entail temporary backward steps to reorganize and reintegrate the self-picture implies the incorporation of this idea in appropriate modifications within each beginning level of the education system. Rather than giving only lip service to the notion of an adjustment period, they will need to anticipate lower available energy levels in the beginning weeks for academic work when little of the original store of energy may be left for school-task-related activity. Flexible *programming for beginnings and transitions* must be an integral part of educational planning for adolescents. However, notwithstanding the conceptual introduction here of a generic set of conditions, the idiosyncratic reactions of students, based in part of their history of reinforcement, must continue to be recognized. Anxiety levels connected with initial adjustments may be differentially manifested. Not all students exhibit a lack of concentration on academic tasks. Academic tasks may be used to withdraw from stimuli. High amounts of energy in fact may be placed on studies. Not all uneven adjustments are immediately observable. Uneven adjustments that become manifest in the latter half of the school year often reflect the early operation of masked defenses to initial difficulties.

Certainly the school is a natural resource for reducing the deprivation quotient of the Adolescent without a Group. For schools whose populations come from widely dispersed areas, as in rural settings, curriculum can be developed so as to include informal peer-group formats within a philosophy of both academic and developmental concerns. In order to estimate the extent of the deprivation, objective measurement instruments to ascertain the amount of peer-group exposure will need development alongside sophisticated probes into the quantity and quality of peer experience.

The peer-arena model of dynamic functional interaction is pregnant with potential for practical applications to (1) identify students who overtly or covertly experience educational distress, identifying the source of discomfort from an expanded perspective, and work toward eliminating active potential dropout; and (2) develop creative programming and planning that functionally serves optimal academic performance through strategies for prevention and amelioration of academic stress and accompanying personal effects.

17

Diagnosis and Therapy: Implementation

Current Modalities

Prevailing therapeutic modalities reflect differing theoretical orientations represented in the adolescent literature, ranging along a continuum from behavior-modification techniques to traditional psychoanalysis. Some of the encountered adolescent resistance to therapy may be in relation to theoretical conceptions that appear less relevant now than when introduced. (For example, the adolescent himself appears much less concerned with separation from parents or adolescent rebellion than does the current generation of therapists. In fact, the preference of adolescents for therapeutic plans that do not include their parents may be due less to hostility, anger, or need for separation than to the desire to concentrate exclusively on issues of immediate relevance to them.) Discussion of faulty family relationships may be of only minor relevance to adolescent concerns but does allow for respite from focusing their energies on the effects of peer-arena interactions.

Theoretical notions of peer relevance did advance the organization of adolescent peer-counseling strategies. Adolescent groups were designed in theoretical allegiance to the acknowledged impact of adolescent peers on one another and the support functions they could offer. However, the potential for offering a "living microcosm" of their real world went unrecognized, and the power of this living microcosm has been ironically underutilized. Verbal interchange in the rap group generally concentrated on relationship problems or interpretations of group dynamics, or on behavior interpretations for feedback purposes of immediately occurring interactions. Because of a lag in theory, the peer-group component of developmental progression went unrecognized, as did the related dynamics activated within the new group, which reenergized AD functions—a replay of original peer-group experiences of trauma. Opportunities for examinations of the functional processes of the peer-group interaction, their affective consequences, and the behavioral responses or defenses were not handled because theory had not yet recognized their presence.

An Alternative Conceptual Framework

The model of sequential peer-group memberships in which adolescents work to construct an integrated self leading to self-definition and self-direction has been presented as a path for healthy adolescent progression in development. Conversely, it suggests a framework within which to identify irregularities or temporary stalemates in development. Introduction of the sequential-peer-arena model within a theory of Dynamic Functional Interaction also offers a conceptual framework within which therapeutic strategies may be operationalized within interactional functions and processes formulated. The major objective is to raise the level of conscious awareness of manifest behaviors, latent AD functions, and their interrelationships. Hence, the first therapeutic objective is the identification of behaviors that manifest cognitive and affective consequences of AD functions. The second objective is the determination of the adaptive or maladaptive nature of the behaviors. Organizing the behaviors within a goal-related framework is the third therapeutic objective. Strengthening the adolescent in decision making and assumption of responsibility is a continuing focus.

The peer-arena model of adolescent social development puts primacy on interaction with adolescent peers as essential to adaptive progression through adolescence. Lack of access to or flight from a sufficiently full progressive experience in the sequential developmental peer-arena forum, in all its component parts of formally and informally assembling peer groups, constitutes developmental deprivation and seriously hinders smooth completion of adolecent tasks. Involvement of primary environmental figures (parents, siblings, relatives, teachers) is for the specific need for information or appropriate secondary support functions.

Central to actualization of this therapeutic model is reactivation of the experience in the peer arena. Lack of accessibility to or flight from the impact of its developmental functions represents a deprivation or an assault. The peer group is the central forum in which adolescent development occurs. The point at which the sequential process was interrupted defines the locus of intervention. Interruption to growth may have occurred in the large primary peer group or in a smaller secondary peer group. A few adolescents may have encountered trauma in leaving the peer group and moving on to individual peers or into intimacy.

Revised Focal Point

The revised focal point for therapeutic intervention is a component of the theoretical model. In departure from earlier theoretical models for intervention with adolescents, in this formulation separation from parents, with its behavioral expression, erratic idiosyncratic is not considered central. Rather, the assumption is that adolescent separation has taken place before the peer-group period becomes relevant and that the idiosyncracies of evident behavior are responses primarily to cognitive and affective consequences of functional interactions with peers. A condition of readiness is a basic assumption consequent to physical, cognitive and affective growth that releases latent dynamic activity in a field-of-force gathering of adolescent peers. Parents and other older reference figures are seen as important environmental figures who are called on for support functions in the service of maintaining primary interactive relations with peers.

Primary Therapeutic Focus

The primary therapeutic focus of the peer-arena model rests in an examination of the progressive status of the target adolescent along the continuum of peer-arena passage. Thus a framework by which to interpret the genesis of adolescent behaviors appearing uncharacteristic or unexpected is available. For example, if the history of one assumed to be in the beginning stages of adolescence reveals regular interactions with only one or two others, an inappropriate developmental posture is flagged, since beginning adolescence corresponds developmentally with the period of primary-peer-group membership—an interlude of many friends, not just one or two. Inquiry can than focus on the manifest deviation and its source; the remediation-planning focus will be toward participation in a primary-peer-group model. As seen from this simple illustration, the propositions of Dynamic Functional Interaction theory suggest effective areas of inquiry that hold potent data for diagnosis and intervention as well as potential research areas—for example, range of deviation from appropriate positions along the continuum of development at the expected time period; supports or assaults that stimulated progression or retrogression; nature of the defensive response as seen within the continuum model of irregularities; the extent of manifest behaviors and the prosocial or antisocial nature of manifest behaviors; the forum selected to express the behavioral response, and so forth.

Peer-Arena Progression Profile (PAPP)

The foregoing data in singular and combined form can be entered into the Peer-Arena Progression Profile (PAPP). Beginning diagnoses or a hypothesis for further inquiry may be formulated. Areas included in the profile and covered in the accompanying question sheets are: (1) peer arena—past and present membership, size of group, extent of involvement, time spent at home with parents and/or siblings relative to time spent with peers, accessibility to peer group, preadolescent social preference choices; *clues* to developmental timing, level of participation, and their intersective nature are thus provided; (2) parental attitudes toward peer-group involvement; a measure of support from the secondary field is garnered; (3) regularity or irregularity of academic pattern; *clues* to stability of and/or selected forums for projection of affect are offered. In order to identify levels of similarity and/or differences in parent and child perceptions, an identical data sheet is administered both to adolescents and to parents. The index to congruity or incongruity of perception may offer generalizable potential to other common concerns. (See table 17-1.)

Data on continuity or change in quality of academic task performance is more currently pertinent information than is the specific academic level achieved. Inconsistency of performance may be a clue to increase in stress and/or evidence of a lag or deficiency of cognitive development. On the other hand, radically better performance could reflect a cognitive spurt or integrations of cognitive or affective growth. Stress levels in home and school are tapped. Congruity of behaviors in the home and school at either extreme provides additional clues to levels of integration or stress. Incongruent reactions afford insight to the preferred and possibly safer arena for expression of stress, or reverse clues to which secondary field may be exacerbating the stress condition. A second form of the Peer-Arena Progression Profile (PAPP-SF) offers this data. (See table 17-2.) Thus data from the two forms of the PAPP provide a primary-peer-arena field panorama, and may in addition picture two relevant secondary fields of the home and school with some dimensions of attitudinal congruity or incongruity.

The Subjective PAPP profile is administered only to the adolescent. It yields subjective data on cognitive awareness levels to AD functions,

Table 17-1

Peer-Arena Progression Profile-Objective Scale (PAPP-A and/or PAPP-P)

Grade

| | Primary Peer Group | | | Secondary Peer Group | | | Special |
	Enter	Mid	Leave	Enter	Mid	Leave	Friend
7							
8							
9							
10							
11							
12							
13							
F							
S							
J							
S							

Note: Identical format for perception of parental attitude, perception of parental active support. PAPP-A scale for adolescent, for perception of parental behaviors. PAPP-P scale for parent, for perception of adolescent behaviors.

Table 17-2
Peer-Arena Progression Profile—Secondary Field (PAPP-SF)

Grade	Field			
	School Performance*		Home Demeanor*	
	Stable	Change (+ or −)	Stable	Change (+ or −)
7				
8				
9				
10				
11				
12				
F				
S				
J				
S				

Note: Measure of past several years provides a general index to stability or change in quality of school work and in the home field. Respondent can also be teacher.

Question Sheet: PAPP-A and PAPP-P and PAPP-SF

Questions to accompany PAPP for Adolescents (PAPP-A)
1. When did you join a group of peers, or peer group? If they say never, ask if they have any special friends.
2. How have your parents felt/do they feel about your having so many friends? or, How do they feel about your having special friends instead of a lot?
3. Do they assist you when you need help in getting to activities?
4. Do you consider your school work to be on the same level as it usually has been or has it gotten better or worse? When did the change start?
5. What do you think of your attitudes/behavior at home? Is it the same as before, or different? When did it start

Questions to accompany PAPP for Parents (PAPP-P) and Secondary Field (PAPP-SF)
(Can be administered individually to each parent if desired for comparative purposes.)
1. When did your child join a peer group? If never, ask if they consider that their child has any special friends?
2. How do you feel about their membership or non-membership or, the special friendships?
3. How do you think your child perceives your attitude about his friends?
4. Are there any ways in which you assist your child in getting to friends? Or, if objection, in which way do you stand in the way?
5. Has your child's school work stayed on the level it was on in the past, or has it changed? How?
6. Is your child's behavior the same or different than it used to be? If different, when did it change?

Responses to these general questions will provide interviewer with necessary data to fill out the PAPP-A, PAPP-P, and the PAPP-SF (secondary field-school and/or home).

responses, and actions. (See table 17-3.)

A data base for diagnosis, further inquiry, therapeutic planning, and research is yielded by descriptive data of the objective and subjective PAPP forms. Data on secondary support resources are collected for potential use in simultaneous but complementary posture.

Table 17-3
Peer-Arena Progression Profile—Subjective (PAPP-SS)

Question	Primary Peer Group			Secondary Peer Group		
	Entry	Middle	End	Entry	Middle	End
1. Engaged in comparative acts						
2. Examined own characteristics						
3. Examined others						
4. Aware of response to $AERR^n$-others						
5. Aware of response to $AERR^n$-self						
6. Examined self in relation to other						
7. Attitudes toward group						
8. Was he there long enough?						
9. Left on own prerogative						
10. Left because of rejection						
11. Time spent with family						
12. Preference						
13. History						
14. Goals set						
15. Self-knowledge						

Note: Subjective Scale—adolescent only.

Question Sheet-PAPP-SS
Questions to Accompany Subjective PAPP-SS
 1. Did you ever think about how you ranked as compared with your friends on different
    characteristics and abilities when you were a member of a peer group?
    a . Was it when you were a member of large group? What grade in school?
    b . Was it when you were a member of a smaller group? What grade in school?
 2. Did you examine your own characteristics?
 3. Did you examine the characteristics of others carefully?
 4. Do you know how you felt about the characteristics of others?
 5. Do you know how you felt about your own characteristics?
 6. Do you know how you felt when you compared yourself with them?
 7. Did you like or dislike being a member?
 8. Do you feel you were a member long enough?
 9. Did you leave because you decided to?
10. Did you leave because you thought you should?
11. Did you spend most of time with your friends or your family (parents, sibs)?
12. Who did you prefer to be with? Friends or family?
13. Is this the same or different than the way it was in grade school?
14. Did you set future goals for yourself? When?
15. Did you settle on aspects of what you were like as a person? When?

Therapeutic Plan

The therapeutic plan of the peer-arena proper combines the experiential impact of this new peer group with didactic analysis and interpretation. Peers
incrementally yield support from fellow adolescent members who have in
the past and are once more currently experiencing similar responses to AD
functions. They engage together with new and reactivated unfinished AD
functions. Achievement of the first therapeutic goal (increased, if not totally
new, cognitive accessibility to latent functions) diffuses an abstract anxiety.

AD developmental functions are set forth as a common experience, not a suspiciously idiosyncratic one. Responses, though unique, are viewed as similar to those of others in the group. As the sense of isolation is reduced, developmental progression—an explicit goal—appears possible. The Dynamic Functional Interaction model varies from the group-dynamics model. The focus is not on how one another's behavior affects respondent behaviors in and toward the group, but on how the verbal and nonverbal behaviors of others in the group affect the internal operations of AD functions such as ESA and $AERR^n$. What adolescents do with *data* from one another is the primary focus. What they do with *one another* is seen as a response to the data and as a means of using the data. Irregularities in development are conceptualized as manifestations of a core peer problem.

The therapeutic model provides for assignment to a group that most closely simulates the peer group of trauma. Treatment strategies are designed to be worked through in the appropriate peer group. Hence, if the irregularity occurred in the period of the primary peer group, the treatment group would be large. If the setback occurred during the secondary-peer-group period, the group would be smaller. Although this latter, smaller group more closely resembles the traditional adolescent rap group, its purposes and the direction of the treatment differs. The focus in both the primary- and the secondary-level peer groups is on AD functions. At the primary-peer-group level the focus is on troubled responses to ESA or $AERR^n$ functions; adolescents whose PAPP profile indicates placement at the secondary level focus on SES and SER functions.

The major therapeutic goal is reinstatement of the adolescent as a well-functioning member of the appropriate peer group so that the adolescent can complete the necessary developmental process. The impact of peers on one another is the primary focus. Reworking the past affront in a current experience is the therapeutic path. Sensitization for cognitive awareness is the first therapeutic step. Achieved insight into latent AD functions as well as skill building in verbal expression of an internal experience is the second step. Developmental assaults experienced in the simulated setting are examined in relation to behavioral response. Strategies are implemented toward realignment of defenses antithetical to smooth progression, to positive behavioral adaptations that will foster retention of membership in the appropriate group and resumption of work with AD functions.

Limitations of the Model

Not all therapeutic interventions will be able immediately to utilize the simulated peer-arena model. Some adolescents can tolerate only a one-to-one model, particularly in the initial phases. Others with a history of peer-relationship difficulties can begin only with an adult. They require adult support and reinforcement as necessary buildup prior to joining a group of peers. Some may continuously resist the peer format. Although an alternative therapy available on a one-to-one basis may not be the therapy of choice for a peer-arena developmental deprivation or irregularity, certain psychological growth or adjustment needs will be served. A goal of eventual participation by the adolescent in the appropriate therapeutic primary or secondary peer group is generally choice. It offers an opportunity for both cognitive comprehension and experiential reexperience and reworking of the original functions and processes that define the peer-arena developmental experience. For the adolescent without a group, this experience may represent the first such invovlement.

Therapeutic Goals

General Goals

1. achievement of cognitive accessibility to AD functions
2. establishment of AD functions as commonly experienced and developmentally proper
3. interpretation of the AD dynamic functions and processes, for example, $AERR^n$ and Adolescent Kinetic
4. establishment of self-definition and self-direction as adolsecent tasks
5. express linkage of adolescent tasks and AD functions

Individual Insight-Oriented Goals

1. isolation of earliest stress
2. identification of possible links between adolescent stress points and individual history; coordination with current social experience
3. identification of defenses
4. identification of customary behavior manifestations of the defenses
5. examination of functional or dysfunctional impact of defense

Individual Future-Oriented Goals

1. allocation of defenses to prosocial/adaptive or antisocial/maladaptive categories
2. determination of plan for incorporation of prosocial, elimination of antisocial defenses

3. methodological plan for completing adolescent tasks
4. incremental goal setting—for example, rejoin primary peer group
5. identification of strategies for achieving incremental goals
6. determination of relationship of secondary fields to intermediate and future goals.

Therapeutic Methodology

Therapeutic Group

Design: approximation of adolescent peer group, primary or secondary

Process: naturally evolving discussions; no specified content

Therapist role: facilitator; direct conceptually oriented focus

Therapeutic goal: Reworking developmental lag

Anticipated outcome: Commitment to rejoin appropriate adolescent peer group; New insights and communication skills

Cooperative Postures of the Home Field

Placing a secondary-support perspective on the home frames parents in a cooperative rather than combative, posture with peers. A focus on the realignments necessary to maintain parents and the home as an ongoing aspect of the adolescent's life replaces notions of rebellion and problems in separation from parents. As adolescents begin to understand that the home may have become a repository for tensions built up elsewhere, they are better able to evaluate the appropriateness or inappropriateness of their own behaviors. Furthermore, the impact of their own actions on the perceived presence or absence of current support from the family field as well as on its future potential become more amenable to consideration. This type of insight in and of itself usually is manifested in a new self-consciousness that acts as an ameliorating force on behavior.

Individual family systems do present different physical and psychological conditions for each individual adolescent. Although improved functioning in the home field is not an explicit therapeutic goal, achievement of insight into the potential of the home as a support system for sustaining developmental progress in the peer group is such a goal. Therapeutic interventions may be recommended—with parents first, or perhaps exclusively.

Educational Innovation

For other parents, educative interventions or discussion-format classes may suffice. For lack of another model, many parents have clung to notions of adolescent rebellion to explain erratic and often mystifying behaviors of their offspring. It will be reassuring for them to understand that the unpredictable adolescent behavior they live with is not necessarily rebellion but, instead, may serve rather than retard growth. Educational foci should emphasize (1) the progressive sequence of adolescent peer groups and (2) the dynamic functions that are operative. A framework by which adolescent behaviors and preferences can be better understood is thus afforded. For example, confusing and even upsetting attitudes and "values" and adolescent friendships may be more easily tolerated through familiarity with the ESA function and the crucial role of available friendships. Knowing that the associations, attitudes, or values may be only temporarily assumed may relieve concern and possibly avert confusing and groundless conflict with offspring. The common complaint, "I can't understand what you are so excited about, Mom and Dad," may well represent the adolescent's sense of a purpose more fundamental than that to which the adult is privy in its manifest act or expression.

Therapeutic Innovation

Therapeutic groups for parents are often comforting for a simple reason—the company of others experiencing a similar situation. Parents of adolescents, in particular, who themselves are experiencing a transition (in relation to at least one child, if not more) experience initial relief in the company of similar others, just as their children have. Empathizing and swapping tales provide temporary relief, perhaps even enough to regroup strengths, but no substantial movement forward. As with their children, support alone does not suffice to meet the transitional crisis.

Seen within a format of incremental reassessment and realignment of functions, the parent is charged with two tasks, both therapeutic goals: (1) extinguishing obsolete primary-nurturer patterns and (2) acquiring secondary-field skills of support and information giving. Within a conception of altering forms in a continuity of parenting change does not portend of inconsistent functioning. A continuing role for parents, but with a new emphasis, fits well within a notion of the centrality of the peer group. Skills that are essential to the new challenge demand openness to relocation of functions.

I have departed from antecedent notions of the place and role of the peer group in adolescent development to structure a theory of the dynamic functional interactions of adolescents within sequential peer-group memberships wherein specific developmental functions are conjointly operative. Models for therapeutic intervention incorporating notions of the theory have also been offered, in rudimentary form.

Part V
Conclusions

18 Summary Views on the Phenomenon of the Peer Arena

Dynamic Functional Interaction considers the peer group the organizing dynamic core of the adolescent period. Furthermore, it holds that without study of the general adolescent-peer-group experience and its specific processes, the essence of the adolescent experience is missed, as is comprehension of the real origins of adolescent adaptation or maladaptation. Just as family relationships are traditionally considered a primary influence, so must primary- and secondary-peer-group experiences be examined. What were the experiences in the adolescent peer group? the emotional response to functional interactions? flight from dissonance? substitute group sought?

Placing the peer-group component central to adolescent passage brings a revised view of adolescent adaptation and maladaptation. Membership and dynamic involvement in an adolescent peer group is seen to be a developmental need. A conceptual framework that includes the quality, character, and approximate length of the sequential peer-group experience defines a vital part of the adolescent passage. Without this framework, adaptation or maladaptation cannot be examined, let alone understood. Each adolescent must idiosyncratically tackle the peer-group growth challenge. The impulse to congregate as peers and to actualize readiness for AD functions may be of a strength close to that of the attachment of infant and mother—a quasi instinct for attachment to peers arising after the nurturance of parents is sated, and eager for release to engage developmental work.

Adolescents want very much to achieve on their own, but they are new at it. They come out of a tradition of years of intake. Cognitively and physically, they now sense a new power to create. The time seems past for mere acquisition of skills. Passive knowledge of ability or talent no longer suffices. The adolescent has some notion of his skills, abilities, and opinions. But these become real only when they are experienced as relevant. Thus a tangible skill becomes real when he sees it in others. Hence, beyond being advised or told, they need to test and to compare themselves with relevant others who will continue with them in their future, with individuals who have trod the same path for the same number of years. These co-travelers are their adolescent peers and future adult peers. What group could be more appropriate for display and measurement? Membership in a group of peers offers opportunities to see what holds water, to take opinions and abilities out of the abstract, and to learn what is real and what is functional.

Membership in a peer group does not represent a rejection of pertinent others. Parents and other reference groups retain their importance to adolescent peers. The affective component of interaction with parents is now balanced with cognitive regard of issues. Parents are sources of information and do influence adolescents. Membership in an adolescent peer group signals a reality-based functional relation to growing up. Peers serve as both mirrors and models—positive and negative—for one another of present functioning and future concerns. Automatic, spontaneous activation of the Adolescent Dialectic (AD) functions offers the ready peer-group congregation avenues of assessments of self and self-skills essential to the identification of realistic, pertinent, and appropriate goals. The positive instance of relevance is not a member of any other reference group but at all times is a member of their own. Areas of relevance do not extend much beyond one another. The first veil of the peer group is escape, fun, and camaraderie. Underneath the seventh veil, however, is a serious assembly, active and complex, with goal-directed functions. In essence, the peer group appears to function as a sorting house, characterized by a pulsating, evaluational tempo, in which adolescents use one another to examine, assess, and evaluate—in service of beginning framework of self.

Developmental psychologists have defined the needs and tasks of adolescence but for the most part have remained loyal to traditional formulations and perspectives. The true interactional dynamics of the period have generally not been clarified. The dedication devoted to meeting the developmental needs of infancy and of early and later childhood should be extended to efforts to ensure that developmental needs are met for peer-group membership over respective sequential periods. A system that provides opportunities for functional interaction for adolescents will serve the distinct adolescent developmental needs of self-definition and self-direction. An understanding of the developmental significance adolescent peers hold for one another can suggest reformulations of policy and practice toward adolescents in major societal institutions. Reforms in child-rearing philosophy and practice, in educational programs and policies, and in mental-health treatment methods have been suggested here. Practical applications can also be extended to the juvenile-justice system and incorporated with greater relevance into sophisticated interventive and preventive strategies for selected adolescent target groups within the family, education, justice, and health systems.

Adolescents have been utilizing assorted attention-getting forms of outward behavior in order to draw attention to their intuitive response to growing up in Western society. The have indeed shrunk the world to include only their fellow travelers as they strive to prepare themselves in relative rather than in absolute fashion. Reflective of their own changing state, the external world appears to change so quickly that they choose to focus on what may appear an isolated, permanently relevant element—their peers.

The adolescent community seems to have taken the matter into its own hands. They have leapfrogged the cultural lag. Adolescent peer groups are their preparatory arena for citizenship in a complex technological society. They will travel with peers now and later. They strive to draw attention to the centrality of peer-group experiences for their development. They ask recognition of the validity and importance of the peer arena.

19 Observations on the Dynamics of the Peer Arena

In the metamorphosis from caterpillar to butterfly, a larval stage is critical. Holistic changes doubtless take place inside the cocoon, for the form that emerges is dramatically different from the one that went in. The human animal undergoes no such dramatic alteration of form, but adolescence does bring the physical, cognitive, and emotional changes necessary to structure an adult mind and body—hardly a metamorphosis, merely progressive change toward the normal adult condition. But in fact Dynamic Functional Interaction infers that a "psychological cocoon" does occur in the form of the peer arena, a semiclosed world in which the chemistry of social growth takes place.

The simile of one of nature's most beguiling magical tricks is not useful beyond symbolism, for the human adolescent's experience involves mechanisms largely under his own control. The tasks adolescents set themselves—from utter frameworklessness to stable self-structure—are akin to the caterpillar's gaining flight as a butterfly. The enormous energies, emotional investments, and difficult obstacles cumulatively overcome are of a magnitude greater than heretofore understood.

Most impressive is the simplicity of the process. The philosophical essence of pragmatism and utilitarianism permeates a functional system of interaction in which the adolescent himself is the primary socializer and other age-mates are instruments and inventory with which to build his own self-structure. The economy and directness of task orientation and performance are sublime. In that crucible of interaction, the peer arena, forces and force fields stimulate and magnetically pull the adolecent onward. Through dissonance, pain, and rapid progression the adolescent's own kinetic energy keeps Adolescent Dialectic (AD) functions in constant motion, in continuous service of selection and evaluation of elements for future building blocks of self-structure. Forces of the Individual Adolescent Dialectic (IAD) and forces in the arena (combinations of forces from the ADs of individual members plus the group's characteristic dynamics) together make up the components of dynamic functional interaction.

I have described the functions of AD and how they each operate in service of each other, how in the primary peer arena they are engaged by the Adolescent Kinetic (Ado K) and alter in subsequent arenas for more careful tasks. What happens inside the arena as the adolescent passes on through stages of development, as well as what does not happen, is crucial to end goals. Maladaptations hold risks for adults long after the adolescent stage is assumed to be finished, testimony to the centrality of the peer-arena experience in healthy development.

Thus Dynamic Functional Interaction argues that an innate readiness for developmental progress is brought by adolescents to and lives within the peer arena. It is a readiness for experiencing dissonance and change, for sampling freely and copiously of elements borrowed from peers, for the necessary involvement with group and step-by-step progression through each stage without omission. By employing the utilitarian approach to all contacts and a dedication to constant information seeking, a skill emerges that is equal to formidable tasks of adolescence. Continuously and inexorably the adolescent sees in interactions new sensations and new questions in a demanding assessment and evaluation, reassessment and reevaluation, over and over until some elements are stored (readied) for eventual integration. Consciously he employs enormous energies toward constructing a self-structure for his own present definition as well as his future identity. Exquisitely sensitive to peers, and not quite aware of what and who he is not, the evolving adolescent respects change and changing perhaps more open-mindedly than adults can hope to understand. Especially in this circumstance, the adolescent's accomplishments and abilities are impressive. What emerges from this progammed building-block progression view of adolescent growth is an enormously attentive organism that is capable of consciously integrating physical, emotional, and cognitive changes over which he has had little control into a wider structure of self that he attempts to control. He does surprisingly well.

Every developmental period has a unique relationship to perception of time as it affects its respective environment. To the adolescent time is discrete in presents and futures; short time frames and longer-range spans juxtapose and compete simultaneously in the adolescent's quest for stability and self-knowledge within a future awareness that borders on urgency. Actually, the present challenges him more urgently; the future he must craft himself. He engages tasks directly within two time frames simultaneously with a facility and relevance that belies the often confused image or unconcerned posture displayed to adults.

Perhaps the overriding characterization emerging from Dynamic Functional Interaction is the dominance and influence of task orientation in adolescent development. The capacity of the adolescent for direct action may give a more simplified panorama of the period precisely because tasks are identifiable and progressive. However, the sheer quantity of energies applied and the number of factors integrated in the quest for each task over a changing terrain he cannot know, the innate drives that fuel his needs, society's demands that he must learn to accommodate, and the socialization challenges that press upon him—all these together hardly constitute a simple experience.

As to the what, why, and how of adolescence, the Dynamic Functional Interaction theory of adolescent social development emphasizes the "how" as the central mechanic of passage through to adulthood. It is in this view of "how" that the adolescent earns the most respected attention. For it is the use of other adolescents as instruments for his own development, the recognition of forces of the group and within the group as tools, the computerlike simplified "mathematics" for digesting thousands of interactions, that give the adolescent his own accomplished construction of self-knowledge and identity toward a self-structure for his adult life to follow. Indeed, the how comes to integrate the what and why of differing theoretical schools, for the how adjusts emphasis as a quality of its mechanic. Thus the functional drive incorporates diverse environmental, historical, and psychological factors in assuming a dynamic quality itself among other dynamics extant throughout adolescence.

Motion and energy characterize, perhaps dominate, the feeling of passage that permeates the adolescent and his peers. It is exemplified particularly in the concept of Adolescent Kinetic (Ado K)—the kinetic energy that builds up out of its own momentums and the force fields through which it travels. This cascading effect accrues more and more energy (based on the electromagnetic-field model) as it powers functions of the AD as drives or forces, themselves movements of productive work. Motion and energy are symbolic of the adolescent. Dynamic Functional Interaction contributes a pattern of travel to that motion and energy over progressive stages of development to a goal via explicit functional forces innately inspired and consciously programmed. Through a socialization process, the adolescent questions where he is and where he wants to go next, with an alert eye on the future. Ironically but logically, this quest is born out of a unique frameworklessness that forces the adolescent into an original organization of his own.

The consequences of inadequate development in the adolescent stage, though not unknown, have not heretofore been traceable to the sequence of the passage itself. Dynamic Functional Interaction permits isolation of the stage within adolescence at which the passage becomes impeded and further suggest how such impedance may be avoided. Although theoretically broad enough to allow departures and returns, the theory suggests maladaptations that occur for those who do not complete the full exercise of the dynamics component to coaction with many peers through the primary and secondary arenas. Consequences and effects of an inadequate peer-arena period are suggested. The implications are extensive. To the extent that these applications may be further researched and understood, thinking on areas as diverse as criminology, productivity, forms of societal participation, educational policy, and human services may conceivably be effected. (Some direct applications are suggested in Part IV.) The generalization that again stands out from this back-door approach to Dynamic Functional Interaction is that the simplicity and logic of its sequential model are applicable to understanding symptomatic behavior that otherwise appears complex and obfuscated.

In the spectrum of different orientations represented in the literature, the posture presented here is essentially neutral, accommodating most theoretical positions now in the existing literature, albeit through a somewhat different prism. It is an action theory, a model of specific interactional processes conceptualized within a sequential time frame of primary- and secondary-peer-group participation. The road from frameworklessness to self-structure is paved with changes and challenges. Dynamic Functional Interaction introduces the notion that each adolescent's road must be traveled not only with peers, but also within peer arenas. The model does not specify the locale or type of group, merely its size and related functions within the time frames of early to late adolescence, as well as those transitional moments that entail some shuttling back and forth. The various concurrently operative adolescent-group experiences in which the adolescent participates converge to effect a Peer Arena. Dynamic Functional Interaction provides a perspective with a new focal point. It offers a theoretical point of departure toward a unifying structural base. Propositions and concepts within the theory hold the potential for creative research and application—and for more theory.

References

Adelson, J. 1975. The development of ideology in adolescence. In S.E. Dragastin and G.H. Elder, Jr., eds., *Adolescence in the life cycle: Psychological change and social context*. New York: Halsted Press, Wiley.

Adelson, J. 1971. The political imagination of the young adolescent. *Daedalus* 100:1013-1050.

Adelson, J., and Doehrman, J. 1980. The psychodynamic approach to adolescence. In J. Adelson, ed., *Handbook of adolescent psychology*, pp. 99-116. New York: Wiley.

Adoni, H. 1979. The functions of mass media in the political socialization of adolescents. *Communication Research—An International Quarterly* 6:84-106.

Ainsworth, M. 1972. Variables influencing the development of attachment. In C. Lavatelli and F. Stendler, eds., *Readings in child behavior and development*, pp. 193-201. New York: Harcourt, Brace, Jovanovich.

Ainsworth, M.; Blehar, M.; Waters, E.; and Wall, S. 1978. *Patterns of attachment*. Hillsdale, N.J.: Lawrence Erlbaum Associates.

Anthony, E. 1975. The reactions of adults to adolescents and their behavior. In A. Esman, ed. *The psychology of adolescence: Essential readings*. New York: International Universities Press.

Aronson, E. 1961. The effect of effort on the attractiveness of rewarded and unrewarded stimuli. *Journal of Abnormal and Social Psychology* 63:375-380.

Arrowood, A., and Friend, R. 1969. Other factors determining the choice of a comparison other. *Journal of Experimental Social Psychology* 5:233-239.

Asch, S. 1956. Studies of independence and conformity: A minority of one against a unanimous majority. *Psychological Monograph* 70, no. 9:177-190.

Atkinson, J., and Feather, N., eds. 1966. *A theory of achievement motivation*. New York: Wiley.

Ausubel, D. 1954. *Theory and problems of adolescent development*. New York: Grune and Stratton.

Ausubel, D., and Ausubel, P. 1966. Cognitive development of adolescence. *Review of educational research* 36:403-413.

Ausubel, D.; Montemayor, R.; and Svajian, P. 1977. *Theory and problems of adolescent development*. New York: Grune and Stratton, 2nd ed.

Ausubel, D., and Sullivan, E. 1970. *Theory and problems of child development*, 2nd ed. New York: Grune and Stratton.

Backman, C.; Secord, P.; and Pierce, J. 1963. Resistance to change in the self concept as a function of consensus among significant others. *Sociometry* 26:102-111.

Baldwin, A. 1967. The theory of Jean Piaget. In A. Baldwin, ed., *Theories of child development*. New York: Wiley.

Bandura, A. 1964. The stormy decade: Fact or fiction? *Psychology in the Schools* 1:224-231.

―――― . 1972. The role of modeling processes in personality development. In C. Lavatelli and F. Stendler, eds., *Readings in child behavior and development*. New York: Harcourt, Brace, Jovanovich.

Bandura, A., and Walters, R. 1963. *Social learning and personality development*. New York: Holt, Rinehart and Winston.

Bar-Tal, D. 1978. Attribution theory and achievement. *Review of educational research* 48:259-271.

Bary, B. 1978. Impact of parents on their adolescent sons' identity crises. *Clinical psychologist* 32:12-13.

Baumrind, D. 1975. Early socialization and adolescent competence. In S.E. Dragistin and G.H. Elder, Jr., eds., *Adolescence in the life cycle*, pp. 117-139. New York: Halsted.

Bealer, R.; Willits, F.; and Maida, P. 1964. The rebellious youth subculture—A myth. *Children* 11:43-45.

Bell, G. 1963. Processes in the formation of adolescents' aspirations. *Social Forces*, pp. 179-195.

Benedict, R. 1938. Continuities in cultural conditioning. *Psychiatry* 1:161-167.

―――― . 1950. *Patterns of culture*. New York: New American Library.

―――― . 1954. Continuities and discontinuities in cultural conditioning. In W. Martin and S. Stendler, eds., *Readings in child development*. New York: Harcourt, Brace.

Berlyne, D. 1954. A theory of human curiousity. *British Journal of Psychiatry* 45:180-191.

Bermant, G., and Davidson, J. 1974. *Biological Bases of Sexual Behavior*. New York: Harper and Row.

Bernard, J. 1964. The adjustment of married mates. In H.T. Christenson, ed., *Handbook of marriage and the family*, pp. 675-739. Chicago: Rand McNally.

Berzonsky, M. 1981. *Adolescent development*. New York: Macmillan.

Bettelheim, B. 1963. The problem of generations. In E. Erikson, ed., *Youth: Change and challenge*. New York: Basic Books.

Biddle, B.J. 1980. Parental and peer influence on adolescents. *Social Forces* 58:1057-1079.

Biller, H. 1968. A multiaspect investigation of masculine development in kindergarten age boys. *Genetic psychology monographs* 76:89-139.

―――― . 1974. *Paternal deprivation: Family, school, sexuality, and society*. Lexington, Mass.: D.C. Heath and Company.

Bloch, H., and Niederhoffer, A. 1958. *The gang: A study of adolescent behavior*. New York: Philosophical Library.

Bloom, B. 1964. *Stability and change in human characteristics*. New York: Wiley.

Blos, P. 1962. *On adolescence: A psychoanalytic interpretation*. New York: Free Press.

———. 1965. The initial stage of male adolescence. In *Psychoanalytic study of the child*, vol. 22. New York: International Universities Press.

———. 1970. *The young adolescent*. New York: Free Press.

Bowlby, J. 1969. *Attachment*. Attachment and loss, vol. 1. New York: Basic Books.

———. 1973. *Separation*. Attachment and loss, vol. 2. New York: Basic Books.

Braham, M. 1965. Peer group deterrents to intellectual development during adolescence. *Educational Theory* 15:251-258.

Brandt, D. 1977. Separation and identity in adolescence: Erikson and Mahler—Similarities. *Contemporary Psychoanalysis* 13:248-258.

Braungart, R. 1980. Youth movements. In J. Adelson, ed., *Handbook of adolescent psychology*, pp. 560-598. New York: Wiley.

Brehm, J. 1959. Increasing cognitive dissonance by a fait accompli. *Journal of Abnormal and Social Psychology* 58:379-382.

———. 1960. Attitudinal consequences of commitment to unpleasant behavior. *Journal of Abnormal and Social Psychology* 60:379-383.

Brehm, J., and Cohen, A. 1959. Choice and chance relative deprivation as determinants of cognitive dissonance. *Journal of Abnormal and Social Psychology* 58:383-387.

———. 1962. *Explorations in cognitive dissonance*. New York: Wiley.

Brickman, P., and Berman, J. 1971. Effects of performance expectancy and outcome certainty on interest in social comparison. *Journal of Experimental Social Psychology* 7:600-609.

Brickman, P., and Bulman, R.J. 1977. Pleasure and pain in social comparison. In J.M. Suls and R.L. Miller, eds., *Social comparison processes: Theoretical and empirical perspectives*. Washington, D.C.: Hemisphere Publishing, Halsted Press, Wiley.

Brittain, C. 1963. Adolescent choices and parent peer pressures. *American Sociological Review* 28:385-419.

———. 1968. An exploration of the bases of peer compliance and parent compliance in adolescence. *Adolescence* 2:445-458.

———. 1969. A comparison of rural and urban adolescence with repect to peer versus parent compliance. *Adolescence* 13:59-68.

Bronfenbrenner, U. 1958. Socialization and social class through time and space. In E. Maccoby, T. Newcomb, and E. Hartley, eds., *Readings in social psychology*, pp. 400-425. New York: Holt, Rinehart and Winston.

———. 1970. *Two worlds of childhood*. New York: Russell Sage.

————— . 1972. Response to pressure from peers versus adults among Soviet and American school children. In C. Lavatelli and F. Stendler, eds., *Readings in child behavior and development*, pp. 513-520. New York: Harcourt, Brace, Jovanovich.

Bruner, J.S. 1962. *A Study of Thinking.* New York: Science Edition.

————— . 1973. *Beyond the Information Given.* New York, Norton.

Burlinghame, W. 1967. An investigation of the correlates of adherence to the adolescent peer culture. Ph.D. diss., University of Washington.

————— . 1970. The youth culture. In E. Evans, ed., *Adolescents: Readings in behavior and development*, pp. 131-150. Hinsdale, Ill.: Dryden Press.

Cartwright, D., ed., 1951. *Field theory in social science: Selected theoretical papers by Kurt Lewin.* New York: Harper and Brothers.

Cartwright, D., and Zander, A. eds., 1968. *Group dynamics: Research and theory*, 3rd ed. New York: Harper and Row.

Chess, S., and Thomas, A. 1977. Temperamental individuality from childhood to adolescence. *Journal of the American Academy of Child Psychiatry* 16:218-226.

Clark, B.R., and Trow, M. 1960. Determinants of college student subculture. Center for the Study of Higher Education, University of California, Berkeley.

Clark, R. 1972. *Reference group theory and delinquency.* New York: Behavioral Publications.

Clausen, J.A. 1968. Perspectives on childhood socialization. In J. Clausen, ed., *Socialization and society.* Boston: Little, Brown.

————— . 1975. The social meaning of differential physical and sexual maturation. In S. Dragastin and G. Elder, Jr., eds., *Adolescence in the life cycle.* New York: Halsted.

Cockram, L., and Beloff, H. 1978. *Rehearsing to be adults.* Leicester, England: National Youth Bureau, April.

Cohen, O.P. 1978. The deaf adolescent: Who am I? *Volta Review* 80:265:274.

Cohen, S. 1976. *Social and personality development in childhood.* New York: Macmillan.

Coleman, J. 1960. The adolescent subculture and academic achievement. *American Journal of Sociology* 65:337-347.

————— . 1961. *The adolescent society: The social life of the teenager and its impact on education.* New York: Free Press.

————— . 1978. Current contradictions in adolescent theory. *Journal of Youth and Adolescence* 7:1-11.

————— . 1980. Friendship and the peer group in adolescence. In J. Adelson, ed., *Handbook of adolescent psychology.* New York: Wiley.

Coleman, J.; Herzberg, J.; and Morris, M. 1977. Identity in adolescence: Present and future self concepts. *Journal of Youth and Adolescence* 6:63-75.

Conant, J. 1959. *The American High School Today.* New York: McGraw-Hill.

Conger, J.J. 1975. *Contemporary issues in adolescent development.* New York: Harper and Row.

———. 1976. Current issues in adolescent development. *JSAS Catalog of Selected Documents in Psychology* 6, no. 4:94.

———. 1977. *Adolescence and youth: Psychological development in a changing world,* 2nd ed. New York: Harper and Row.

———. 1977. *Adolescence and youth.* New York: Harper and Row.

Constantinople, A. 1969. An Eriksonian measure of personality development in college students. *Developmental Psychology* 1:357-372.

Costanzo, P., and Shaw, M. 1966. Conformity as a function of age level. *Child Development* 37:967-975.

Csikszenmihalyi, M., 1977. The ecology of adolescent activity and experience. *Journal of Youth and Adolescence* 6:281-294.

Darley, J., and Aronson, E. 1966. Self evaluation vs. direct anxiety reduction as determinants of the fear affiliation relationship. *Journal of Experimental Social Psychology,* Supp.:66-79.

Darwin, C. 1859. *On the origin of the species by means of natural selection.* London: John Murray.

Deutsch, M. 1949. A theory of competition and cooperation. *Human Relations* 2:129-151.

Douvan, E., and Adelson, J. 1966. *The adolescent experience.* New York: Wiley.

Dozier, J.; Lewis, S.; Kersey, A.; and Charping, J. 1978. Sports group: An alternative treatment modality for emotionally disturbed adolescents. *Adolescence* 13:483-488.

Dragastin, S., and Elder, G. eds., 1975. *Adolescence in the life cycle.* New York: Halsted.

Eichorn, D. 1975. Asynchronizations in adolescent development. In S. Dragastin and G. Elder, Jr., eds., *Adolescence in the life cycle.* New York: Halsted.

Eiseley, L. 1946. *The immense journey.* New York: Random House.

Elder, G. 1975. Adolescence in the life cycle: An introduction. In S. Dragastin and G. Elder, eds., *Adolescence in the life cycle,* pp. 1-19. New York: Halsted.

———. 1980. Adolescence in historical perspective. In J. Adelson, ed., *Handbook of adolescent psychology,* pp. 3-46. New York: Wiley.

Elkind, D. 1970. *Children and Adolescents: Interpretive Essays on Jean Piaget.* New York: Oxford University Press.

———. 1974. *Children and adolescents: Interpretive essays on Jean Piaget,* 2nd ed. New York: Oxford University Press.

———. 1975. Recent research on cognitive development in adolescence. In S. Dragastin and G. Elder, eds., *Adolescence in the life cycle,* pp. 49-59. New York: Halsted.

Elkind, D., and J.H. Flavell, eds. 1971. *Studies in Cognitive Development: Essays in Honor of Jean Piaget.* New York: Oxford University Press.

Elkin, F., and Westley, W. 1955. The myth of adolescent culture. *American Sociological Review* 20:680-684.

Epperson, D. 1964. A reassessment of the indices of parental influence on the adolescent society. *American Sociological Review* (February):93-96.

Erikson, E. 1956. The problem of ego identity. *Journal of American Psychoanalytic Association* 4, no. 1:56-121.

———. 1950, 1963. *Childhood and Society.* New York: Norton.

———. 1963. *Youth Change and Challenge.* New York: Basic Books.

———. 1968a. *Identity and the life cycle.* New York: Norton.

———. 1968b. *Identity: Youth and crisis.* New York: Norton.

———. 1974. *Dimensions of a New Identity.* New York: Norton.

Erikson, M., and Jensen, G. 1977. Delinquency is still group behavior: Toward revitalizing the group premise in the sociology of deviance. *Journal of Criminal Law and Criminology* 68:262-273.

Esman, A. 1975. *The psychology of adolescence.* New York: International Universities Press.

Faust, M.S. 1960. Developmental maturity as a determinant in prestige of adolescent girls. *Child development* 31:173-184.

Feather, N. 1980. Values in adolescence. In J. Adelson, ed., *Handbook of adolescent psychology,* pp. 247-294. New York: Wiley.

Ferguson, G. 1971. *Statistical analysis in psychology and education,* 3rd ed. New York: McGraw Hill.

Festinger, L. 1950. Informal social communication. *Psychological Review* 57:271-282.

———. 1954. A theory of social comparison processes. *Human Relations* 5:117-139.

———. 1957. *Theory of cognitive dissonance.* New York: Harper and Row.

———. 1964. *Conflict, decision, and dissonance.* Stanford, Calif.: Stanford University Press.

———, ed., 1980. *Retrospections on social psychology.* New York: Oxford University Press.

Festinger, L.; Torrey, J.; and Willerman, B. 1954. Self evaluation as a function of attraction to the group. *Human Relations* 7:161-173.

Flacks, R. 1967. The liberated generation: An exploration of the roots of student protest. *Journal of Social Issues* 23:52-75.

———. 1971. *Youth and social change*. Chicago: Markham.

Freud, A. 1936. Instinctual anxiety during puberty. In *The Writings of Anna Freud*, vol. II. New York: International Universities Press.

———. 1948, 1966. *The ego and the mechanisms of defense*. New York: International Universities Press.

———. 1958. Adolescence. In *Psychoanalytic study of the child*, vol. 13, pp. 255-278. New York: International Universities Press.

Freud, S. 1905a. The transformations of puberty. In J. Strachey, ed., *The standard edition of the complete psychological works of Sigmund Freud*, vol. 7. London: Hogarth, 1953 ed.

———. 1905b. Three essays in the theory of sexuality. *Standard Edition*, vol. 7. London: Hogarth Press, 1961 ed.

———. 1917. *A general introduction to psychoanalysis*. Garden City, N.Y.: Doubleday, 1953 ed.

———. 1921. Ego and the Id. *Standard Edition*, vol. 19, p. 12. London: Hogarth Press, 1961 ed.

———. 1932. New introductory lectures on psychoanalysis. *Standard Edition*, vol. 22, pp. 5-182. London: Hogarth Press, 1964 ed.

———. 1936. *The Problem of Anxiety*. New York: Norton.

———. 1938. *An outline of psychoanalysis*. New York: Norton, 1949 ed.

———. 1950. *The Ego and the Id*. London, Hogarth.

Friedenberg, E. 1959. *The vanishing adolescent*. Boston: Beacon Press.

———. 1963. *Coming of age in America: Growth and acquiescence*. New York: Random House.

Furth, H.G. and Piaget, J.Q. 1973. The nature-nurture controversy. *Development* 16, no. 1, 61-73.

Gallatin, J. 1980. Political thinking in adolescence. In J. Adelson, ed., *Handbook of adolescent psychology*, pp. 344-382. New York: Wiley.

Gesell, A. 1933. Maturation and patterning of behavior. In C. Murchison, ed., *A handbook of child psychology*, 2nd ed. rev. Worcester, Mass.: Clark University Press.

Gesell, A.; Ilg, F.; and Ames, L. 1956. *Youth: The years from ten to sixteen*. New York: Harper and Row.

Getzels, J.W., and Jackson, P.W. 1962. *Creativity and intelligence*. New York: Wiley.

Goethals, G., and Darley, J. 1977. Social comparison: An attributional approach. In J.M. Suls and R.L. Miller, eds., *Social comparison processes: Theoretical and empirical perspectives*. Washington, D.C.: Hemisphere Publishing Corporation, Halsted Press.

Goodman, P. 1956. *Growing up absurd*. New York: Random House.

Gordon, B. 1966. Influence and social comparison as motives of affiliation. *Journal of Experimental Social Psychology*, Supp. 1:55-65.

Grinder, R. 1969. The concept of adolescence in the genetic psychology of G. Stanley Hall. *Child Development* 40:355-369.

———— . 1975. *Studies in adolescence*, 3rd ed. New York: Macmillan.

Hakmiller, K. 1966a. Need for self evaluation, perceived similarity, and comparison choice. *Journal of Experimental Social Psychology*, Supp. 1:49-55.

———— . 1966b. Threat as a determinant of downward comparison. *Journal of Experimental Social Psychology*, Supp. 1:32-39.

Hall, G.S. 1916. *Adolescence* 2 vols. New York: Appleton.

Hart, C.W.M. 1974. Contrasts between prepubertal and postpubertal education. In G. Spindler, ed., *Education and cultural process: Toward an anthropology of education*, pp. 342-360. New York: Holt, Rinehart and Winston.

Hartley, R. 1968. Norm compatibility, norm preference, and the acceptance of new reference groups. In H. Hyman and E. Singer, *Readings in reference group theory and research*. New York: Free Press.

Hartshorne, H., and May, M. 1928-1930. *Studies in the nature of character: Studies in deceit*, vol. 1. New York: Macmillan.

Havighurst, R. 1973, A cross cultural view of adolescence. In J.F. Adams, ed., *Understanding adolescence: Current developments in adolescent psychology*, 2nd ed. Boston: Allyn and Bacon.

Havighurst, R., and Taba, H. 1949. *Adolescent character and personality*. New York: Wiley.

Hebb, D. 1949. *Organization of behavior*. New York: Wiley.

Heider, F. 1946. Attitudes and cognitive organization. *Journal of Psychology* 21:107-112.

Hill, J.P., and Palmquist, W. 1978. Social cognition and social relations in early adolescence. *International Journal of Behavior Development* 1:1-36.

Hoffman, M. 1970. Moral development. In P.H. Mussen, ed. *Carmichael's handbook of child psychology*, vol. 2, New York: Wiley.

———— .1980. Moral development in adolescence. In J. Adelson, ed., *Handbook of adolescent psychology*, pp. 295-343. New York: Wiley.

Hollingsworth, L. 1928. *The psychology of the adolescent*. New York: Appleton-Century.

Honess, T. 1980. Self reference in children's descriptions of peers: Egocentricity or collaboration. *Child Development* 51:476-480.

House, E.A.; Durfee, M.; Bryan, C. 1979. A survey of psychological and social concerns of rural adolescents. *Adolescence* 14:361-376.

Huba, G.; Wingard, J.; Bentler, P. 1979. Beginning adolescent drug use and peer and adult interaction patterns. *Journal of Consulting and Clinical Psychology* 47:265-276.

Hunt, J. McV. 1961. *Intelligence and Experience*. New York: Ronald Press.

Hyman, H. 1942. The psychology of status. *Archives of psychology* 269:5-38; 80-86.

Hyman, H., and Singer, E. 1968. *Readings in reference group theory and research.* New York: Free Press.

Inhelder, B., and Piaget, J. 1958. *The growth of logical thinking in children and adolescents.* New York: Basic Books.

James, S. 1977. Living with children in transition: Resources for parents of pre and early adolescents. *Research in Education* (October).

Jessor, R., and Jessor, J. 1977. *Problem behavior and psychosocial development.* New York: Academic Press.

Jones, E., and Gerard, H. 1967. *Foundations of social psychology.* New York: Wiley.

Jones, S., and Regan, D. 1974. Ability evaluation through social comparison. *Journal of Experimental Social Psychology* 10:133-146.

Josselson, R. 1980. Ego development in adolescence. In J. Adelson, ed., *Handbook of adolescent psychology,* pp. 133-210. New York: Wiley.

Josselyn, I.M. 1952. *The Adolescent and his world.* New York: Family Service Association of America.

————. 1954. The ego in adolescence. *American Journal of Orthopsychiatry* 24:223-227.

Justice, B., and Duncan, D. 1976. Running away: An epidemic problem of adolescence. *Adolescence* 43:365-371.

Kandel, D. 1978a. Homophily, selection, and socialization in adolescent friendships. *American Journal of Sociology* 84:427-436.

————. 1978b. On variations in adolescent subcultures. *Youth and Society* 9:373-384.

Keating, D. 1980. Thinking processes in adolescence. In Adelson, J., *Handbook of adolescent psychology.* New York: John Wiley.

Kelley, H. 1952. Two functions of reference groups. In G. Swanson, T. Newcomb, and E. Hartley, eds., *Readings in social psychology,* rev. ed. New York: Holt, Rinehart and Winston.

Keniston, K. 1965. *The uncommitted: Alienated youth in American society.* New York: Harcourt, Brace and World.

————. 1967. The sources of student dissent. *Journal of Social Issues* 22:108-137.

————. 1968. *Young Radicals.* New York: Harcourt, Brace and World.

————. 1971. *Youth and dissent: The rise of a new opposition.* New York: Harcourt, Brace, Jovanovich.

Kerlinger, F. 1966. *Foundations of behavioral research.* New York: Wiley.

Kohlberg, L. 1964. Development of moral character and moral ideology. In M. Hoffman and L. Hoffman, eds. *Review of child development research,* vol. 1. New York: Russell Sage Foundation.

————. 1970. Moral development and the education of adolescents. In E.

Evans, ed., *Adolescents: Readings in behavior and development.* Hinsdale, Ill.: Dryden Press.

———. 1976. Stage and sequence: The cognitive development approach. In T. Lickona, ed., *Moral development and behavior: Theory, research, and social issues.* New York: Holt, Rinehart and Winston.

Kohlberg, L., and Gilligan, C. 1971. The adolescent as philosopher: The discovery of the self in a post conventional world. *Daedalus* 100: 1051-1086.

Kohlberg, L., and Kramer, R. 1969. Continuities and discontinuities in childhood and adult moral development. *Human Development* 12:93-120.

Konopka, G. 1966. *The adolescent girl in conflict.* Englewood Cliffs, N.J.: Prentice-Hall.

Kraus, J. 1977. Causes of delinquency as perceived by juveniles. International Journal of Offender Therapy and Comparative Criminology 21:79-86.

Landsbaum, J., and Willis, R. 1971. Conformity in early and late adolescence. *Developmental Psychology* 4:334-337.

Langer, J. 1969. Disequilibrium as a source of development. In P. Mussen, J. Langer, and M. Covington, eds., *Trends and issues in developmental psychology.* New York: Holt, Rinehart and Winston.

Larson, Lyle E. 1975. The process of learning parental and sex role identification. In R. Grinder, *Studies in adolescence,* pp. 257-268. 3rd ed., New York: Macmillian.

Latane, B., ed. 1966. Studies in social comparison. *Journal of Experimental Social Psychology,* Supp. 1.

Leslie, G. 1979. *The family in social context.* New York: Oxford University Press, 4th edition.

Lesser, G., and Kandel, D. 1969. Parental and peer influences on educational plans of adolescence. *American Sociological Review* 34:213-223.

Levine, E., and Kozak, C. 1979. Drug and alcohol use, delinquency, and vandalism among upper middle class pre and post adolescents. *Journal of Youth and Adolescence* 8:91-101.

Levy, N. 1968. The use of drugs by teenagers for sanctuary and illusion. *American Journal of Psychoanalysis* 28:48-56.

Lewin, K. 1935. *Dynamic theory of personality.* New York: McGraw Hill.

———. 1936. *Principles of topological psychology.* New York: McGraw Hill.

———. 1939. Field theory and experiment in social psychology; Concepts and methods. *American Journal of Sociology* 44:868-897.

———. 1943. Defining the field at a given time. *Psychological Review* 50:292-310.

———. 1951. *Field theory and social science.* New York: Harper & Row.

Lieberman, J. 1977. *Playfulness,* pp. 107-122. New York: Academic Press.

Litwack, E. 1960. Reference group theory, bureaucratic career, and neighborhood primary group cohesion. *Sociometry* 23:72-73.

Looft, W. 1975. Egocentrism and social interaction in adolescence. In R. Grinder, *Studies in adolescence,* pp. 556-561. New York: Macmillan.

Lorenz, K. 1965. *Evolution and modification in behavior.* Chicago: University of Chicago Press.

Maccoby, E., and Jacklin, C.N.N. 1974. *The psychology of sex differences.* Stanford, Calif.: Stanford University Press.

Marcia, J. 1980. Identity in adolescence. In J. Adelson, ed., *Handbook of adolescent psychology,* pp. 159-187. New York: Wiley.

Masterson, J. 1968. The psychiatric significance of adolescent turmoil. *American Journal of Psychiatry* 124:1549-1554.

Maswud, M. 1980. Transition from objective to subjective responsibility in Nigerian adolescents. *Adolescence* 15:341-354.

McCleland, D. 1965. Toward a theory of motive acquisition. *American Psychologist* 20:321-333.

Mead, M. 1928. *Coming of age in Samoa.* New York: Morrow.

——— . 1958. Adolescence in primitive and modern society. In G. Swanson, T. Newcomb, and E. Hartley, eds., *Readings in social psychology.* New York: Holt, Rinehart and Winston.

——— . 1962. *Growing Up in New Guinea.* New York: Morrow.

——— .1963. Why is education obsolete? In R. Gross, *The teacher and the taught.* New York: Dell.

——— . 1970. *Culture and commitment: A study of the generation gap.* New York: Doubleday.

Merton, R. 1957. *Social theory and social structure.* Glencoe, Ill.: Free Press.

Merton, R., and Rossi, A. 1950. Contributions to the theory of reference group behavior. In R. Merton, *Social theory and social structure,* pp. 225-275. New York: Free Press, 1957 ed.

Mettee, D., and Smith, G. 1977. Social comparison and interpersonal attraction. The case for dissimilarity. In J. Suls and R. Miller, eds., *Social comparison processes: Theoretical and empirical perspectives.* Washington, D.C.: Hemisphere Publishing, Halsted Press, Wiley.

Mincer, J. 1975. Youth, education, and work. In R. Grinder, *Studies in adolescence,* 3rd ed., pp. 79-86. New York: Macmillan.

Molinaro, J. 1978. The social fate of children disfigured by burns. *American Journal of Psychiatry* 135:979-980.

Mussen, P.; Conger, J.; and Kagan, J. 1974. *Child Development and Personality* (4th ed.). New York: Harper and Row.

Mussen, P., and Jones, M. 1957. Self conceptions, motivation and interpersonal attitudes of late and early maturing boys. *Child Development* 28:243-256.

Muus, R. 1975. *Theories of adolescence,* 3rd ed. New York: Random House.

Nelsen, E., and Rosenbaum, E. 1975. Language patterns within the youth subculture: Development of slang vocabularies. In R. Grinder, *Studies in adolescence,* pp. 273-284. New York: Macmillan.

Newcomb, T. 1943, *Personality and social change.* New York: Holt, Rinehart and Winston.

––––––. 1948. Attitude development as a function of reference groups: The Bennington study. In E. Maccoby, T. Newcomb, and E. Hartley, eds., *Readings in social psychology,* 3rd ed. pp. 265-275. New York: Holt, 1958 ed.

––––––. 1968. Interpersonal balance. In R. Abelson, E. Aronson, W. McGuire, T. Newcomb, M. Rosenberg, and P. Tannenbaum, eds., *Theories of cognitive consistency: A sourcebook.* Chicago: Rand McNally.

––––––. 1978. Youth in colleges and in corrections: Institutional influences. *American Psychologist* 33:114-124.

Newman, P., and Newman, B. 1976. Early adolescence and its conflict: Group identity vs. alienation. *Adolescence* 9:261-274.

Niles, F. 1979. The adolescent girls' perception of parents and peers. *Adolescence* 14:591-597.

Noblit, G. 1976. The adolescent experience and delinquency: School versus subcultural effects. *Youth and Society* 8:27-44.

O'Donnell, W. 1976. Adolescent self esteem related to feelings toward parents and friends. *Journal of Youth and Adolescence* 5:179-185.

Offer, D. 1969. *The psychological world of the teen-ager,* New York: Basic Books.

––––––. 1974. Three developmental routes through normal adolescence. Paper presented at Second Annual Friends Hospital Clinical Conference, Philadelphia, Pa., October.

Offer, D.; Marcus, D.; and Offer, J. 1970. A longitudinal study of normal adolescent boys. *American Journal of Psychiatry* 126:917-924.

Offer, D., and Offer, J.B. 1975. *From teenage to young manhood.* New York: Basic Books.

Otto, L. 1977. Girl friends as significant others: Their influence on young men's career aspirations and achievements. *Sociometry* 40:287-293.

Parsons, T. 1955. Family structure and the socialization of the child. In T. Parsons and R. Bales, eds., *Family socialization and interaction processes.* Glencoe, Ill.: Free Press.

Parsons, T., and Bales, R.F. 1955. *Family, socialization and interaction process.* Glencoe, Illinois: Free Press.

Pascal, R. 1967. *The German strum und drang.* Manchester: Manchester University Press.

Patchen, M. 1961. A conceptual framework and some empirical date regarding comparisons of social rewards. *Sociometry* 24:136-156.

Pearson, G. 1958. *Conflict of the generations.* New York: Norton.

Pepitone, A. 1976. Toward a nonmative and comparative biocultural social psychology. *Journal of Personality and Social Psychology* 34:641-653.

Pepitone, E.A. 1972. Comparison behavior in elementary school children. *American Education Research Journal* 9:45-62.

———. 1980. *Children in cooperation and competition.* Lexington, Mass.: Lexington Books, D.C. Heath and Company.

Petersen, A., and Taylor, B. 1980. The biological approach to adolescence. In J. Adelson, ed., *Handbook of adolescent psychology,* pp. 117-155. New York: Wiley.

Piaget, J. 1932. *The moral judgment of the child.* New York: Free Press, 1965 ed.

———. 1952. *The origins of intelligence in children.* New York: International Universities Press.

———. 1954. *The construction of reality in the child.* New York: Basic Books.

———. 1972. Intellectual Evolution from Adolescence to Adulthood. *Human Development* 14:1-12.

———. 1973. *The child and reality: Problems of a genetic psychology.* New York: Grossman Publishers.

Piaget, J., and Inhelder, B. 1958. *The growth of logical thinking.* London: Routledge.

———. 1969. *The psychology of the child.* New York: Basic Books.

Piaget, J. 1969. The intellectual development of the adolescent. In G. Caplan and S. Lebovici, eds. *Adolescence: Psychological Perspective.* New York, Basic Books, pp. 22-26.

Porter-Gehrie, C. 1979. Models of adulthood: An ethnographic study of an adolescent peer group. *Journal of Youth and Adolescence* 8:253-267.

Radloff, R. 1961. Opinion evaluation and affiliation. *Journal of Abnormal and Social Psychology* 62:578-585.

———. 1966. Social comparison and ability evaluation. *Journal of Experimental Social Psychology,* Supp. 1:6-26.

Rainwater, L. 1972. Crucible of identity: The Negro lower class family. In C. Lavatelli and F. Stendler, eds., *Readings in child behavior and development,* pp. 112-126. New York: Harcourt, Brace, Jovanovich.

Redl, F. 1974. Something new has been added on the way to the forum. Paper presented at Second Annual Friends Hospital Clinical Conference, Philadelphia, Pa., October.

———. 1975. Emigration, immigration, and the imaginary group. *Adolescent Psychiatry* 4:6-12.

Redl, F., and Wineman, D. 1962. *Controls from within.* Glencoe, Ill.: Free Press.

Reinhard, D. 1977. The reaction of adolescent boys and girls to the divorce of their parents. *Journal of Clinical Child Psychology* 6:21-23.

Research for Better Schools. 1967. *Sequential Analysis of Verbal Interaction (SAVI)*. Philadelphia: Research for Better Schools.

Ritter, E. 1979. Social Perspective taking ability, cognitive complexity and listener adapted communication in early and late adolescence. *Communication Monographs* 46:40-51.

Rokeach, M. 1973. *The nature of human values*. New York: Free Press.

Rosen, B. 1955. Conflicting group membership: A study of parent peer cross pressures. *American Sociological Review* 20:155-161.

Rosenberg, M. 1975. The dissonant context and the adolescent self concept. In S. Dragistin and G. Elder, Jr., eds., *Adolescence in the life cycles,* pp. 97-114. New York: Halsted.

Rosenthal, T., and Zimmerman, B. 1978. *Social learning and cognition*. New York: Academic.

Rossi, A.; Kagan, J.; and Harevon, T.K. 1978. *The family*. New York: W.W. Norton.

Schachter, S. 1951. Deviation, rejection, and communication. *Journal of Abnormal and Social Psychology* 46:190-207.

_____ . 1959. *The psychology of affiliation*. Stanford, Calif.: Stanford University Press.

_____ . 1964. The interactions of cognitive and physiological determinants of emotional state. In L. Berkowitz, ed., *Advances in experimental and social psychology,* vol. 1. New York: Academic.

Schachter, S., and Singer, J. 1962. Cognitive, social and physiological determinants of emotional state. *Psychological Review* 69:379-399.

Schiamberg, L. 1972. Some socio cultural factors in adolescent parent conflict: A cross cultural comparison of selected cultures. In W. Looft, ed., *Developmental psychology: A book of readings,* pp. 176-195. Hinsdale, Ill.: Dryden Press.

Schmitt, R. 1972. *The reference other orientation: An extension of reference group concept*. Carbondale: Southern Illinois University Press.

Schonfeld, W. 1966. Body-image disturbances in adolescents: Influence of family attitudes and psychopathology. *Archives of General Psychiatry*. 15:15-2.

Schwartz, G., and Merten, D. 1975. The language of adolescence: An anthropological approach to the youth culture. In R. Grinder, *Studies in adolescence,* pp. 315-333. New York: Macmillan.

Sears, R. 1951. Social behavior and personality development. In T. Parsons and E. Shills, *Toward a General Theory of Action*. Cambridge, Mass.: Harvard University Press, pp. 465-478.

Sears, R. 1957. *Patterns of Child Rearing*. New York: Harper and Row.

Sears, R.; Maccoby, E.; and Levin, H. 1957. *Patterns of child rearing*. Evanston, Ill.: Row, Peterson.

Seltzer, V. 1975. An exploratory study of the adolescent reference field and of the processes of social comparison with specific regard to their function in development. Ph.D. diss., Bryn Mawr College, 1975.

_____ . 1978. Social comparison processes among adolescents in peer groups. *Research in Education* (May).

_____ . 1980 Social comparison behaviors of adolescents. In E. Pepitone, *Children in cooperation and competition.* Lexington, Mass.: Lexington Books, D.C. Heath and Company.

Shrauger, S., and Jones, S. 1968. Social validation and interpersonal evaluation. *Journal of Experimental Social Psychology* 4:315-323.

Sherif, M. 1954. Reference groups in human relations. In M. Sherif and M. Wilson, eds., *Group relations at the crossroads.* New York: Harper and Brothers.

Sherif, M., and Sherif, C. 1964. *Reference groups.* New York: Harper and Row.

_____ . 1969. *Social psychology.* New York: Harper and Row.

Simmons, R.; Rosenberg, F.; and Rosenberg, M. 1975. Disturbance in the self image at adolescence. In R. Grinder, *Studies in adolescence,* pp. 200-218. New York: Macmillan.

Smith, B. 1976. Adolescent and parent: Interaction between developmental stages. *Center quarterly Focus* (Fall).

Smith, T. 1916. Push versus pull: Intra family versus peer group variables as possible determinants of adolescent orientations towards parents. *Youth and Society* 8:5-26.

Spindler, G. 1974. The transmission of culture. In G. Spindler, ed., *Education and cultural process: Toward an anthropology of education,* pp. 279-310. New York: Holt, Rinehart and Winston.

Stein, K.; Soskin, W.; and Korchin, S. 1975. Drug use among disaffected high school youth. *Journal of Drug Education* 5:193-203.

Stone, L.; Miranne, A.; and Ellis, G. 1979. Parent peer influence as a predicator of marijuana use. *Adolescence* 14:115-122.

Suls, J., and Miller, R., eds. 1977. *Social comparison processes: theoretical and empirical perspectives.* Washington, D.C.: Hemisphere Publishing, Halsted, Wiley.

Tanner, J. 1962. *Growth and adolescence,* 2nd ed. Springfield, Ill.: Thomas.

_____ . 1972. Sequence, tempo and individual variation of growth and development of boys and girls aged twelve to sixteen. In J. Kagan and R. Coles, eds., *Twelve to sixteen: Early adolescence.* New York: Norton.

Teicher, J. 1972. The alienated, older male adolescent. *American Journal of Psychotherapy* 26:401-407.

Thibaut, J., and Kelley, H. 1959. *The social psychology of groups.* New York: Wiley.

Thornburgh, H. 1973. *Adolescent development.* Dubuque, Iowa: W.C. Brown.

———. 1975. *Contemporary adolescence: Readings,* 2nd ed. Monterey, Calif.: Brooks Cole.

Thorton, D., and Arrowood, A. 1966. Self evaluation, self enhancement and the locus of social comparison. *Journal of Experimental Social Psychology,* Supp. 1:40-48.

Turiel, E. 1966. An experimental test of the sequentiality of developmental stages in the child's moral judgments. *Journal of Personality and Social Psychology* 3:611-618.

———. 1974. Conflict and transition in adolescent moral development. *Child Development* 45:14-29.

Turner, R. 1955. Reference groups of future oriented men. *Social Forces* 34:130-136.

———. 1956. Role taking, role standpoint, and reference group behavior. *American Journal of Sociology* (January): 316-318.

———. 1964. Upward mobility and class values. *Social Problems* 11: 359-374.

Vorrath, H., and Brewdtro, L. 1974. *Positive peer culture.* Chicago: Aldine Publishing Company.

Vygotsky, L. 1962. *Thought and Language,* Cambridge, Mass.: MIT Press.

Wagner, H. 1978. *The social psychology of adolescence.* Washington, D.C.: University Press of America.

Wallach, M., and Kogan, N. 1965. *Modes of thinking in young children.* New York: Holt, Rinehart and Winston.

Weatherley, D. 1964. Self-perceived rate of physical maturation and personality in late adolescence. *Child Development* 35:1197-1210.

Webb, R. 1978. *Social development in childhood.* Baltimore, Md.: Johns Hopkins University Press.

Weick, K. 1969. Systematic observational methods. In G. Lindzey and E. Aronson, eds., *The handbook of social psychology,* vol. 2. Reading, Mass.: Addison-Wesley.

Westby, D., and Braungart, R. 1966. Class and politics in the family backgrounds of student political activitists. *American Social Review* 31:690-692.

Wheeler, L. 1966. Motivation as a determinant of comparison upward. *Journal of Experimental Social Psychology,* Supp. 1:27-32.

———. 1970. *Interpersonal influence.* Boston: Allyn and Bacon.

Wheeler, L., and Latane, B. 1966. Emotional reactions to disaster. *Journal of Experimental Social Psychology,* Supp. 1:95-103.

Wheeler, L.; Kelley, R.; Shaver, L.; Jones, R.; Goethals, G.; Cooper, J.; Robinson, J.; Gruder, C.; and Butzine, K. 1969. Factors determining the choice of a comparison other. *Journal of Experimental Social Psychology* 5:219-232.

Wheelis, A. 1958. *The quest for identity.* New York: Norton.

White, R. 1959. Motivation reconsidered: The Concept of competence. *Psychological Review* 5:297-333.

Williamson, R. 1977. Variables in adjustment and life goals among high school students. *Adolescence* 12:213-225.

Wrightsman, L. 1960. Effects of waiting with others on changes in level of felt anxiety. *Journal of Abnormal and Social Psychology* 61:216-222.

Young, J., and Ferguson, L. 1979. Developmental changes through adolescence in the spontaneous nomination of reference groups as a function of decision content. *Journal of Youth and Adolescence* 8:239-252.

Zajonc, R. 1968. Cognitive theories of social psychology. In G. Lindzey and E. Aronson, eds., *The handbook of social psychology,* vol. 1. Reading, Mass.: Addison-Wesley.

Zellermayer, J., and Marcus, J. 1972. Kibbutz adolescence: Relevance to personality development theory. *Journal of Youth and Adolescence* 1:143-153.

Ziajka, A. 1972. The black youth's self concept. In W. Looft, ed., *Developmental psychology: A book of readings,* pp. 249-268. Hinsdale, Ill.: Dryden Press.

Glossary

AD	Adolescent Dialectic
Ado K	Adolescent Kinetic (primary group)
Ado k	Adolescent kinetic (secondary group)
AERR^n	Assessment-Evaluation-Reassessment-Reevaluation (n = infinity)
AERR^n-IF	Assessment-Evaluation-Reassessment-Reevaluation - Integration and Flexibility
AERR^n-f	Assessment-Evaluation-Reassessment-Reevaluation future (primary group)
AERR^n-fg	Assessment-Evaluation-Reassessment-Reevaluation future goal (primary group)
AERR^n-g	Assessment-Evaluation-Reassessment-Reevaluation goal (primary group)
AERR^n-F	Assessment-Evaluation-Reassessment-Reevaluation Future (secondary group)
AERR^n-FG	Assessment-Evaluation-Reassessment-Reevaluation Future Goal (secondary group)
AERR^n-G	Assessment-Evaluation-Reassessment-Reevaluation Goal (secondary group)
ARGI	Adolescent Reference Group Index
CHAD	Child-Adult
DFI	Dynamic Functional Interaction
ESA	Element Substituting Action
IA	Individual Attribute (Score)
IAD	Individual Adolescent Dialectic
IRA	Initial Relative Assessment
IRA/R	Initial Relative Assessment/Rank
PAPP	Peer Arena Progression Profile
PAPP-SF	Peer-Arena Progression Profile - Secondary Field
PAPP-SS	Peer-Arena Progression Profile - Subjective Scale
PFF	Peer Field of Force
SER	Selected Element Refinement
SER-G	Selected Element Refinement - Goal
SER-IF	Selected Element Refinement - Integration and Felxibility
SES	Specific Element Selection
SS	Self-Structure
TI	Total Individual (Score)

Indexes

Index of Names

Index of Subjects

About the Author

Vivian Center Seltzer received the B.A. at the University of Minnesota; the M.S.W. at The University of Pennsylvania; and the Ph.D. in child development and clinical evaluation, with subfields in social psychology and learning theory, at Bryn Mawr College. Dr. Seltzer is an associate professor at The University of Pennsylvania, Graduate School of Social Work. Her major teaching areas are psychological growth and social functioning, child and adolescent development, and research methodology. Dr. Seltzer's focus on the process of adolescent social development represents an area of theoretical interest of long standing. Her preparation in several disciplines served to stimulate questions of theoretical integrations. Considerable clinical exposure yielded licensing and certifications in clinical psychology, school psychology, social work, and family therapy; as well as serving as consultant to schools on structural programming, behavior and learning problems and remediation, and family-school relations. The functional analysis of interactional processes in adolescent social growth, the benchmark of her contextual theory, is in part a product of this background both in theory and practice. Dr. Seltzer recently served as a University of Pennsylvania exchange professor at the University of Edinburgh. She is currently curricular head of the Individual and Social Processes course of study sequence.